DOWNWARDLY
GLOBAL

LALAIE AMEERIAR

DOWNWARDLY GLOBAL

Women, Work,
and Citizenship in the
Pakistani Diaspora

Duke University Press   Durham and London   2017

Printed in the United States of America on acid-free paper ∞
Text designed by Courtney Leigh Baker
Typeset in Garamond Premier Pro by Westchester Publishing Services

Library of Congress Cataloging-in-Publication Data
Names: Ameeriar, Lalaie, author.
Title: Downwardly global :
women, work, and citizenship in the Pakistani diaspora /
Lalaie Ameeriar.
Description: Durham : Duke University Press, 2017. |
Includes bibliographical references and index.
Identifiers: LCCN 2016033439 (print)
LCCN 2016034172 (ebook)
ISBN 9780822363019 (hardcover : alk. paper)
ISBN 9780822363163 (pbk. : alk. paper)
ISBN 9780822373407 (e-book)
Subjects: LCSH: Pakistanis—Canada. |
Women immigrants—Employment—Canada. |
Pakistani diaspora. | Cultural pluralism—Canada.
Classification: LCC F1035.P34 A44 2017 (print) |
LCC F1035.P34 (ebook) | DDC 305.8914/122071—dc23
LC record available at https://lccn.loc.gov/2016033439

COVER ART: Sausan Saulat, *Maybe tomorrow* / (details). Private collection.
Courtesy of the artist.

Duke University Press gratefully acknowledges the support of the
Hellman Foundation, at the University of California Santa Barbara,
which provided funds toward the publication of this book.

CONTENTS

ACKNOWLEDGMENTS

I would like to begin by thanking all the people in Toronto, Lahore, and Karachi who shared their lives and their stories with me. In order to protect their confidentiality, I cannot name them here, but I am forever indebted to them. I also wish to thank the numerous organizations that allowed me to conduct research within their walls, and the patience they had in answering my unending questions. A special thanks goes to Mazeena.

I am also grateful for several institutions and centers whose generosity made this research and writing possible. This research was supported by funding from the Woodrow Wilson Foundation; the UC President's Faculty Research Fellowship in the Humanities; the National Bureau of Economic Research at Harvard University; the Department of Anthropology at Stanford University; the Institute for International Studies at Stanford University; the Research Institute for Comparative Studies in Race and Ethnicity at Stanford University; the Clayman Institute for Gender Research at Stanford University; the Department of Asian American Studies at the University of California, Santa Barbara; the University of California Academic Senate; the UCSB Interdisciplinary Humanities Center; the UC Center for New Racial Studies; and the Hellman Fellows Program.

My thinking has been deeply inspired by James Ferguson and Akhil Gupta, who introduced me to critical studies of globalization long before I arrived at Stanford University. James Ferguson's willingness to read drafts at every stage and his critical engagement with my work has been invaluable. Akhil Gupta's mentorship, guidance, and writings helped inspire me throughout my time at Stanford, and I thank him for helping me conceptualize this project. I thank Purnima Mankekar for her constant encouragement of my work in South Asian diaspora studies and her critical engagement with my research and writing. I also wish to thank Shahzad Bashir, Renato

Rosaldo, S. Lochlann Jain, Sylvia Yanagisako, Miyako Inoue, and David Palumbo-Liu, for their support and guidance throughout my dissertation research and write-up. I wish to thank Ellen Christensen and Shelly Coughlin for their administrative and emotional support in the Department of Cultural and Social Anthropology and the Department of Anthropology. I cannot thank Ellen and Shelly enough.

I owe a debt of gratitude to my friends and colleagues at Stanford University for their critical insights, observations, feedback, and support during my time there: Tania Ahmad, Nikhil Anand, Hanna Appel, Elif Babul, Falu Bakrania, Aisha Beliso-de Jesus, Jocelyn Chua, Maya Dodd, Maura Finkelstein, Kelly Freidenfelds, Patrick Gallagher, Rachael Joo, Yoon-Jung Lee, Bakirathi Mani, Tomas Matza, Ramah McKay, Jisha Menon, Zhanara Nauruzbayeva, Marcia Ochoa, Bruce O'Neill, Kevin O'Neill, Flavio Paniagua, Natalia Roudakova, Robert Samet, Peter Samuels, Sima Shakhsari, and Thet Win. Thank you to Tania Ahmad, Rachael Joo, Zhanara Nauruzbayeva, and Kevin O'Neill for their unwavering support, incisive feedback, and for believing in my work. Thank you to Maura Finkelstein for being a close friend and supporter during my years in San Francisco and beyond. My research also benefitted from my time as an IHUM postdoctoral fellow and the colleagues and compatriots I met there: Renu Cappelli, Kathleen Coll, Matthew Daube, Michael Hunter, Tomas Matza, Christy Pichichero, Jeremy Sabol, Candace West, and Joshua Wright. A special thank you to Abigail Heald and Uzma Rizvi, who sustained me with Little Star Pizza and *Project Runway* in San Francisco after long teaching days. For our friendship, I will always be grateful.

New colleagues at the University of California, Santa Barbara, have helped shape this book at critical moments. My colleagues in the Department of Asian American Studies, Feminist Studies, Anthropology and Global Studies offered productive feedback and provided critical support when I needed it. I thank my colleagues Diane Fujino, erin Ninh, John Park, Lisa Park, Sameer Pandya, Celine Parreñas Shimizu, Xiaojian Zhao, Sucheng Chan, Paul Amar, Kum-Kum Bhavnani, Eileen Boris, Eve Darian-Smith, Brian Donnelly, Bishnupriya Ghosh, Mary Hancock, Zaveeni Khan-Marcus, George Lipsitz, Kate McDonald, Ross Melnick, Dean Melvin Oliver, Leila Rupp, Bhaskar Sarkar, Barbara Walker, and Casey Walsh. I want to thank in particular senior faculty members who have shown me steadfast support and guidance and have taught me what it means to live one's politics. Thank you to Leila Rupp who is an incredible mentor and role model for feminist scholars. Thank you to Eileen Boris for her unwavering support for my research and writing, reading drafts at critical stages in the writing process. Thank you to George Lipsitz for reading drafts and offering incisive feedback which has helped shape this book. Thank you to Dean Melvin Oliver for his support and guidance as I navigated the intricacies of assistant professor life. Thank you to Eve Darian-Smith for her support and encouragement and for drawing me into the world of Global Studies at UCSB. Thank you to Lisa Park who was a new addition to the department, but has helped me in ways I will always be immensely grateful for. I want to thank Sucheng Chan for her careful reading and insightful feedback on the introduction. A special thanks goes to Kum-Kum Bhavnani for her amazing mentorship and guidance as I navigated life as a junior faculty member. Our friendship has been invaluable. I would also like to thank Arlene Phillips, Elizabeth Guerrero, Redilyn Mesa, Paula Ryan, and Gary Colmenar for their administrative support.

I am grateful to my friends and colleagues across the UC and beyond: Attiya Ahmad, Jessica Cattelino, Aisha Finch, Inderpal Grewal, Sarah Haley, Sunaina Maira, Minoo Moallem, Kalindi Vora, and Neha Vora. In my first year at UCSB, I was fortunate enough to be invited by Eileen Boris to join her in the intellectually stimulating environment of the UC-wide working group Working at Precarity. There I met Aisha Finch, whose kindness and encouragement have sustained me as I navigated junior faculty life and Kalindi Vora, who read drafts and offered support and friendship, showing me how to live a progressive feminist politics. Sarah Haley, my fellow Woodrow Wilson cohort member who taught me the value of a well-timed drink and who provided support in critical moments. To my Woodrow Wilson mentor Minoo Moallem, thank you for your guidance and critical readings of my work, for which it is stronger. Thank you to Inderpal Grewal for offering comments and insights on my work as well as encouragement and mentorship.

Thank you to my friends and accomplices in San Francisco and Los Angeles, in particular Hannah Appel, Nicole Duffy, Jason Freidenfelds, Katie Hasson, Abigail Heald, Anna Krakus, Flavio Paniagua, and Brian Yarish, who have been great friends and allies during the long dark days of writing. I also wish to say thank you to Kelly Freidenfelds for her intellectual engagement at all stages of my research and her steadfast support throughout my years at Stanford, without which I would not have made it. Thank you to Katie Hasson for friendship and late-night drinks and who always offered a friendly ear. Hannah Appel has been an amazing thinking partner throughout, reading drafts and helping to move the project forward. Thank you to Abigail Heald for being the sister I always wanted.

I have had the opportunity to present this research at a range of venues and I thank the audiences for their rigorous engagement of my work. I presented drafts of chapters in the Department of Comparative Human Development at the University of Chicago, the Center for Research on Women at Barnard College, in Sociology and Equity Studies at the University of Toronto, in the Department of Gender and Women's Studies at UC Berkeley, in the Department of Anthropology at UCLA, at the Pacific Basin Institute at Pomona College, in the Department of Anthropology at Santa Clara University, and in the Department of Asian American Studies at UC Santa Barbara, and at the annual meetings of the American Anthropological Association, the American Studies Association, the Association of Asian American Studies, the Society for Cultural Anthropology, and the Canadian Anthropological Association.

Duke University Press has been a dream to work with. Thank you to Courtney Berger who believed in this project from the beginning, gearing my book toward production with the utmost integrity for the work. I also thank her for the numerous pep talks and drinks at conferences around the country as she helped guide me through the process of turning a dissertation into a book. I also want to thank the anonymous reviewers. It was a pleasure receiving comments from readers who engaged with my research in a way that helped me strengthen and refine the arguments I am making. The manuscript is stronger because of this process. I also want to thank Sandra Korn for her astute editorial assistance. I also want to thank the production and design team at Duke, in particular Danielle Houtz and Amy Buchanan, for seeing the book to completion. I want to thank Basit Iqbal for creating an excellent index. I am also grateful to Anitra Grisales for her meticulous editing of this manuscript. Parts of chapter 2 appeared as "Pedagogies of Affect: Docility and Deference and the Making of Immigrant Women Subjects," in *Signs* 40, no. 2. Portions of chapter 3 appeared as "The Sanitized Sensorium" in *American Anthropologist* 114, no. 3: 509–20. Both are reprinted with permission.

This project really began when I was an undergraduate at the University of Toronto and first learned of the world of social theory and ethnographic method. The scholars who helped guide my thinking and inspire this work include Richard Lee, Bonnie McElhinny, Stuart Philpott, Kerry Rittich, and Gavin Smith. A special thanks goes to Bonnie McElhinny who changed my life. She has not only been a trusted mentor since my days as an undergraduate, but has also become a friend. Bonnie saw promise in my work before I could see it myself, encouraging me to apply to Stanford, the possibility of which seemed preposterous at the time for a kid from Scarborough, and yet was wonderfully possible. She has helped shaped my career by offering me possibilities that had been unimaginable. I wouldn't be where I am today without her. Thank you, Bonnie.

Finally to my mother, the inspiration of this study, who made more sacrifices for me than I'll ever know. This book wouldn't exist without her. Thank you, mom.

Lalaie Ameeriar
Los Angeles, 2016

The Sanitized Sensorium

The fluorescent bulb flickered as it always did, emitting an unrelenting, low, and persistent buzzing that filled the space. The windowless room and harsh institutional lighting made all the participants feel uneasy. Everyone shuddered and fidgeted—physical manifestations of the anxiety, panic, anger, fatigue, and desperation that filled them. As the class got under way, some participants taking notes and others seemingly distracted, a cascade of proscriptions filled the room: "Don't show up smelling like foods that are foreign to us," "Don't wear a shalwar cameeze," "Change your name if it's hard to pronounce," and "Don't wear a hijab if you want to get a job." This was the core curriculum (and moral imperative) delivered to a room full of professional Pakistani, Indian, and Bangladeshi women seeking work in Toronto. I looked around at the fifteen participants in this government-funded workshop, trying to gauge their reactions. The instructions seemed astonishingly dissonant for a workshop aimed at foreign-trained professionals with advanced levels of education, skills, and experience.

The strangeness of it all was not lost on the participants. As one attendee, Saima, remarked to me later, "It's different back home. At home there's more importance stressed on qualifications." I met numerous Pakistani immigrant women like Saima in settlement-services agencies, many of whom were unemployed or underemployed. The majority of these women lived in relative poverty in government housing projects in peripheral parts of the city. Despite having migrated as "skilled workers,"[1] most of them will never enter their chosen fields again. In fact, 44 percent of the Pakistani population of Toronto lives below Canada's low income cut-off.[2] And yet, in this pedagogical effort to facilitate their entry into the workforce, immigrant women were subjected to intimate instructions concerning their sartorial ^{—clothes/style of dress} and hygiene practices.[3] Rather than the skills-focused conversation the participants had expected, they received a barrage of regulatory proscriptions aimed at the immigrant body.

This unemployment workshop took place in a government-funded, privately run settlement-services agency for new immigrants that specifically worked with South Asian women, and that I will call "the Center." It was located in a small building in the emerging Little India—or Little Pakistan, depending on whom you ask—in the West End of Toronto. The neighborhood was economically marginal and populated by a large immigrant community because of the availability of difficult-to-find low-cost housing there. The main street was filled with small Indian and Pakistani restaurants, grocery stores, dollar stores, and a storefront mosque. Many of the city's settlement services were located nearby, but the center of the social world for many Indian and Pakistani women was the Center. Women sat in the waiting room, much like a doctor's office, but one that opened up to the rest of the Center. The large storefront windows in the waiting area put the attendees on display for anyone passing by. Counselors had their offices in cubicles that dotted the space, which ended in a large fluorescent-lit back room where classes and workshops were held. As a first stop for many new immigrants, settlement agencies provide services ranging from help finding a home, to understanding healthcare, to unemployment workshops. Such agencies and organizations form part of the bureaucratic matrix put in place to settle new immigrants. More than one hundred of these settlement-services agencies in the greater Toronto area are aimed at "immigrant integration"—a catchphrase the federal government uses in its emerging agenda for managing immigrants. These centers are a critical site for examining the interface between immigrant bodies and bureaucratic structures.[4]

These South Asian nonprofit organizations also actively participate in numerous cultural festivals that take place throughout the city during South Asian Heritage Month, which happens every May in Ontario. I attended these festivals throughout my time in Toronto, sometimes participating as a volunteer with South Asian organizations and sometimes as a consumer, drinking mango lassi and eating chicken tikka masala and samosas under the blazing sun of a Toronto summer. South Asian cultural festivals are staged throughout the city and display a commodified form of culture, including dance performances, art, and *mehndi* parlors; cooking demonstrations; and stalls selling clothing, jewelry, and food, all presenting a simulacrum of South Asia. The festivals attempt to engage the senses: the sight of beautiful sari fabric, the sounds of Bollywood music, and the smells of pan-Indian food fill the air. But in other contexts, like those discussed in the employment-training event, these same exotic markers of difference are a barrier to employability and even citizenship. How can this be reconciled with the fact that at the cultural festival, which is also situated squarely within the state's practice and logic of multiculturalism, these same people are encouraged to highlight their difference? Here, the smell of citizenship changes.

The classroom encounter, the cultural festival, and Pakistani women's downward mobility all provide a meaningful introduction to the issues this book explores. They help demonstrate how integration in Canada represents not the erasure of all differences, but the celebration of some alongside the eradication of others. Publicly and internationally, the Canadian nation-state has built a reputation of openly abdicating its right to impose a single culture on its citizens. However, in reality, culture is in fact a primary domain of action on the part of the state. The Canadian nation-state relinquishes cultural imperialism and celebrates multi-ness through cultural festivals or state-sanctioned forms of difference, yet uses semi-governmental agencies to impose a particular Canadian mode of bodily comportment on new immigrants. This dual mode of interpellation puts immigrants in an impossible situation in which they must sometimes suitably display their Otherness, but otherwise cannot be culturally different. In the Canadian multicultural state, an implicit process of moralizing is taking place through a politics of multiculturalism that simultaneously attempts to produce, celebrate, and erase differences. These performances have lasting effects, conditioning immigrants to understand themselves as Other.

This book theorizes what I call the "sanitized sensorium" as a means to understand the ways that foreign bodies become legible and recognizable through particular kinds of sensorial and affective registers. The sanitized sensorium signals the forms of embodiment (smell, appearance, and bodily comportment) necessary for inclusion in the public sphere of multicultural Toronto. The daily practices in agencies such as the one described above serve to construct a sanitized body, and sensory perception becomes a crucial means by which that body is judged. The imagined smelly, sweaty, unhygienic immigrant body is central here. In these contexts, many senses are engaged, but in this book I focus primarily on sight (appearance and dress) and smell (bodily odors). These processes are located within intersensorial junctures and thus concern the kinds of affects that such bodily differences evoke for workshop leaders, potential employers, and the larger Canadian public. But rather than just smelling or seeing, this book is also concerned with the experience of being seen and smelled in a particular way. Immigrant women, too, have their own sensorial experience of difference and Otherness. While many of the ways the sanitized sensorium operates has to do with perception, this book also explores how these women perceive themselves in light of their racialization and interpellation as immigrant women. This work then makes central the affective encounter between immigrant women and the greater public to examine the spaces in which race and citizenship are made. The sanitized sensorium contains within it both the promise of citizenship and the damage done to it by the threat of alterity.

By bringing together anthropological debates concerning multiculturalism and the anthropology of the senses, this book examines the sanitized sensorium to understand how the *same* sensorial phenomena (smells, tastes, forms of dress, and embodiment) can be a means of both *exclusion* and *inclusion*, signifying both racialized Otherness and belonging. The way the liberal multicultural state manages these sensorial phenomena is an important part of its so-called project of immigrant integration. Taken together, the economic marginalization of Pakistani Muslim immigrant women and the state's presumed solution to that problem render a landscape of downward mobility built on a terrain of bureaucratic entanglements and multicultural ideologies. Since the 1970s, there has been a large-scale migration of professionals from Asia to North America, facilitated by the easing of immigration regulations and the implementation of a points system that favored professional skills when granting visas to incoming immigrants. Unfortunately, and somewhat paradoxically, these global processes have contributed to increasing social inequality. Skilled immigrant workers are drawn into the global economy with the promise of upward mobility, but most often end up downwardly mobile and unemployed or working in survival jobs. Put simply, while the Canadian government actively recruits professionals from abroad, and the economy relies on such immigration for growth, once in Toronto immigrants are often unable to find work in their fields.

For a city that prides itself on multicultural inclusion, the unemployment and underemployment of highly skilled foreign workers have become an immense social problem, earning its own moniker in daily news accounts and government think tanks as "the foreign-trained-professionals problem." The government, public, and media have been immersed in the very vocal and ongoing debate around this unemployment, recognized most readily on the global stage through the gendered stereotype of the Indian taxicab driver who was a "doctor in his home country."[5] But the fact that this is also a crisis for highly skilled, professional women is often overlooked in Canadian public discourse on the problem. When I asked who is to blame for the foreign-trained-professionals problem, the most commonly stated answer was bureaucracy. As the narrative goes, the federal government regulates immigration, while the provincial government regulates labor, but there is little coordination between the two. Thus, skilled immigrant workers are admitted with little consideration of provincial labor-market needs; further, upon arrival they enter a local bureaucratic system that rejects their foreign credentials. This macro understanding of bureaucracy fails to take into account just how intimate and personally targeted this social problem can be.

The experiences, perceptions, and frustrations of Pakistani Muslim immigrant women in Toronto reveal these otherwise-occluded dimensions of multiculturalism and governance. Seemingly small sites like employment counseling centers and cultural festivals reverberate with larger issues, as the women in this study encounter a Canadian society rife with contradictions: It famously promises immigrants universal inclusion while it actually practices differentiated exclusion. It deploys racial projects yet disavows them. And it denies them meaningful state action against discrimination, yet uses the powers of state licensing to deskill them from professional careers and compel them to become service workers. These are not merely the personal problems of one aggrieved group. They are part of a pattern in metropolitan countries where the unfettered movement of capital across borders requires the denial of racial distinctions in order to assert the universality of the market and its subjects, while it also exploits racial differences to make surplus profits. At the same time, to maintain the political coherence of nations that were founded through settler colonialism, new racial identities and hierarchies must proliferate constantly. In the end, the race (or gender, or cultural difference) of aggrieved people is used to scapegoat them for the failures of neoliberal programs. Their unemployment is not understood as a failure of economic or immigration policy at the state level, but rather as a failure of the immigrant workers themselves.

This book brings together the political economy of labor regimes with intimate affective economies to examine how they have become mutually constitutive features of late capitalism. What I describe in this book is a global story, a story of immigration; but it is also a story of racialization and gendering in the context of state-making and national identity. In this context, the binding of smells, habits, and bodily gestures to skilled immigrant professionals is not exclusively about molding foreign bodies to the demands of late capitalist production; it is a state-based naturalization of immigration policy. The practices of agencies such as the one described at the beginning of this introduction ultimately contradict Canadian models of multiculturalism by teaching a Canadian mode of bodily comportment to new immigrants, thus reinscribing colonial notions of the uncivilized and wild Other in need of domestication. Though the specter of the state looms large, the responsibility for becoming settled, and becoming Canadian, now lies with the individual and her body. As I demonstrate, the practice of multiculturalism as it pertains to the integration of foreign labor and bodies is ultimately not about getting employers or the larger public not to discriminate; rather, it is about making oneself into someone who will not be discriminated against. This phenomenon contributes to the changing character of the Canadian multicultural state, which focuses on culture while ignoring the real material interests of minority groups. Paradoxically, then, liberal Canadian governance in the postcolonial, globalized world continues to attempt to colonize and discipline the immigrant brown body.

Cartographies of Downward Mobility

Asma was in her early thirties and had been living in Toronto for two years when we first met at the Center. Her brother, who was also in Toronto and formerly worked as a computer scientist, was working at Value Village, a used clothing store similar to Goodwill. She was a lawyer, but had not worked as one since she arrived. She often hung around the Center and was known as nervous but kind; every time I encountered her she expressed interest in helping me with my project. She had attended unemployment workshops for about eight or nine months, but was unable to find work. Eventually she gave up looking for something in her field and started taking various survival jobs, such as cashiering, as they arose.

Focusing on the intimate spaces in which this unemployment or under-employment occurs, I conducted ethnographic fieldwork in various sites throughout urban Toronto.[6] I spoke with immigrant women like Asma in a range of regulated professions (those in which a license is required to work) including medicine, engineering, law, and education.[7] Through this research I learned that it is highly unlikely that any professional would be able to work in her field without returning to school for extensive reeducation, but many do not have the resources to do so. Asma was heading down the typical track that skilled immigrant workers are often forced to travel: she entered the country under the skilled-worker class, her foreign credentials were then misrecognized or not recognized at all, and eventually she began taking survival jobs. The women's stories you will read here are typical not only of Pakistani women but also of immigrant professionals from other countries, although the ways the sanitized sensorium operates here is particular to Pakistani women.

The impact of this problem is troubling for men and women, but the state, the market, and even scholars have a blind spot when it comes to the experiences of women, which prevents us from fully understanding how this downward mobility operates. For instance, the kinds of work opportunities typically available to women earn them less money. Thus, if women are funneled into feminized jobs that pay less, despite the fact that they entered the country with the *same* professional credentials as men, then the liberal rhetoric of "equal pay for equal work" does not apply. In the United States context, a study using census data from 1950–2000 found that occupations began paying less once women entered them in large numbers (e.g., professions including housekeepers, designers, and biologists). This phenomenon works the other way as well, as evidenced by the field of computer programming. When more men entered the profession, it began paying more and became more prestigious.[8] Thus, this process of transnationalism not only de-skills professional Pakistani Muslim women but also serves to gender them as workers. Accounts of their experiences provide an intimate look at how global processes impact women's individual lives.

Pakistani women in Canada have very high rates of unemployment (20 percent) and part-time employment (36.3 percent), and very low rates of participation in the labor force (below 50 percent). By comparison, only 10 percent of those listing "European" as their race/ethnicity were living below the low income cut-off, and for some European groups the figure was only 5 percent (Ornstein 2006: 72).[9] Immigrant women aged twenty-five to fifty-four had much higher unemployment rates than both immigrant men and Canadian-born women (Chui 2011: 24). Immigrant women of color only make 48.7 cents for each dollar that a white, male immigrant makes (Block and Galabuzi 2011: 12). In 2006, immigrants were more likely to have a university education than Canadian-born women and men; however, the unemployment rate for recent immigrants (2001–2006) was more than double for those born in Canada (Zietsma 2006). This unemployment is particularly pressing in Canada, which has the highest immigration rate in the world. It is projected that by 2020, 100 percent of the net growth of Canada's labor force will be due to immigration, and by 2030, 100 percent of Canada's net population growth will be due to immigration.[10]

In the context of multicultural Toronto, South Asian immigrants have been the largest minority group since 2006,[11] and thus are key players in the politics and practice of multiculturalism. In some ways they are an indicator of its successes and failures, and they are often invoked in government brochures as the success story of multicultural integration. But in contrast to the highly mobile South Asian high-tech workers that often underpin accounts of globalization and upward mobility, 44 percent of the Pakistani population of Toronto lives in housing projects on the city's periphery, meaning they fall below Canada's low income cut-off.[12] Different segments of the Pakistani community, including officials in the Pakistani embassy, members of the Canada-Pakistan Business Council, and local community workers and members, each (and independently of one another) reported to me rates of poverty at 80 percent. This varies dramatically from the state's official figure, which is significant on its own, but the community's perception that nearly twice as many live in poverty indicates an even more overwhelming sense of social decline. Regardless of the discrepancy, it is unquestionable that the economic and political conditions of Pakistani immigrants in Toronto contradict the state's rhetoric of equality within a model of difference.

These figures offer a glimpse into what has become a national concern. Foreign-educated immigrants earn over two billion dollars less than their Canadian-born counterparts do, mainly because they end up working below their educational and skill level.[13] Nonprofit agencies and government offices commonly acknowledge that it is very unlikely new Canadian immigrants will ever use their educational training again.[14] According to Statistics Canada, fewer than 25 percent of foreign-trained professionals in 2007 were working in their professions. Many authors have documented the ways foreign credentials and work experience become devalued, while others have considered the particular obstacles women encounter (Akbari

1999; Basran and Li 1998; Bauder 2003; Chakkalalkal and Harvey 2001; Ng 2006). However, what remains largely unacknowledged within this scholarship and within governmental agencies is the correlation between the nature and availability of jobs for highly trained immigrant workers, and the sustained perception that those workers are unsuited to such employment because of their foreignness.

Within Canadian vernacular practice, South Asians are called "visible minorities." According to Canadian sociologist Himani Bannerji (1993), the term visible minority emerged when Canadian immigration policy was reformed in the 1960s and 1970s. The concept developed from the federal Employment Equity Act, which defines visible minorities as "persons, other than Aboriginal peoples, who are non-Caucasian in race or non-white in color." According to Statistics Canada, "The visible minority population consists mainly of the following groups: Chinese South Asian, Black, Arab, West Asian, Filipino, Southeast Asian, Latin American, Japanese and Korean" (Statistics Canada 2009b). Bannerji (1993) argues that unlike the sister term, people of color, used in the United States, visible minority translates color into visibility, stressing both being non-white and politically minor actors. While the categories of "immigrant women" and "third-world women" are part of Canadian political-cultural language, "visible minority" emerged as the most common descriptor.

The race politics of the term have not escaped international scrutiny. In 2013, the United Nations Council on the Elimination of Racial Discrimination asked Canada to "reflect upon its use of the term visible minority," because it was perceived to be outdated and discriminatory.[15] In Toronto, I found that local community activists and organizers work with the concept of "racialized persons" in an attempt to draw attention to the process by which visible minorities become understood as racially Other. This rhetorical shift is described as a form of resistance to the term "visible minority," which activists understand as a state-produced category of belonging that centers a white subject to the exclusion of nonwhite people. In this book I use the term racialized person rather than visible minority, in an effort to move away from the language of state institutions and to align my critique with the concerns raised by activists and nonprofit workers. It is an important move as well because the term "racialized person" draws attention to the class dimensions of the processes of racialization, particularly in the case of foreign-trained professionals, which reconfigures their socioeconomic status and makes them downwardly mobile.[16]

I encountered this process during my time in Toronto. While doing research, I traveled by subway to both ends of the city—Scarborough to the east and Mississauga to the west—where many Pakistanis lived in government housing projects. In 2002, the Metro Toronto Housing Authority (MTHA) merged with other public-housing providers to form the Toronto Community Housing Corporation. The MTHA was established in the 1950s to house the economically marginal in an effort to eliminate the development of slums. Now the largest social housing provider in Canada and the second largest in North America, Toronto Community Housing accommodates 164,000 low- and moderate-income tenants in 58,500 households in 360 high-rise and low-rise apartment buildings in the city.[17] However, there is still an intense shortage of affordable housing, evidenced by the fact that as of July 2014 there were 170,000 people on the waiting list for Toronto Community Housing. Increasingly, within government housing projects there is a hierarchy whereby nonwhite people live in the more secluded, less safe, peripheral projects.[18] In an interview with the *Toronto Star*, Abdul Sheikh, president of the Scarborough Muslim Association, said that poor immigrants have very few housing options because they cannot provide local references for employment or past rentals. He cited ten apartment complexes in Scarborough in which Pakistanis and Indians form the majority of the tenants. In one, elderly and disabled tenants were trapped when the elevator was out of order for a month.[19]

In Toronto as it is across the globe, poverty is highly racialized and spatialized. According to a study conducted by Michael Ornstein of the Institute for Social Research (ISR) at York University, all twenty of the most economically disadvantaged ethno-racial groups in the Toronto census metropolitan area (CMA) are non-European (Ornstein 2006). According to Ornstein's study, more than half of the Bangladeshi, Somali, Afghan, and Ethiopian populations live below Statistics Canada's low income cutoff. The gap between those of European and non-European descent has been increasing over the past thirty years,[20] and the racialization of poverty has simultaneously increased; fourteen of the top twenty most economically marginal population categories have poverty rates between 30 and 40 percent (Ornstein 2006: vi). Ornstein puts the numbers in perspective: "For groups with 20 or 25 percent of people below the poverty line, we have to think in structural terms: about kids not completing high school, the low level of the minimum wage, the expense of good daycare, the problems of finding a job that uses their skills and credentials, the very high cost of housing and our governments' retreat from social housing over the last twenty years, and the effects of discrimination."[21] As of 2012, the poverty rate for racialized Canadians was three times that of other Canadians (19.8 percent versus 6.4 percent).[22] Despite all these facts including evidence of the racialization of poverty, the Canadian model of multiculturalism has been acclaimed as an international success story.

Sensing Multiculturalism

This book offers an ethnographic analysis of a multicultural state in crisis.[23] Since September 11, 2001, and in response to the intensification of anti-Muslim sentiment and violence against Muslims throughout the Western world, political leaders of purported multicultural states have attempted to understand the position of Muslims in the imagined West. Heads of state and citizens alike in the United States, Britain, France, Germany, and Canada (to name a few) are currently struggling to place minority culture within the politics of multiculturalism, identity, and difference. In 2009, French President Nicholas Sarkozy declared that the Islamic burqa was "not welcome,"[24] while in October 2010, German Chancellor Angela Merkel said that the attempt to build a multicultural society in Germany "has utterly failed."[25] In February 2011, during a security conference in Munich, British Prime Minister David Cameron argued that the United Kingdom needed a stronger national identity to prevent extremism, saying, "Frankly, we need a lot less of the passive tolerance of recent years and much more active, muscular liberalism,"[26] essentially calling for a return to a Westernized, patriarchal vision of citizenship.

Although multiculturalism is often touted as the foundation of Canadian society, it has never been an entirely coherent category, existing more as rhetoric and ideology than in policy and legislation. Canada was the first country in the world to adopt multiculturalism as an official policy, in promotion of Prime Minister Trudeau's "just society." Multiculturalism broadened the definition of Canadian citizenship by outlining a more inclusive model. However, when Trudeau first introduced it in 1971, multicultural policy did not have any enabling legislation. When it was eventually passed in 1988, the Canadian Multiculturalism Act outlined the tenets of multiculturalism, including to "promote the understanding that multiculturalism reflects the cultural and racial diversity of Canadian society and acknowledges the freedom of all members of Canadian society to preserve, enhance and share their cultural heritage"[27] The Department of Canadian Heritage further asserts, "Multiculturalism is a central feature of Canadian citizenship, in which every Canadian has the freedom to choose to enjoy, enhance or share his or her heritage, and the federal government has the responsibility to promote multiculturalism throughout its departments and agencies" (2007). Rather than a feature of Canadian society, multiculturalism became central to it.

Multiculturalism is a process, rather than an already determined social fact. Therefore, I do not use the terms "multiculturalism," "difference," and "identity politics" interchangeably. Instead, multiculturalism is understood as a state policy that directs social practices and interactions between diverse actors including governmental workers, nonprofit workers, and immigrant workers. These issues are examined from four perspectives: global trends of transnational labor migrations in late capitalism, the national context of a politics of multiculturalism, the local context of Toronto immigration policy and the foreign-trained professionals problem, and the everyday life experiences of Pakistani immigrants living in Toronto. These areas allow for an exploration of the relationship between processes of globalization and transnationalism and processes of subject formation and belonging.[28]

Until the 1960s, Canadian immigration policy was designed to create a "white settler" population, admitting those mainly from Britain, Europe, and the United States (Stasiulis 1999).[29] In the 1960s, there was a shift from assimilationist strategies—known as the anglo-conformity model, in which some immigrant groups were denied entry because it was believed they could not assimilate—toward the model of integration that prioritized preserving culture, known locally through the metaphor of the "mosaic" and later the "salad bowl." In a single generation, the city of Toronto was transformed from the "Belfast of the North" to one of the most racially and ethnically diverse cities in the world.[30] In 1998 it adopted the motto "Diversity Our Strength."

Scholarly writing about multiculturalism in Canada (outside of Québec) can be divided into three broad categories: multiculturalism as serving assimilationist goals, multiculturalism as a tool that co-opts the real interests of Canada's minority groups, and multicultural policy as meeting the needs of minority groups (Abu-Laban and Stasiulis 1992). The second category is crucial for my analysis here in its suggestion that multicultural policy focuses on culture while ignoring real material interests. For instance, Kogila Moodley argues that the ideology of multiculturalism focuses on the expressive parts of culture (such as food, clothing, and music), and therefore is not threatening because it "trivializes, neutralizes and absorbs social and economic inequalities" (1983: 326). The public discourse of multiculturalism acknowledges inclusion and creates a body politic that imagines itself to be accepting and tolerant of cultural difference, while in reality it ignores how immigrant bodies are being raced, gendered, sexualized, and then excluded on the basis of those differences. Within a structure of racial inequality, the inclusion of expressive parts of culture is contextually specific and occurs in tandem with economic marginalization (or exclusion).

This is clear in the operationalization of the sanitized sensorium. Cooking smells, for example, are acceptable in certain contexts and not others. A recent example in the province of Québec illustrates this. While in some ways Québec forms a kind of exception in the context of Canada, in that it is both inside and outside of the state project of multiculturalism, this rhetoric is not unfamiliar in national debates concerning immigration. In 2011, the city of Gatineau published a "statement of values" to try to help newcomers integrate. The councilor for cultural diversity, Mireille Apollon, a Haitian immigrant herself, said, "We receive immigrants from diverse horizons and cultures . . . behaviors aren't uniform around the globe. There can be irritants."[31] The document outlined a range of behaviors and expectations, including the importance of punctuality, that bribing officials is not okay, that violence is not justified even in "safeguarding honour," and that children should not be subjected to forced labor. Under "hygiene, cleanliness and quality of life," it suggests that it is important to curtail smells like "strong odors emanating from cooking."[32] Here, citizenship and legibility are encoded in bodily comportment ranging from a diverse series of factors including punctuality and smell, demonstrating the ways that the sanitized sensorium mediates belonging. Building on the work of scholars who have focused on the role of smell in excluding immigrant bodies (Manalansan 2006; Ong 2003; Walcott 2003), this example demonstrates the ways that food smells become signifiers of difference; they represent the uncontainable and unfamiliar, becoming indicative of an immigrant community's inability to assimilate.

My development of the concept of the sanitized sensorium follows the work of anthropologist Paul Stoller (1989), who has critiqued the overreliance on vision and text, advocating instead for embodied analyses that take the human sensorium into account. Building on this notion of engaging the human sensorium, Constance Classen (1993) has argued that sensory perception itself is a social and cultural phenomenon; thus "sign, hearing, touch, taste and smell are not only means of apprehending physical phenomena, but also avenues for the transmission of cultural values" (401). It follows, then, that the meanings of different kinds of sensorial phenomena—particular colors, smells, or tastes—will vary contextually and connect people to their environment. As Charles Hirschkind (2006) writes, "an inquiry into the senses directs us beyond the faculties of a subject to the transfers, exchanges and attachments that hinge a body to its environment" (29). Thus, exploring the senses demonstrates that sensation is not only an individual but also a social experience, one that connects the individual not only to others but also to their larger surroundings.

As I conceptualize it, the sanitized sensorium also pays attention to place and environment, signaling a broader range of phenomena. I follow Seremetakis (1994), who argues, "The sensory is not only encapsulated within the body as an internal capacity or power, but is also dispersed out there on the surface of things as the latter's autonomous characteristics, which then can invade the body as perceptual experience. Here sensory interiors and exteriors constantly pass into each other in the creation of extra-personal significance" (6). In this way, being attuned to the sensorium means also paying attention to the relationship between bodies, spaces, and objects. Food, music recordings, and clothing alone are material artifacts of specific cultures and cultural practices, but in relation to particular bodies they become a marker of their difference. Rather than just focusing on the experience of smelling, for example, being attuned to the sensorium makes us think about the broader environment in which particular bodies are located.

How do we understand the feelings invoked in the encounter between immigrant women and the greater public, in the response to bodily smells, the sight of headscarves or shalwar cameeze suits, or the sound of a foreign name? I use the term affect here, or what Massumi (2002) has called intensity, to map a terrain of bodily difference and sensorial readings of and by those marked as Other. Rather than spending time here differentiating between affect, emotion, feeling, and sentiment, which other scholars have done very well (e.g., Lutz and White 1986; McElhinny 2010; Sedgwick 2003), I instead look at the social work that these affects do. I am interested in the *encounter* part of the affective encounter. How do sensory and affective experiences serve to racialize and gender immigrant workers as more

and less fit to be citizens? Studies of the South Asian diaspora often explicitly or implicitly contend with questions of affective sensibilities, as they
bind people to their imagined homelands while simultaneously engender-
ing new forms of belonging (e.g., Grewal 2005; Maira 2002; Mankekar
2014).[33] Building on those and other studies of the racialization of South
Asian diasporic workers (Rana 2011), I explore the ways that sensory and
affective encounters shape processes of racialization and, in turn, delineate
the parameters of belonging.

This book explores the production of a South Asian global worker for
whom culture is a site of contestation (e.g., Radhakrishnan 2011; Upadhya
2008). For instance, Upadhya (2008) explores the ways "culture" is mobilized
to construct Indian IT professionals into competent global professionals,
which is also a means to continue to mark them as different. Radhakrishnan
(2011) looks at how Indian IT workers create a "global Indianness" by employing Indian cultural practices and transforming them into generic, mobile, Indian norms. Bringing together theories of multiculturalism, affect,
and the senses, I contribute to these studies of transnationalism, bodies, and
culture by theorizing how sensory-based perceptions of South Asian–ness
become signifiers of both inclusion and exclusion. This is demonstrated by
the different values certain things hold in distinct contexts; for example,
what is exotic and fragrant in the cultural festival becomes repugnant on
the job market. These kinds of embodied differences are critical in understanding the relationship between multiculturalism and colonial civilizing
projects. By focusing on women in the South Asian diaspora, I examine the
ways that perceptions of gender function as structuring devices and ideological constructs that delineate proper behavior for immigrant women and
their bodies. These perceptions become further complicated when com-
bined with other identity markers, including race and class, as I explore in
the chapters that follow.

Cultural Logics of the Body and Work

In Toronto there are more than one hundred settlement-services agencies
organized around ethnic identities (e.g., family services for South Asians,
or the Portuguese community women's center). Many of the women I interviewed revealed that they were given a series of flyers about settlement
services when they first arrived at the airport. During the course of fieldwork, I visited all of the agencies for South Asians and Muslims as well as

those specializing in labor. In general, I went to the most popular workshops for new immigrants and attended a total of fifty unemployment workshops over the course of eighteen months. I attended workshops that were profession-specific, such as those for nursing and engineering, as well as some that were organized around particular ethnic and religious identities (e.g., South Asian, Muslim). I found a serious discrepancy between the mandates of the centers, the expectations of participants, and what actually happens in the space of the workshops, as many participants had understood them to be placement centers. I also followed my interviewees as they navigated the politics and practice of multiculturalism in Toronto, which included numerous cultural festivals organized for what turned out to be the contested category of "South Asians," an issue I discuss in detail later in the book.

I spent a lot of my time in Toronto at the Center in the West End of the city on Bloor Street. From 1999 to 2000, they provided services to nearly five thousand women and children in the form of information, counseling, and advocacy; by 2011–2012, they provided services to 10,300 women. Founded in 1982, the Center caters to South Asian women immigrants at their first level of what nonprofits call integration; therefore, many of the clients are very new immigrants. Nonprofits use the term "newcomer" to denote an immigrant or refugee who has been in Canada for a short period of time (typically less than three to five years), and settlement services are often specifically geared toward newcomers. The Center held many types of educational workshops, from healthcare initiatives to social groups for senior women. I attended all the workshops for foreign-trained professionals. As time went by, settlement workers would ask me to sit in the front row to demonstrate to visiting instructors the seriousness of their pupils, as I was known for taking abundant notes. I sat in many lectures learning about pay equity and regulated professions, as well as how to fill out application forms for survival jobs such as cashiering.

These agencies occupy a critical place in relation to the state, for they are not state bodies—in that the workers are not considered governmental workers, and there is no government oversight concerning their practices—but they are state-funded and state-sanctioned, and thus are critical sites to witness the emergence of new forms of governance. The unemployment workshop leaders were overwhelmingly middle-class white women (all but one of the instructors I met were white women) who had followed a very similar trajectory of being stay-at-home moms just reentering the workforce after their children left for college. In some ways the placement of these white women, as mediators of culture and belonging, mirrors colonial-era practices in which the wives of administrators were tasked with "civilizing" colonized women by teaching them how to be good spouses and mothers. That women perform this reeducation is not coincidental and aligns with gendered notions of care and the feminization of care labor itself. The decline of the welfare state has led to new forms of governance that depend on the underpaid and undervalued labor of women.

As I discovered, settlement services agencies unemployment workshops focus on the cultivation of a particular kind of self, and the production (or attempts at the production) of a specific kind of body or racial erasure. Thus, the body becomes central in debates surrounding the lived experience of immigration as well as in the process of constructing citizenship. Within contemporary debates surrounding multiculturalism, struggles of identity are waged on immigrant bodies. These struggles remake ideas of citizenship and the nation in an era of global migrations and demonstrate a social order in which citizenship itself is based on bodily performance. Rethinking immigrant bodies as central to the making of national identity, rather than as a challenge to it, contradicts the whiteness naturalized as the center and subject of liberal multicultural discourse. As Aihwa Ong (2003) argues, "Women's bodies become the site, and the female gender the form, in a biopolitics of citizenship" (13). In this context, the female, immigrant body becomes a site of discipline for cultivating ideals of normative citizenship and appropriate modern womanhood. The white subject becomes dominant by defining himself against the subjugated person of color. In this sense, there is continuity with racialized attempts to incorporate the Other through the colonial enterprise, as anthropologists such as Ann Stoler (2002) have documented. In earlier historical moments, the smell of the low-wage immigrant was a mark of one's Otherness. This mark of the Other has not fully dissipated today.

These indicators of Otherness, along with accompanying bodily performances, are signifiers of one's ability to participate in the modern project. Modernity is an enlightenment discourse of progress and civility, and in this case it is written onto the bodies of immigrant women. This book explores modernity in its sensory and affective terms as embodied practice. As Shah (2001) contends, "The entanglement of race in modern science, governance and morality reveals a paradox at the core of modernity itself. Modernity, on the one hand, promotes ideas of universality and, on the other hand,

obsessively objectifies difference. In nineteenth- and twentieth-century science, social science, law and political systems, this contradictory process employed race as a category to explain the bodies, behavior, and cultures that
deviate from and defy presumably universal norms and standards" (5). Thus
for Shah, and in my own research, this tension between the modern, rational
state imposing seeming order on disorderly subjects is not an aberrant practice, but is in fact constitutive of modernity and the modern project itself.

In the contemporary moment, race, bodily difference, and hygiene
are sites of governance in the management and regulation of immigrant
women workers. Social theorists have long been concerned with questions
of the body and culture, from Marcel Mauss (1934) and *les techniques du
corps* to Pierre Bourdieu's (1984) formulation of habitus. Historically, hygiene and bodily smell have been tied to the intimate and embodied aspects
of modernity and the construction of the modern subject. As Timothy
Burke (1996) has argued in the case of colonial Africa:

> Changes in sanitation, personal cleanliness, and collective hygiene . . .
> were also brokered by a much more pervasive and subtle field of ide-
> ologies and institutions. . . . The intimate materiality of these readings
> of race through images of hygiene and appearance were reflected in a
> number of particular obsessions of whites in colonial society. Odor,
> for example, was a regular feature of white representation of their
> interactions with Africans, not only in Zimbabwe but throughout
> southern Africa. One Southern African ethnographer commented,
> "No description of the outward appearance of the Kafirs would be
> complete if we failed to refer to the omnipresent odour which streams
> from these people." (18, 21)

Burke also shows how hygiene has been tied to the production of a particular kind of citizen-worker as well: "When the English working classes
were hegemonically portrayed to be 'unwashed' or to have deformed bodies, these characterizations were always dialectically related to depictions
of colonial subjects as also having dirty or undesirable bodies" (18). The
sanitized sensorium has its historical legacies in such colonial civilizing mis-
sions that sought to discipline and cultivate a modern subject through the
regulation of bodily and affective sensations.

Sensory perceptions of bodies and hygiene influence ideals of what constitutes a good and modern worker in multicultural contexts. These sites
exist on a continuum of affective disaggregation that marks some bodies

as fit to be citizens and workers, while others are to be excluded from the national project. In the contemporary multicultural moment, the marking of immigrants' bodies as Other happens not only through a politics of erasure, but also through selective incorporation and the demand for a radical form of difference. Women are not, however, passive recipients of these sensorial regimes and embodied requirements for citizenship. While there are constraints on the possibilities for action (that is, women do need to work in order to survive), I found that they do find ways to exercise agency. For instance, as chapters 4 and 5 illustrate, Pakistani women resist state-produced categories of multicultural inclusion as "South Asian," while also positioning themselves as full citizens despite their current socioeconomic exclusion. Despite living in a state of precarity, they position themselves as Canadian subjects. Thus, the sanitized sensorium is not simply imposed onto immigrant subjects but is also a site of contest and protestation.

The Vulnerable Observer

This is a very personal story.[34] This work is animated by my own subject position as the daughter of a Pakistani Muslim, foreign-trained worker who spent her life in survival jobs and was eventually forced into retirement because of her inability to ever be fully integrated into the global market economy. I grew up in a housing project in Scarborough that was known colloquially as Ghetto-ridge, a cluster of three large, concrete buildings that had the dubious distinction of being one of the less dangerous government housing projects in the Greater Toronto area. Returning to those projects was difficult. I was confronted with the reminders of a childhood filled with the constant threat of home invasions, kidnapping, and rape that kept me largely confined to our small one-bedroom apartment and in the toxicity of the government-housing buildings themselves, which were filled with mold and cockroaches. As a child, I would stay up late—much later than my mother—partly for the quiet, since earlier evenings were often punctured by the neighbor's loud and bloody fights with her young child behind my bedroom wall. A nightly event, it never occurred to me to report them to the security guards permanently posted downstairs, since I had learned to keep my head down and not get involved.

Late into the night, I watched movies that promised some kind of escape from everyday life and what it meant to live in the projects. I would watch Audrey Hepburn and Cary Grant and dream of that kind of love and adventure. I also developed a love of horror movies; I liked to be scared by something that, for once, was knowable or understandable. These escapes were often interrupted by the realities of everyday life. Hungry one night, and in a roller-skating phase, I glided into the kitchen of the small apartment my mother and I shared. When I turned on the light millions of cockroaches scattered; they covered the walls, invaded the stove, and crunched under my skates. I had found them on my body and even in my mouth before, but somehow being faced with this many all at once was something I will never forget. I also remember with great clarity the night I heard rustling in the hallway, responded to a knock, and was confronted with the Canadian equivalent of the SWAT team about to descend on my neighbor, a known drug dealer. "Stay away from the door," the kind officer urged. I went to bed.

Growing up Other in a multicultural city has also had some lasting effects. A few nights ago I realized I hadn't been wearing deodorant all day. In bed, as my head rested against my arm, I could smell my body. The real smell of my body. A smell that I had worked really hard to fight against and that had always been a preoccupation of mine. And when I say preoccupation, I mean all-encompassing obsession. Going to a public high school with a large South Asian population, I was hyper-aware of the ways the smell of my body would codify my belonging. I used to bring deodorant with me in my school backpack, just in case my morning application was not enough to last the day. The ESL kids, the English-as-a-second-language students, were largely South Asian, or at least that's the way I remember it: young men with struggling facial hair, pressed shirts, and nice pants, but who my high school classmates talked about as smelling like "a mix of body odor and South Asian food." I didn't know, and didn't want to know the ESL kids. I kept my distance. I didn't really want anything to do with them because in high school, one false move, even a kind move like talking to a new student, could ruin your reputation forever. My mother would generally cook once a week and freeze food for us to defrost and eat. Those weekend cooking sessions often resulted in long, protracted arguments between us; she couldn't understand why I might be upset that my hair would smell like garam masala on Monday morning. I learned then that smell could racialize me.

I ran fast and far from Ghetto-ridge as soon as I could, to California, where I went to graduate school and then stayed for my own promise of a better life. Coming from an elite institution was not a problem while doing fieldwork in Toronto, since the women I interviewed were themselves well educated. Like my mother, the subjects of this book were professionals who had worked as doctors, engineers, or lawyers, and through their transnational migration were forced into poverty. Now I grapple with my own class status in the American academy, where the typical subject position of a South Asian living in the United States, and certainly in academia, is one of relative wealth and privilege. This means that I find myself constantly confronting the assumption that my parents are wealthy and that I grew up in a middle-class suburb. In Toronto, there was no shock that I myself had come from the projects; and in some ways, it is possible that to some of the women I met, my upward mobility represented what their own sacrifice could mean for their children.

It was hard to bear witness to another generation of immigrants living and growing up in these kinds of conditions when I returned. Faced again with the place that I had tried so hard to escape, I found myself over-identifying with some of my interviewees as I remembered my own experiences growing up. My childhood was not the same as that of my interviewees, and I am not the subject of my study; but it is important to acknowledge my own subject position. I bring this up in respect to those ethnographers writing during the reflexive turn in anthropology (e.g., Behar 1997; Rosaldo 1993) who asked scholars to question the objectivity of ethnographic methods, practices, and observations, and showed us that ethnography never happens outside the space of life experience or the lens of the ethnographer. As much as being an insider-ethnographer allowed me special access to the community, it also undoubtedly led me to take certain things for granted. The act of observing is not a neutral one; we are all vulnerable observers.

An Education

I begin this story of embodied downward mobility by addressing the question I received most in the field, "How does this happen?" To attempt an answer, chapter 1 examines the tension between two explanations for the sustained unemployment of foreign trained professionals: bureaucratic miscommunication versus bodily difference. In numerous conversations with a range of social actors in Toronto, the unemployment of foreign workers is universally understood as a problem of bureaucracy, while my fieldwork demonstrated that at the level of the everyday, unemployment is treated as a problem of the body. This chapter juxtaposes these two kinds of explanations to explore the space of contact between an imagined immigrant Other and an equally imagined sanitized West, and what it means to be a flexible or adaptable worker in late capitalism. Regulatory regimes that can be traced historically to colonial modernist projects of empire and civilization are still relevant in the contemporary sanitized sensorium, where certain aspects of Otherness have become a personalized deficiency to be trained away. Even so, in the current reality of global capitalism, there are some aspects of Otherness that should not be unlearned—for instance, the fact that women are undervalued as workers and thus can be paid less, or that there are appropriate affects encoded onto certain kinds of labor that are understood as "women's work."

Taking up this question of affective labor and embodiment, chapter 2 examines the colonization of the intimate labor that women do, in particular the notion of "care work" in a global perspective. Here I trace the ways that intimacy and affect become a pedagogical focus in training foreign nurses, which uses an affective register to attempt to produce docile bodies. This chapter focuses on a government-funded pilot project designed to help foreign-trained nurses become licensed in Ontario. These classes for foreign-educated nurses employ what I call "pedagogies of affect," which reproduce a racialized notion of femininity predicated on Westernized ideas about docility and deference. While other accounts of affect and labor have considered the role of gender, I seek to bring these important studies into conversation with race and gender-making in global contexts. As the training of foreign nurses demonstrates, when performing intimate labor immigrant women are expected to present themselves as docile and deferential. However, these expectations change yet again when women perform a distinct type of gendered cultural labor as the exotic representatives of radical, acceptable difference.

In the multicultural state, performances of cultural Otherness (during circumscribed moments such as cultural festivals) are necessary in order to validate state claims to liberalism and inclusivity, while real economic and material claims to inclusion are marginalized. Chapter 3 explores this disjuncture between what is vilified in the public space of government-funded nonprofit classrooms and what is valued in public celebrations of multiculturalism. Bridging the two contexts, the classroom encounter and the multicultural festival, brings the Janus-faced sanitized sensorium into relief. This chapter examines the contradictory calls for embodiment, focusing on a politics of the senses to try to understand the erasure of difference with regard to immigrant bodies, which must be cleansed and sanitized, and the simultaneous recognition of that very difference. I argue that these contexts say more about Western notions of both femininity and the Other than about the immigrant women themselves, who must negotiate this dual mode of interpellation.

How do women react to these sensorial regimes, to the multicultural state's requirements for citizenship? The last two chapters explore women's affective and sensorial experiences of racialization and precarity, and how they manage and move forward. Chapter 4 discusses the ways that multicultural state ideologies about citizenship exclude Pakistani women who refuse liberal constructions of "South Asia." This category is produced through a process of racialization that includes a range of actors and institutions at multiple scales, including the state, grassroots organizations, and even the practice of racism itself. The Pakistani women I spoke with often felt misidentified when culture is understood purely in terms of food, music, and clothing because it glosses them as Indian. The demand for recognizable difference, a radical alterity, rendered them invisible as Pakistani and hypervisible as South Asian. This chapter traces the discursive construction of "South Asia" in multicultural Toronto and how women distance themselves from a state-produced category that has done little to mitigate the precarious social and economic position they must deal with.

Precarity is not only an economic condition, but also a sensorial experience. This last chapter explores the sensorial and affective registers by which people come to understand their belonging (or not), how they respond to that sensation, and the incommensurability that marks them and attempts to interpellate them as second-class citizens. Like the uneven distribution of resources, precarity is also dealt unevenly, as the life histories I detail in this final chapter demonstrate. I explore women's understandings of citizenship, identity, place, and belonging, examining the ways women invoke discourses of a promising future in order to understand their liminal and marginal position. In so doing, they position themselves as good citizens deserving of full participation in the nation-state. Embedded in the narratives presented here are strains of hope and optimism, which illuminate important features of the affective dimension of precarity. Hope or promises of a better life provide a means out of the catastrophic present.

This is a story of what it means to live as a poor immigrant in Toronto—the hopelessness, the desperation, the lived experience of not being able to make ends meet. How does one maintain a sense of dignity when one's house feels unsafe, or one's daughter is not able to eat well? This book presents cartographies of impoverishment with the conviction that careful attention to seemingly intractable life circumstances offers new insights for the anthropology of the state and neoliberalism, critical studies of multiculturalism, the anthropology of the senses, the South Asian diaspora, and the performance of a global body. At its heart, this book seeks to understand what it means to live in a state of precarity and liminality as a subject of globalization and late capitalism.

CHAPTER ONE

BODIES AND BUREAUCRACIES

Moving to Ontario is one of the most important choices you will ever make. Ontario is a land of opportunity. It is a prosperous, democratic society built by the hard work of generations of immigrants. We hope that you will decide to make Ontario your new home. Our people are our greatest asset, and we welcome the talent and energy that newcomers bring to our province. In return, we offer opportunities and a quality of life that are second to none.—GLOBAL EXPERIENCE ONTARIO

Canada has the highest educated taxi drivers in the world.—INTERVIEW WITH FAISAL, president of a Pakistani-Canadian organization for businessmen

Khudija had been called to the front of the class by June, the instructor, and was told to sit as if she were at a job interview. June looked at her and said, "Always dress in plain clothes and in plain colors," which Khudija was wearing. An audience member called out that she needed to be more relaxed. Khudija shifted in her seat. June began calling out various instructions in the style of a drill sergeant: "Never put your bag on the table because it's not your table—put it on the floor, it's a sign of respect." Khudija fidgeted with her bag before putting it at her feet. June continued focusing on what Khudija was doing wrong. "It's alright to put your arm on the table, but don't lean on it; there is no right or wrong, but just don't be too forward; women can cross their legs, but don't switch crossing them too often, and don't tap your feet; be on time, get there early, take off your jacket because your appearance is very important; prepare your language, do not translate in your head; use simple sentences; have a firm handshake; change your

[handwritten margin note: disciplining the body]

name if it's hard to pronounce; be aware of nonverbal behavior; don't wear bright colors, and keep your traditional dress at home." Another member of the class called out, "It's like being a robot."

When class was dismissed, the participants shuffled out for lunch, but Khudija stayed and began eating her sandwich at the table. I didn't want to intrude, so I gathered my belongings and started to leave. "You know what they need to do?" she said suddenly. I turned around and asked, "No, what?" "The government needs to tell us we need to go through cycles [meaning that assimilation or integration takes time], and embassies back home should guide us better. I came to Canada because Canada said they wanted engineers. Here I am without a job." Despite the workshop's advertised focus of helping foreign-trained engineers find jobs, none of the instruction had considered the role of professional regulating bodies, how to get one's foreign credentials recognized, or even how to retrain for a different job in engineering. As Khudija and I learned that day, finding work meant learning what to wear and how to move one's body. These seminar instructors seem to imply that bodies can be rehabilitated—albeit piecemeal—by removing the shalwar cameeze, taking a shower, rehearsing an effective seven-second first impression, and making eye contact.

Khudija seemed small in that big room. The classroom had all the referents of institutional architecture and style—a brownish façade, polyester and metal chairs, large functional tables, and a blackboard. Khudija was in her thirties and had migrated alone from Karachi under the skilled-worker class. She had been living with her parents in Pakistan and was unsure if she wanted to get married; instead, she chose a life abroad as a potential escape from their expectations. But life in Toronto was not what she had expected. Despite being a professional engineer, she was working full-time at a large theme park on the border of the Greater Toronto area selling fast food. Further demoralizing to her was that the government had required her to prove she had $10,000 before she could enter the country, which left her feeling exploited. She explained, "To get a license [as an engineer] you need one year [of] experience in Canada; to get experience you need a license. The PEO [Professional Engineers of Ontario] requires engineers to apply for a license, and if you don't have experience you take four courses at $800 each plus $200 for the exam. I was invited to come here. Australia, New Zealand, Canada all have half-page ads in papers." Khudija's entry into the Canadian workforce had been tumultuous. Two different times she accepted work for which she was paid under the table, meaning it was undocumented; the first time was for a public transportation company conducting research and the second time it was teaching computer programs to engineers. In both cases they accepted her work but ultimately did not pay her, and she found herself with no recourse because all payment arrangements were to be under the table. Khudija was a victim of precarious employment and increasing "flexibility" in global labor regimes (Harvey 1990). While she may have qualified for welfare, she told me, "I don't want government funds. I want to work." Later she admitted, "It's hard for me to think of myself as unemployed. Every day I get up and I have nothing to do."

In numerous conversations with Torontonians approaching this issue from different angles—government agents, nonprofit workers, activists, journalists, and everyday citizens—the foreign-trained-professionals problem is universally understood as a problem of bureaucracy. For instance, one afternoon in August I was invited to the home of Kate, a local nonprofit worker and activist who had collaborated with a local employment-equity organization to author a document on flexible labor. She was also part of a study that examined the racial politics of hiring practices for temporary work agencies. They found that some local employers were trying to get temporary agencies to send them candidates with specific racial characteristics; in other words, they wanted white workers. As we sat in her backyard garden sipping lemonade, Kate pegged the unemployment of skilled immigrant workers as a problem that starts with the bureaucratic lack of coordination between the federal government's management of immigration and the provincial government's management of labor. Immigrants are funneled into settlement services, where they often find they need to be retrained because regulatory bodies, which control access to licensed professions, will not accept their foreign credentials. This bureaucratic miscommunication results in many taking survival jobs. This narrative, first told to me by Kate, was one I heard repeatedly and was provided as an almost self-evident explanation of how this could happen. These people, the story goes, were tragically caught in bureaucratic entanglements.

Over time I came to interpret this narrative of bureaucratic inefficiency as symbolic of the struggle to understand the role of government in the context of the rolling back of the welfare state. In these accounts, bureaucracy is impersonal and painfully rational. Foreign-trained professionals are mere casualties of this efficiency. Rather than addressing these bureaucratic shortcomings, the government has further intensified the bureaucratic matrix by funneling money into settlement-services agencies, which treat unemployment as a problem of the body and attempt to remold foreign bodies into modern global workers. The body is stripped bare to the skin, whereby its color, adornments, and movements mark the condition of one's belonging—and this happens when people are at their most vulnerable.

In this context, classrooms are the site of affective encounters between strange bodies and those who serve as gatekeepers of inclusion, illuminating the legacy of colonialism and the failures of the multicultural project. As Sara Ahmed suggests, "Through strange encounters, the figure of the 'stranger' is produced, not as that which we fail to recognize, but as that which we have already recognized as 'a stranger.' . . . The alien stranger is hence, not beyond human, but a mechanism *for allowing us to face that which we have already designated as the beyond*" (2000: 3; original emphasis). The rehabilitation of the immigrant body is based on the fantasy projection of an ideal worker who is to be constructed in the space of these workshops, where what constitutes appropriate bodily comportment for women is a racialized and gendered imagining of a global worker. Here we see the reinscription of Orientalist and colonial conceptions of a wild Other in need of domestication. I use the word "domestication" rather than "disciplining" because it references the taming of something wild, a kind of breaking in, like the training of a pet. To domesticate something is to make it housebroken, with broken being the operative word, involving the breaking down and rebuilding of bodies in the name of modernity and progress. From the seat of sensation, immigrant women's bodies are measured, deciphered, and codified as part of the metric of belonging.

Government-funded workshops are a critical site for racializing immigrant bodies as those refusing to conform to global economic standards. In the context of the global market, Pakistanis are decent workers as long as they stay in Pakistan; as immigrants to Toronto, they are matter out of place. These racial projects always and already see markers of race as problematic, and in these contexts, race is read as an obstacle regardless of skills. On the ground, culture or racialized difference is still an obstacle in a skilled immigrant worker's search for employment in Canada. Thus, *culture* and racialized bodily difference become barriers to full inclusion in the multicultural nation-state, which is predicated on accepting cultural difference. This is not simply a critique of multiculturalism—that Canada is not multicultural enough—but rather a demonstration of the contradiction that lies at the heart of multiculturalism when it operates as it is supposed to. In practice, multiculturalism concerns questions of food, music, and clothing, but not economic integration. This process leaves untouched not only social inequities in Canadian society, but deep-rooted inequalities in global capitalism.

These processes of domestication, these strange encounters, have a fundamental flaw: they are doomed to fail. Regardless of whether Pakistani women change their names, clothes, or smells, there are systemic barriers to their unemployment; some are easier to see, such as the nonrecognition of their foreign credentials, and some are less apparent, such as the inherent racism in discriminatory hiring practices. While racist imaginings of the ideal worker are still prevalent in contemporary Canada, as illustrated by Kate's study, these concerns are never explicitly addressed at the level of the everyday. As Kate illustrated, the most discussed explanation of the persistence of the foreign-trained-professionals problem is that of bureaucratic entanglements. These popular narratives, however, do not link bureaucratic functioning with racist ideologies. This chapter works to do just that by juxtaposing transformations in governance with their real-life implications in places like settlement-services agencies, painting a picture of the material and ideological barriers foreign-trained professionals face. I begin by explaining the bureaucratic matrix in place, including shifts in immigration policy as they pertain to labor and the role of regulatory bodies as gatekeepers. I then take a close look at the changing nature of work as expectations shift toward models of flexibility and adaptability in late capitalism, which themselves undergird transformations in immigration policy. Within that context, I situate and examine the practices of settlement services agencies as sites of strange encounters. Ultimately, we see how bureaucracy in Canada is not neutral, rational, or hygienic, but rather bureaucratic practice is a performance of neutrality and rationality. When faced with the irrationality of Other bodies, the constructedness of this performance becomes apparent and throws into stark relief the contradictions between multicultural policy and practice.

Bureaucratic Entanglements

Zubeidah is the person I had the most contact with in the field. She was my ally and friend. She was a counselor at the Center and in contrast to the unemployment workshop leaders, she understood the particular challenges and obstacles her clients faced. Her expertise was in one on one counseling. When we met she had been in Toronto for four years and had yet to feel established. Her husband had applied for entry hoping for a better life for the family, and ultimately left behind his job as an engineer in Pakistan. Before moving to Canada, Zubeidah ran a charity school for the underprivileged, worked in fundraising, and volunteered at a women's organization. She told me that she had a different picture of Canada before arriving. She thought it would be "a life without worries," but that they could always change their mind and go back if it did not work out. The process of immigration took two years, which is relatively fast compared to the average of six. Ultimately, she told me, it was the political situation that compelled them to leave Pakistan permanently, though she was reluctant to go into detail, perhaps wanting to leave the past in the past. For the first eight months her husband was unemployed and heard repeatedly that he was overqualified and possessed no Canadian experience, an exclusionary tactic that makes it almost impossible for new immigrants to establish themselves. One needs Canadian experience to find a job, but one needs a job to get Canadian experience.

Zubeidah said she felt disappointed in Canada because her life had completely changed. Her husband was working in sales and telemarketing to make ends meet, but still hoping one day to be able to return to engineering. Because of their financial difficulties in the first few years, she worked at Walmart as a sales associate in cosmetics and jewelry during the day, while her husband's job in telemarketing had him working at night. When she worked for Walmart she would leave home at 7:30 AM and get back by 6 PM, while her husband worked from 3 PM to 1 AM, which only allowed them to communicate through phone calls and notes. In my conversations with Zubeidah it was clear that different axes of identity including race, gender, class, and religion exacerbated her feelings of marginalization and increasing precarity. She said, "We felt things that all newcomers feel, only, at the time we thought it was just us, but now I know that all newcomers feel these things." They felt frustrated, desperate, and not fully established, waiting and hoping for better opportunities to materialize.

As Zubeidah's situation illustrates, contrary to a teleology of progress and improvement endemic to global processes, things have actually gotten substantially worse for skilled immigrant workers. Until 1980, new immigrants earned approximately 80 percent of the wage of a Canadian-born worker (Grady 2009: 28). Foreign-trained doctors and engineers arriving in the 1980s were more likely to find work in their professions than those arriving in the 1990s. For instance, a foreign-trained doctor arriving before

1980 had a 92 percent chance of working in medicine (not necessarily as a doctor) in Canada, but only 55 percent had that chance in 2001. Only 26 percent of foreign-trained engineers currently work as engineers (Boyd and Schellenberg 2008: 4, 5, 6). The trend is overwhelmingly one of decline.

In order to understand the downward mobility of foreign-trained professionals, it is important to situate this moment in longer histories of Canadian immigration policies, which over time have both helped and hindered transnational labor migration while also encouraging models of flexibility and adaptability.[1] In 1967, Canada introduced the points system in order to relieve the burdens of sponsored immigration, which resulted in the targeting of highly skilled and educated immigrants. The new system afforded immigrants points on a scale that marked their ability to "fit in" in Canada.[2] Since the 1970s, immigration to Canada from Asia, the Middle East, South America, and Africa has increased dramatically. Over time, the criteria under the points system have changed, as has the focus on occupational needs for skilled workers in the economy. In the 1967 model, the occupational categories comprised demand for one's occupation and a pre-arranged employment offer totaled twenty-five out of the possible 100 points. These criteria have shifted toward models of adaptability, as outlined below. Until the mid-1980s, Ottawa had been permitted to regulate immigration based on economic growth or decline in Canada. At that point, Brian Mulroney's government reformed immigration, resulting in increased immigration levels. His government kept the family-reunification class open in order to win votes from minority populations, but added the investor stream[3] for those with a net personal worth of more than $500,000 (Abu-Laban and Gabriel 2002).

Throughout that decade, the Canadian government allocated funding for a number of "settlement services" aimed at integrating Canada's immigrant, ethnic, and minority groups. Around this time, multicultural policy came into practice, which changed the framework for immigrant integration in Toronto. In addition to Indigenous people and the notion of the two "founding nations" (British and French), new cultural groups began to make claims on the multicultural state (Abu-Laban 2004). Thus, multiculturalism was developing at the same time that the welfare state was unraveling, but it was an ineffective solution to the material changes in citizens' lives.

During the 1990s, the postwar Keynesian welfare state dissolved and brought a shift from short-term changes to a more long-term understanding of economic growth.[4] The government of Canada's Liberal Party of Jean

Chretien, who served as prime minister from 1993–2003, created a new age of immigration by shifting toward neoliberal logics of integration and immigrant self-sufficiency (Abu-Laban 2004). Reinforced by the events of September 11, 2001, immigration policy was defined by three factors: the promotion of immigrant integration, attracting self-sufficient immigrants, and increased border security. While integration is a term that predates Chretien's government, it became a crucial hallmark of his mandate.[5]

In the 1990s, the government allowed more skilled workers to enter the country in an attempt to improve labor-market performance. The source countries for immigration also changed, as did language and work experience, resulting in a dramatic deterioration of the success of immigrant workers (Grady 2009). Increased immigration from Asia, Africa, and the Middle East (i.e., more nonwhite immigrants), and the less successful integration of those new immigrants, exacerbated the issue of legibility and drew attention to the practice of multiculturalism, in which inclusion did not seem to include economic integration for racialized people. Rather than acknowledging structural problems, the state put the responsibility on the individual worker to be entrepreneurial so that her individual failure was not seen as a failure of multicultural integration. Rhetorics of flexibility and adaptability in immigration policy have also been critical to the increasing marginalization of foreign-trained workers. A crucial shift that dramatically impacted the foreign-trained-professionals problem occurred in 1993, when the points system was modified to emphasize education over specific job skills; this shift was called the "human capital" approach, in contrast to the "occupational needs" approach, which finds immigrants to fill particular job needs (Grady 2009). Also privileged in the human-capital model is the ability of well-educated immigrants to adapt to the changing environment. Instead of points being allocated on the basis of profession, potential immigrants are now assessed in terms of their adaptability.

According to Citizenship and Immigration Canada, the "Adaptability Factor" was introduced in 2002 with the intention of affording points for personal features that may enhance one's ability to become successfully established in Canada, such as a partner's education, previous work in Canada, previous study in Canada, or arranged employment (Immigration and Refugee Protection Act 2002). Instead of points awarded on the basis of education or profession, now new immigrants would be assessed in terms of adaptability. However, in practice many immigrants who proved their potential to adapt were never given the opportunity to work in their field.

While the human-capital model has been used in Canada, in other countries skilled migrants arrive for specific types of work, and those with skills that are in high demand are given preference (Keung 2008). Under the current Canadian system, there is no correlation between the points system, the need for an immigrant's skills in the current job market, and the chance that Canadian employers and the professional regulatory bodies will recognize the immigrant's credentials.[6] These issues are exacerbated by the fact that there are three levels of bureaucracy that affect immigrants, yet none work together.

First, through a division of the federal government called Citizenship and Immigration Canada, the federal government manages immigration with stringent rules and high costs for admitting migrants. At this federal level, responsibilities are divided between this department and Human Resources and Social Development Canada. The first handles selection and settlement, while the latter is responsible for the labor market in general, though not specifically the labor of immigrants. Therefore, there is no federal department that handles the integration of immigrants into the labor market (Alboim and McIsaac 2007).

At the provincial level, the government manages job and language training. But because there is little communication between the federal and provincial governments, immigrants are recruited without a sense of provincial needs. In addition, there are approximately 400 self-regulated professional and trade regulatory bodies—thirty-five in Ontario—that set entry and training requirements, determine standards, and decide on the information they need to assess qualifications and credentials. Each regulatory body in Ontario is responsible for determining whether candidates may enter particular professions. As Kate and others believe, miscommunication between bureaucrats at different levels of government spins a web of bureaucratic entanglements in which individuals get caught.

Finally, at the municipal or local level, there is the intricate network of settlement services. The result is a model of governance in which both nonprofit governmental organizations and charitable organizations step in to fill the gaps left by the decline of the welfare state. Responsibility for the settlement of new immigrants now lies with state-funded, privately run organizations that have the task of integration—itself a politically charged concept utilized in government policy. Further, this practice of governance demonstrates a disjuncture between the rhetoric, policy, and daily practice of multiculturalism in Canada, which promises universal inclusion and yet marginalizes new immigrants.

Thus, the unemployment and underemployment of skilled immigrant workers in Toronto is sustained and naturalized at the intersection of different modes of governance and attitudes about race. Currently, there is a neoliberal scenario in which the state is still very much present: Canadian ideals of multiculturalism (including of openness to immigrants and cultural inclusion) still shape some parts of Canada's immigration policies, but these coexist with contradictory labor policies. This inconsistency creates the conditions within which immigrants can enter the country and try to find work, but then realize that once they arrive any failures at acculturation are understood as private and personal. Regulatory bodies have a deeply problematic role here; though they hold a disproportionate amount of control over the process, they are, themselves, unregulated. Thus, barriers to their employment, such as discriminatory practices by regulatory bodies that are detailed below, become recast as an individual failure and leave people like Zubeidah and her husband in a holding pattern waiting for something to materialize. In this system, the presumption is that employment is granted through a system of meritocracy, which ignores the material (nonrecognition of their credentials) and ideological (racism) barriers immigrants seeking work may face.

Regulating Professions

I met Sana at the same engineering session where I met Khudija. Sana firmly believed that only local engineers get internships because companies only want those locally trained. "The only useful part of these workshops," she asserted, "is the résumé component." She felt that if someone was taking a course in a settlement-services agency, that person should qualify for employment through federal labor programs, or that it would be more useful for them to update their knowledge of professional software programs instead of learning how to shake hands. She revealed to me that she had recently stopped friends from migrating to Canada. In fact, she admitted, "I was told not to come, too—they don't need skilled labor here, you just immigrate for low-level jobs. If they want people for cashiers, they should recruit these people." Sana had worked for a multinational corporation in Pakistan, but this experience did not count in Canada, so she had begun taking equivalency courses at the University of Toronto. She said, "The courses at U of T are the same as I took back home. WES [World Education Services] has their own equivalency; everyone has their own equivalency.

What's the use if there's no standard? They just want to take money from you." While the majority of skilled workers who apply for jobs are trained for regulated professions, the regulating process is as frustrating and myste-rious to new immigrants as it is to the nonprofit workers charged with the task of helping them through it.

In order to work in one of the regulated professions in Ontario, skilled immigrant workers are required to submit their credentials to provincial regulatory bodies to be licensed. To acquire such recognition, they are often required to take further courses, like Sana was doing, complete exams, and work under supervision for a set amount of time. Approximately 20 percent of the Canadian workforce consists of regulated professions,[7] yet regulations vary among provinces and professions. According to the government of Ontario, that means that "professions themselves set their own standards and register members of the profession." There is no univer-sal definition for a self-regulated profession, yet the government of Ontario has given thirty-five regulatory bodies the authority to approve who can practice in certain fields. Those regulatory bodies serve as gatekeepers to professions such as dental surgery, nursing, optometry, midwifery, occupa-tional therapy, architecture, law, social work, and teaching.[8] Twenty-two of them are in healthcare. The regulatory bodies vary considerably in size, capacity, and methodology; some conduct academic and other assessments internally, while others rely on national bodies to assess qualifications. Often there are no specific provisions on how to address the credentials of foreign-trained professionals.[9]

The shift to adaptability in immigration policy—from particular profes-sions to transferable skills—has made credentialing even more difficult.[10] There is no single government agency or department (at the provincial or federal level) that deals with accreditation, and there is no universal system in place to evaluate foreign credentials. Further, they often do not have the knowledge or experience to deal with educational systems in other coun-tries (Zaman 2006). The issues with accreditation that I identified involve skill utilization on the labor market, recognition of foreign credentials, in-tegration of skills, and discrimination. Vague terms circulate throughout the credentialing process, such as "ensuring a candidate's education is equiv-alent" or "substantially equivalent" or "comparable to Canadian trained" (Ontario Immigration 2005b).

Engineering is one of the few fields that has been well researched. It has the largest group of immigrant professionals waiting to become licensed, and exemplifies the difficulties new immigrants encounter when dealing with regulatory bodies. The Ontario Society of Professional Engineers, a professional advocacy organization, reported over 40,000 foreign-trained engineers in Ontario between 1996 and 2002.[11] Since 1937, the Professional Engineers of Ontario (PEO) has had exclusive rights to license engineers to practice in Ontario. This self-governing association is the largest engineering regulatory body in Canada, with more than 66,000 licensed members. The PEO has the power to develop prerequisites (including training and experience criteria) as well as establish a code of ethics for all engineers in Ontario, a final criterion being that they must be "of good character and reputation" as determined by the PEO (Girard and Bauder 2007: 41–42).[12]

As early as 1989, a provincial task force determined that access to regulated professions in Ontario was unfair and unequal, stemming from the fact that academic credentials and work experience were devalued, exclusionary tactics were being used, unnecessary testing was required, and requirements were constantly changing (Cumming et al. 1989). In response, the Ontario government contracted an independent organization, World Education Services (WES), to assess credentials, which were more often that not described as useless by the women with whom I spoke. As Sana pointed out, the results were not always accepted by different employers, who insisted on their own assessments. I spoke with Dennis, a representative of WES, to get another perspective on the service.

There are currently three organizations designated by the Canadian government that can assess foreign credentials: Comparative Education Service at the University of Toronto School of Continuing Studies, International Credential Assessment Service of Canada, and World Education Services. I focus on the latter because it was the one most often used by the women with whom I spoke and the one almost exclusively recommended by the workshops in which I participated. WES is a nonprofit agency founded in 1974 in the United States and has been in Canada since 2000. It is designated by the minister of Citizenship and Immigration Canada to provide assessments of foreign education and credentials. Each assessment costs $180 or $280 for those wanting a course-by-course analysis, which WES requires for education licensing and regulation.[13] When I asked Dennis how people hear about WES, he said, "Outside of Ontario, we're referred to by Visa offices." It was difficult to get Dennis to explain their credentialing process. In response to questions, he would continually hand me another brochure describing a different aspect of their service. For example, WES will consider whether the degree-granting institution in one's home country is recognized by the Ministry of Education in that person's home country. If not, the report that WES produces to assess one's credentials will be written differently. According to Dennis, "For example, considering a bachelor of civil engineering from China, what were the admission requirements? Exams taken, high school finished? But it varies from institution to institution. When it comes to evaluation, it's not based on course matching, if you're missing one course, [that] doesn't mean you can't get the equivalent; we look into the scope of programs, the depth of programs. We give equivalency when we can find similar programs of study in the Canadian system." The widespread problem is that their findings are not accepted everywhere, effectively making them of little value.

Each time an evaluation occurs, it is a subjective review of an individual's credentials—and of the individual herself, particularly noted in the fact that the final criterion by which engineers (among those in other professions) are accredited is that they must be "of good character and reputation," an inherently subjective assessment. When Sana arrived in Canada, she found that recruiters would not even accept her résumé. She had recently attended a job fair organized by a settlement-services agency, but she said it was "a waste of time for engineers," as not a single engineering firm attended. "Why can't we work here?" she asked. The Canadian multicultural rhetoric of adaptability and transferability comes into stark relief through the discrepancy between the system as envisioned and the real-life actions of the people responsible for implementing it. Transferability implies the ability to transfer skills, credentials, and accomplishments from one cultural context to another. What occurs, however, is a global hierarchy of class and accomplishment in which skills and achievements cultivated in a different cultural context are rendered not just inadequate, but incommensurable in Toronto.[14]

An example from the Center demonstrates the bureaucratic obstacles concerning regulatory bodies that these women encounter. One day early in July I attended a workshop on teaching qualifications, more specifically what a group of South Asian women could do with foreign teacher training. There were two representatives from the Ontario College of Teachers, which regulates the profession. One of the attendees that day, Uma, had been working as a teacher in India for eighteen years and was upset at the prospect of paying $10,000 more for training. To teach in Ontario, at the time of my fieldwork, one needed at least a three-year university degree and one year of teacher training. There were approximately fourteen requirements that people needed to fulfill in order to have their foreign credentials evaluated. During the workshop there was a debate over the need for official documents from institutions where one received their training. Uma argued that it is difficult to get documents from India, which is why she paid the embassy a large amount of money to have her documents translated and stamped with an official seal before migrating. Zubeidah, in her role as counselor, added that an adverse political situation may also make it difficult to get documents mailed out of a country. The two presenters asserted that there was no flexibility in this policy. After they left, the participants spoke with frustration about how it would take about two years to get those kinds of documents from India or Pakistan. The Ontario College of Teachers charged $409 for evaluations, $100 of which was the membership fee to the organization, which is not refunded if an application is rejected. When I asked the representative about that, she assured me that the women would get a tax break, which to her was a substantial benefit. There was little understanding of the injury these roadblocks created. A tax break would not offer someone back her time or resources if she were to be denied, let alone remunerate her for the loss of wages during that time.

The regulating bodies operate with a logic of bureaucratic efficiency that fails to take into account the everyday obstacles people can encounter and the urgency of their situations. Part of the bureaucratic present consists of rationalizing logics that are inconsistent with real-world realities. The fact that it would take two years to get documents sent from India or Pakistan is incommensurate with bureaucratic logics in place to understand them as foreign workers. Hage (2009) theorizes that there is an "existential mobility," the "sense that one is going somewhere," that is a feature of the contemporary moment. "Even when the bus does not come, even when people are feeling stuck in a queue that is not moving, they heroically keep on queuing. And this is self-reproducing: the more one waits and invests in waiting, the more reluctant one is to stop waiting." Thus, Hage points to the way people must bargain with themselves and with larger social forces at play to justify their life choices. The more time one puts in, the more likely one is to put more in—a phenomenon I witnessed in the space of settlement centers, as women came in day after day to work on résumés, send them to potential employers, and attend workshops and social gatherings. Always and ever present in their minds was their unemployment and the wait for something to materialize. Workers participate in this waiting, and different modalities of governance work in tandem to discipline subjects in

this task. The two years it might take to get documents mailed from Pakistan or India is inconsequential to regulating bodies, but that length of wait
time has the effect of slowing the settlement process, using up savings, and
forcing workers into temporary, contingent labor.

The systematic mistreatment and devaluation of immigrant women
workers is overlooked because of the ways neoliberal logics individualize
success or failure on the job market, which are actually indicative of state
failures under late capitalism, but which do not erase racial politics that came
before. Instead of addressing social inequality, the Adaptability Factor in
Canadian immigration policy calls for the increasing flexibility of workers.
The imperative to be a "flexible worker" (and the failure to perform as one)
becomes a site of individualized failure. This kind of performance, or willingness to be flexible, while being central to contemporary configurations
of work, has historical precedents.

Adapting to Late Capitalism

The discourse of adaptability-as-flexibility has famously been theorized as a
condition of postmodernity endemic to transformations in labor, from the
factory to flexible accumulation. David Harvey's (1990) work on flexibility
is widely used in anthropological theory to understand the changing nature
of work since the 1970s. Characterized by "flexibility with respect to labor
processes, labor markets, products, and patterns of consumption," flexible
accumulation, in Harvey's terms, arose in contrast to the rigidities of Fordism (Harvey 1990: 147). Fordism refers to a system of labor exemplified by
the emergence of factory-line assembly labor as a system of mass production. While it took hold in the post–World War II period (from the late
1940s to 1960), its roots were in Henry Ford's early-1900s Dearborn, Mich-
igan, assembly plant. There, Ford developed a system that deskilled labor so
that the people who performed it could be interchangeable. Workers had to
be socialized into this form of labor, which required long hours of tedious
movements. For their work, laborers would receive a middle-class income
to be able to live a middle-class lifestyle (Lewellen 2002). This system transformed through the intensification of the circulation of capital and goods
across national boundaries and is what Harvey calls flexible accumulation.
Some have articulated this transition as one in response to the rigidities
of Fordism. For example, Emily Martin (1994) has written of this transition: "Gone is the linear work sequence of the moving assembly line, its

machinery dedicated to mass production and mass marketing. Instead, the organization is a fleeting, fluid network of alliances, a highly decoupled and dynamic form with great organizational flexibility" (209). Flexible accumulation "is characterized by the emergence of entirely new sectors of production, new ways of providing financial services, new markets, and above all, greatly intensified rates of commercial, technological, and organizational innovation" (209). This flexibility moved beyond the circulation of capital and goods and led to transformations in the nature of labor itself.

As discourses of flexible labor regimes suggest, flexibility in the new global economy calls for accepting temporary, contract, or part-time work for low wages, no benefits, no sick leave, no pension, and no insurance. According to Henry and Franzway (1993), flexibility refers to a number of different practices (some potentially competing): financial flexibility (wages); numerical flexibility (hours, workloads, or numbers of workers); and functional flexibility (multi-skilling and broad-banding). The area of numerical flexibility has posed the most problems for women workers and for unions, as it is associated with casual, part-time, and nontraditional working arrangements. Almost all labor battles of the 1990s focused not on wage issues, but on the enforced casualization of labor (e.g., the United Postal Service workers' stand against "part-time America") (Klein 2000). Corporate logic is increasingly geared toward a reserve of part-time, temporary, and freelance workers. Production is increasingly relegated to contractors, but clerks are still used to sell products at points of purchase. This corporate logic has been successful in delegitimating clerks as workers in need of job security, livable wages, and benefits. Retail and service employees are infantilized as those earning pocket money over those relying on paychecks. In the United States, service and retail work now account for at least 75 percent of total employment and Walmart is the largest private employer in the United States. Many of the same corporations not offering livable wages to their clerks are also the same corporations that do business in export processing zones (areas that are sealed from local governments, where goods are manufactured with no import or export duties), reducing their obligations to workers at both the production and service ends. In Canada, one third of part-time workers want but cannot find full-time work. The part-time classification is often a technicality, such that workers are kept just under the forty-hour mark so companies do not have to pay overtime benefits or even guarantee full-time hours.

Women have suffered the impact of global transformations, as they have become the model flexible worker. On the global market, precarity emerges through various practices that promote adaptability and result in making women into cheap workers. Anthropologists have problematized the ways multinational corporations have incorporated women as a reserve pool of labor (Fernandez-Kelly 1983; Ong 1987). As Freeman (2000) argues, "Why and how women's labor comes to be defined as cheap is, in fact, a complex process in which gender is created, contested, and refashioned in particular, culturally specific ways. Women are no more 'naturally' cheap labor than they are 'naturally' docile or nimble fingered relative to men" (106). Thus, the devaluation of women's work is a result of social and cultural practices that systematically devalue women themselves.

There is a significant body of literature on women in increasingly feminized labor regimes, ranging from care work as nannies or nurses to the service industry, due to what is understood to be women's inherent patience and motherly abilities (Boris and Parreñas 2010; Calliste 1993; Das Gupta 2009; Flynn 2009). Women are understood to be perfect for work in underpaid and undervalued offices as part-time, temporary, or casual workers. Seen as wives and mothers, their work is not considered a priority in their lives, but instead is a way to supplement the income of their husbands or provide pocket money. Professional immigrant women enter survival jobs that they will likely never leave—an adaptation that appears to be aberrant but is actually intrinsic to the racial regime that deskills workers. This turn toward adaptable labor regimes exists within a neoliberal logic of self-care, so that not only is responsibility for success relegated to the individual (with little risk to governmental processes), but it is to blame for what is perceived as the immigrant's own inability to succeed. Immigrant women also face additional financial and time constraints, such as supporting their families while paying to upgrade their skills (Zaman 2006), what Hochschild (2012) has called "the second shift." Thus flexibility in this process means waiting; tolerating bureaucracy; and adapting to little work, few benefits, and inequitable treatment, all of which ultimately leads to precarity. A lived experience illustrates the frustration of these demands to be flexible.

One cold afternoon I went to meet Saima, a particularly disheartened participant from one of the many unemployment workshops I attended. Her story is indicative of those of other women I met through centers for foreign-trained professionals. Saima was a pharmacist from Karachi who had earned her Bachelor of Science in Pharmacy from the University of Sindh in Hyderabad. She had a raspy voice and was in her mid-thirties. When we met, she had been unemployed for three years while she actively searched for work, sending her résumé to any and all organizations that seemed possible. She had even decided to return to school and had received her diploma as a pharmacy technician. She was very talkative and outspoken about her experiences looking for a job, at times becoming passionate about them. She asserted, "I have the education, and experience, and yet no one will hire me." She now believes that "in Canada you have to complain about your problems openly or everyone will think you are all right," an affective sensibility she was uncomfortable with, accustomed as she was to keeping her problems to herself.

Saima had moved to Toronto alone as a single applicant. She waited at length in Pakistan for a visa, which was followed by the rush to get to Canada and find work immediately upon arrival. She had not returned to Pakistan to visit since she left. She said she would visit one day, but would never live there again because she considered it to be politically unstable. Saima had spoken to me as if I was a bureaucrat until she learned that my mother is Pakistani, at which point she began talking to me more like a friend and less like a government worker. She said it "feels like Indians and Pakistanis don't stick together in Canada—they're scared, we need unity." Although she said she feels Canada is her country, she believes "they don't like our people," pointing to the systemic and sustained racial discrimination she felt. She went on to say, "I was independent in Pakistan. It doesn't feel good here because I don't have a job." She, like Zubeida, expressed feelings of boredom and of having nothing to do, seemingly waiting for work to materialize. She asked me if her experience was similar to those of other women, and when I told her that yes, sadly, her experiences did resonate with others, she seemed almost relieved.

Most of the women I met participated in numerous workshops at a range of different settlement-services agencies. I found, somewhat surprisingly, that the inability to find work after participating in these workshops did not necessarily mean that participants found them unhelpful. For instance, Saima vacillated between blaming Toronto for her struggles and blaming herself. She attended numerous workshops in settlement-services agencies, but rather than blaming their content or the bureaucracy of regulatory bodies, she argued that she was not prepared enough and that she should have studied more. She seemed to be internalizing her inability to get a job. This sentiment was echoed repeatedly by women who felt that their qualifications did not matter as much as how they presented themselves as middle-class Canadians. "There's diversity here," Saima said, "but in a sense of dress, people don't accept you. I only wear shalwar and cover my head at home."

Foreign-trained professionals are disciplined to the rhythms of late capitalism, which unevenly distributes what were once imagined to be rights and entitlements, and are taught to inhabit precarity as a regular feature of social life. Thus, these kinds of classes maintain deep inequities in global capitalism by enabling the prospering of some to the detriment of others. An attention to the everyday encounters with governmental and nongovernmental agencies illustrates the mundane ways that such calls for adaptability are sustained, stretching out one's sense of time in diaspora, trapped in a purgatorial bureaucratic matrix that strips people of their former identities as professional workers and refashions them into downwardly mobile subjects.

Saima's narrative illustrates the complicated dynamic of time and space in processes of migration. Saima is in a state of waiting, feeling like she is doing everything she can on a day-to-day basis, with little result. Saima was frustrated, unhappy, and vulnerable to these global transformations in the meaning and exercise of work. Her waiting is representative of enduring unequal relations of power in late capitalism, which has reconfigured her from a successful pharmacist to an unemployed woman of color, a downward mobility made possible by immigration practices and seeming bureaucratic error, and yet treated as a result of her Otherness. She once imagined herself to be a mobile worker, but found herself stuck in time, a flexible subject at the mercy of bureaucracy. As she waits she is made only too aware of disparate power relations that reproduce her social location. In this context of calls for increasing flexibility or adaptability, bureaucracy and new modes of governance have intensified to take up the challenges of a devolving welfare state.

Settling Bodies

On a trip to Toronto in February 2010, I saw countless advertisements in subways announcing government-funded employment services. A new set of advertisements had appeared that were seemingly directed toward Canadian employers—advertisements about hiring foreign-trained women workers, but not speaking with or to them. In the most popular advertisement, colorful images of women's faces sat above text that read, "You could look all over the world to find star employees. Or you could look at your employees from all over the world." The smaller text read, "Internationally trained businesswomen are a valuable resource, yet often overlooked in the workplace. . . . This Program is designed to help them overcome the cultural challenges they face in Canadian business and turn them into powerhouse employees." The voices of women disappear completely in these advertisements, as business and government interests converge regarding how best to use these women and their skills. In fine print, the ad had a logo for the province of Ontario, under which was written that this program of skills training was funded by the provincial and federal government.

Rather than address bureaucratic shortcomings having to do with foreign accreditation or the practices of regulatory bodies, the bureaucratic matrix in Toronto has become intensified. A major transformation in Canadian society in the 1990s was the formation of the "shadow state" (Mitchell 2004), referring to the increasing scope and power of voluntary organizations located between the state and its citizens. These shadow-state institutions, such as settlement services, are rapidly increasing, as is the degree of control they have over the space between the state and its citizens. In Toronto, settlement services have historically been constituted through voluntary self-help organizations focused on ethnic and religious categories. The government used the pre-existing settlement-service infrastructure at the community level in order to channel funding to private providers (Siemiatycki et al. 2003).

These institutions are not particular to Canada, but are found in many different cultural contexts. In India there has been the emergence of "GONGOS," or governmental non-governmental agencies, charged with the task of women's empowerment (Sharma 2008). Similarly, Rose (1996a) has described the "quango-ization" of the state, referring to quasi-autonomous non-governmental organizations. Quangos have proliferated to take over numerous governmental activities such as regulatory, planning, and (crucial in this discussion) educative functions (Rose 1996a: 56). Instead of decreasing government involvement, the growth of these organizations introduces a new mode of governance marked by the creation of mechanisms that operate on their own.

The growth of the shadow state in Canada has been accompanied by a redefinition of the role of the state and its obligations in providing welfare.

This neoliberal turn corresponded with a decline in direct social services provided by the government as the state began to contract services to institutions. The government of former Prime Minister Brian Mulroney (1984–1993) used this model to limit the role of the Canadian welfare state dramatically, while still maintaining legitimacy despite a direct decline in social services (Mitchell 2001: 167). Borrowing from former U.S. President Ronald Reagan, Mulroney and the Progressive Conservative Party used the liberal rhetoric of freedom and choice to mark this shift in the way services were provided. Mirroring the British Conservative Party Manifesto of 1979, the new state proclaimed, "In the community, we must do more to help people to help themselves and the family to look after their own. We must also encourage the voluntary movement and self-help groups acting in partnership with statutory services" (Mitchell 2001: 167). The rhetoric of "freedom" and "individual choice" entered the Canadian vernacular of social services as citizens were instructed to help themselves. On the ground, government resources have been funneled into settlement services to resolve the problem of unemployment, rather than directly addressing issues related to the credentialing process or the structural problems inherent in immigration policy.

Market logic has been extended to key state functions, such that even if direct services have not been contracted out, state bodies are organized around an enterprise model. Risk becomes the problem not of the state but of the individual, who is now "the entrepreneur of his or her own 'firm,'" meaning individuals are responsible for governing themselves (Gupta and Ferguson 2002: 989). Liberal democracies provide examples of neoliberal forms of governmentality in which power is decentered so that citizens will participate in their own self-governance. Michel Foucault (1991) theorized the concept of "governmentality" to refer to the processes through which the conduct of a population is governed. This involves not only the state in the form of institutions, agencies, and their accompanying discourses, but also techniques of self-regulation and discipline. Within modes of liberal governance, there is a critical connection between the government of the state and the governance of the self. I follow Gupta and Ferguson's (2002) assertion that governmentality explores mechanisms of government that "cut across domains that we would regard as separate: the state, civil society, the family, down to the intimate details of what we regard as personal life" (989).

Two policy shifts occurred in 1995 that changed the ways social services are administered in Ontario, one at the federal and one at the provincial level; in effect, these changes delegate responsibility to lower levels of government (Ontario Council of Agencies Serving Immigrants 2008). First, former Prime Minister Jean Chretien's government transferred responsibility for settlement to the provincial governments via a "settlement renewal" process, and second, the Progressive Conservative government of Ontario dramatically reduced funding to settlement services, relegating responsibility to provincial and municipal governments (Richmond 1996). Since 1995 the majority of Ontario settlement services have been administered through purchase-of-service agreements, primarily between the Ontario government and nonprofit organizations; Citizenship and Immigration Canada only provides funding to a few settlement services through the Ontario Administration of Settlement and Integration Service (Richmond and Shields 2004). This transfer of responsibility to the private sector was formalized in the early 2000s.[15]

Settlement services are primary sites in which new immigrants attempt to become settled and acclimatized; they are even advertised to new immigrants at customs and immigration upon arrival at Pearson International Airport in Toronto. Women repeatedly told me about how they were quickly funneled into settlement services as the acceptable (and expected) next step in their immigration process. These services include employment workshops, language training, interpretation and translation services, housing services, and legal services. Broadly conceived, there are now two types of settlement services: large agencies that provide multiple services, and smaller settlement services that often target specific ethnic or religious identities. There are more than one hundred of these small settlement-service agencies, including Family Services for South Asians, the Portuguese Community Women's Centre, and the Welfare Center for Muslims. In Toronto, I visited all the South Asian and Muslim organizations available, interviewing nonprofit workers as well as women who came into the centers, and made it a priority to seek out and participate in all the unemployment workshops. There were three types—those that lasted months, those that lasted a few weeks, and those that lasted a few days—and I participated in many of each. I attended workshops that were geared toward specific professions as well as those for immigrants from particular countries. While I visited all of these agencies during the course of my time in Toronto, I spent a lot of time at the Center.

As I critique the shadow state in the form of these agencies, it is important to say that while any analysis of the contemporary state must contend with questions of bureaucracy and neoliberalism, as Julia Elyachar (2012) argues, "neoliberalism has become a shorthand way of signaling all that is wrong in the ethnographic present" (76). Rather than offer a simple critique of bureaucracy and the neoliberal state, I want to engage with these forms of governance by asking empirical questions about the specific geographical, political, and historical configuration of neoliberalism and its *particular* effects. So while some macro critiques of neoliberalism (e.g., Barry, Osborne, and Rose 1996) tend to imagine bodies in universal modes (such as white and male), here I take up questions of multiculturalism, race, and gender in the making of subjects. In this context, though the specter of the state looms large, the responsibility for becoming settled, and becoming Canadian, now lies with the individual and her body.

Racialized Otherness Is a Deficiency to Be Trained Away

During fieldwork, I discovered that what underlies transformations in the governance and the nature of work is the production of a particular kind of laboring body. In the space of these workshops, immigrant women are trained to be modern, flexible workers and to erase traces of their Otherness to be marketable on the global stage. What flexibility means in this context is the production of a flexible body. Instructions regarding dress codes and bodily practice (including a range of factors from hygiene to eye contact) direct the question of unemployment away from systemic disjunctures (e.g., immigration policy changes, bureaucratic miscommunication, and discriminatory hiring practices) and present them as containable within individualized logics of self-improvement and domestication, seemingly suggesting that it will all work out if one adheres to the directive to learn how to be culturally appropriate, which effectively recolonizes the bodies of immigrant women.

One such workshop, through the Job-Search Training (JST) program, illustrates this. The program houses workshops for ethnically diverse audiences consisting of both men and women who were skilled immigrant workers in a variety of professions. JST was run through a local center housed in a community college and was started after the center was approached by a government body called Human Resources Development Canada. Although the program is government-funded and -initiated, the content is entirely determined by the workers at the center. JST has a four-week program and a four-day program; the goal is for the latter to be a workshop that can be presented at a number of different centers throughout the city. Stacey, the project manager, described the four-week workshop as a more intense version of the four-day workshop. Both are meant to cover accreditation and certification, cultural expectations in the workplace (including inappropriate behavior), employment standards, and networking. The four-week workshop was held Monday to Friday from 9 AM to 3 PM with a maximum of twenty pupils. The four-day workshop is three hours a day and takes twenty-five students. Participants are mainly engineers, teachers, and lawyers, and included both men and women.

The account I offer below was from day three of a four-week workshop that was unexpectedly low in enrollment, at only fifteen participants, roughly evenly divided between men and women; the majority were South Asian, with two Mexican women and one Iranian man. The leader, Sharon, started with "Cultural Expectations" and encouraged us to think about what kinds of skills and expectations we would want if we hired someone. Her list included the following: be respectful, work in a team, have a positive attitude,[16] work under pressure, be punctual (which she added was one of the most difficult issues for foreign-trained professionals not used to Canadian standards of time management), be independent, adhere to dress codes, and be flexible. This need to be flexible is, as I describe above, a result of transformations in governance and policy that have made it almost impossible to be recognized as a skilled worker, and yet in practice is projected onto the bodies of immigrant women. This call for a race-neutral bodily and cultural practice also highlights the ways that racism is perhaps implicitly understood to be part of the problem (and one that transcends transformations in governance), and yet this form of instruction is never taught as anti-racism training. Rather, it is about how to manage oneself to best avoid discrimination.

The participants furiously took notes as Sharon immediately launched into another list—this one concerning the interview in particular. "You must express confidence," she stressed. "Be prepared, be able to discuss your skills, watch your behavior, and be sure to make eye contact, even though it may not be part of your culture." In response to a question by a woman about dress, Sharon suggested, "It's always better to overdress than under-dress." Another woman raised the question of eye contact: "When you deal with older people in our culture, you don't look them in the eye. It's disrespectful." Sharon quickly responded, "Here, eye contact is a sign of respect. It gives people attention; it lets them know that you're listening.

It makes you seem credible and sincere." With these instructions Sharon illustrated that "home country" conventions must be cast aside in the performance of a confident global worker, who must express respect, attention, credibility, sincerity, and the appearance that one is listening. The control of one's body, dress, and culture is critical in the immigrant rehabilitation or domestication project. That immigrants must be taught these qualities suggests that they do not possess them. They will be judged inadequate until they demonstrate their domestication and effectively reposition themselves in terms of their relationship to culture.

Sharon was a white Canadian woman secure in her own articulations of business culture and confidence, which were presented as self-evident truths even though they were entrenched in whiteness and masculinity. Her positioning was made apparent to me in another workshop in which the leader was not a white woman (one of only two I encountered, and the only one who was an immigrant woman of color) and had a different attitude toward eye contact and affect. Liana was a Filipina woman leading a workshop for engineers. She was articulating the same issue of confidence and eye contact when a woman participant asked the same question about eye contact signaling disrespect in her cultural experience. Rather than sweep aside her concerns, Liana revealed that she shared this woman's hesitation because of her own upbringing outside of Canada. Her strategy was to find a spot on an interlocutor's forehead and focus there instead of making eye contact, which fulfilled the conventions of masculinized business culture while allowing her to maintain her own ideals of respect and bodily practice.

In understanding this sensorial mode of governance, it is important to note that it is not carried out by faceless agents of the state, but rather by authorities who, as Aihwa Ong (2003) argues, "translate the problematics of government into everyday operations" (16). For instance, Liana's sensitivity to her students' concerns demonstrates that while she is an authority, she brings her own experiences and attitudes to the way she exercises it. Nikolas Rose calls these authorities "experts of subjectivity" who "transfigure existentialist questions . . . and the meaning of suffering into technical problems about the most effective ways of managing malfunction and improving 'quality of life'" (cited in Ong 2003: 16), as Liana did through her suggestions around the practice of eye contact. Her cultural training resonated with her students, which allowed her to problem-solve this cultural dilemma. Further, Ong argues, such actors "translate dominant discourses into micropractices that allocate, classify, categorize, and formalize categories of the human . . . then try to mold their subjects into exemplars of the desirable categories" (17). Thus, while the interpretations, particular instructions, and beliefs of workshop leaders were subjective, they did overwhelmingly manage to reproduce particular ideologies and practices concerning whiteness and masculinity, which were presented as "neutrality." That moment in Liana's workshop was the only time I witnessed an immigrant woman's subjective experience of culture and practice taken seriously, and not cast aside as a cultural tradition to be overcome.

The logic of the workshops also seems to suggest that people are unemployed by choice. One can choose to change one's name, clothes, body, and self to find a job in Canada, or one can keep those things—essentially markers of racialized difference and culture—and remain unemployed. At the level of everyday life, the choice is to hold onto race and bodily difference and forsake employment or to become more Canadian (i.e. race-neutral) and thus more employable. Further, the kinds of choices participants are asked to make almost exclusively deal with their bodies—how to smell, what to wear, and how to move. These kinds of choices erase the fact that their unemployment is also part of a systemic problem of the misrecognition of foreign qualifications and miscommunication between different levels of Canadian government.

In their approach to training, settlement services suggest that the possibility of full belonging—or first-class citizenship—in the form of employment and financial stability is primarily contingent upon one's ability to perform a kind of cultural flexibility and what might be considered a race-neutral bodily practice. But in reality, for foreign-trained professionals, as demonstrated here, professional work is essentially a structural impossibility. What settlement-services workers would say to me privately, but would never convey to the women they were trying to assist, was that it was highly unlikely that they would ever work in their fields again. In practice, these workshop leaders assumed a particular kind of unemployed subjectivity. Considering that the participating women were both skilled and unemployed, the workshop leaders assumed that there must be some other problem. The points system of immigration prioritized professional skills, and yet workers are somehow unemployable once they arrive. The problem of their unemployment was not understood to be located in labor markets or the regulation of professional labor, but in their bodies, which were marked as too culturally different for inclusion in the public sphere of employment and which had to be remolded as global citizen-workers. The responsibility for unemployment was placed on these women's bodies—they smelled bad and looked different; in other words, they presented a form of racialized Otherness that was a detriment to their employability. This unemployment of foreign-trained professionals is built into different levels of governance and seeps into every area of government, but at the level of the everyday it is articulated as a personal failure to perform the modern, flexible, global worker.

Yet, this question of responsibility for one's own racialized difference is interesting in this context because it presumes the possibility of race-neutral bodily practice. In actuality, this is not race-neutral at all. Rather, direct eye contact, how to cross one's legs, having a firm handshake, and wearing dark neutral clothing all represent a particular kind of worker predicated on white, North American male business culture.[17] Presenting these performances as race-neutral sets women up for failure and once again demonstrates that this process is an impossibility because immigrant women will never be able to overcome their racialized Otherness.

The participants also misunderstood or were misinformed regarding the goals of the workshops. Though the stated purpose of the workshops is to assist new immigrants in acquiring the tools (e.g., résumé writing or networking skills) to find work on their own, many participants thought the workshops would ultimately place them in jobs. It is critical here that the participants interacted with the workshops as though they were extensions of the state. Women often described recruitment for the workshops as part of their immigration process. These centers represent a form of governance that is prevalent in contemporary Toronto and is indeed crucial to managing immigrant populations, but it is not their responsibility to find anyone work. Therefore, a center is not held accountable for the rates at which participants manage to find employment. While, as we have seen, the welfare state has been declining in Canada (Coulter 2009; Mitchell 2004), the character of the state is distinct from that of other neoliberal contexts in reference to immigrant populations because of Canada's institutionalized commitment to multiculturalism. Canadian multiculturalism posits an equality that cuts across racial and ethnic boundaries, but unemployment workshops demonstrate the existence of an unmarked category of belonging. These practices produce marginalized citizens and political subjects within changing forms of governance. The (neo)liberal multicultural state becomes a detriment to the lives of immigrant and minority women because it equates questions of human security (including food, shelter, employment) with questions of responsibility, choice, and the incommensurability of their bodies and work.

These workplace ideologies place the burden of knowing how to perform on the worker, and by the time the Canadian state steps in with advice about clothing and comportment, the women have, to a large extent, already failed to perform as required for the global economy. So important is this performance that the professional degrees once used to certify these women as experts now become secondary to their skills as expert performers of the model flexible citizen-worker, as judged by potential employers and the government. It follows, then, that the kinds of instructions given to these women workers varied according to the tasks they were expected to perform. The next chapter takes up this question in more detail, focusing on training for foreign nurses and healthcare workers in which the pedagogical emphasis on controlling one's affects and emotions reveals racialized notions of gender and care.

CHAPTER TWO

PEDAGOGIES OF AFFECT

A notable exception to this failure to integrate skilled immigrant women workers into regulated professions is the feminized field of nursing. This chapter draws on fieldwork conducted with a government-funded pilot project (referred to here as "Nurture") to help foreign-trained nurses become licensed in Ontario, in order to examine a special case in which extensive reeducation was not required to reenter one's field in Canada. While locally, the high rate of reentry for nurses has been attributed to the success of this resettlement program, I assert that its practitioners can enter into Canadian venues because of the way nursing is understood as gendered labor.[1] After all, nursing is a feminized profession—that is, it is understood as "women's work"—and so workplace ideologies surrounding masculinized performances of a global modern worker are not applicable. The logics imposed in these classrooms, and the pedagogies employed, are rife with racial and gendered ideologies of appropriate citizenship and appropriate womanhood in a model of care.

During classes at Nurture, a group of foreign-trained nurses and I learned how to control our affect for legibility on the job market, including how to manage conflict. The instructor, Libby, a Black Canadian nurse, had been working with the program as part of her service to the professional nursing association. Conflict, she explained, could consist of "disagreement, crisis, clash, fight, or an argument" that could manifest both internally (guilt, anger, frustration) and externally (yelling at a colleague). In handling "one's own anger management," the first strategy she offered was to "stop being angry." She suggested "breathing deeply," "walking away," and "not cursing" or "yelling." Libby offered her own strategy of singing to herself in order to avoid cursing. In effect, her pedagogy focused on self-management of one's affect, seemingly geared toward the production of a docile and deferent subject who would be legible in the professional world of the global economy.

This chapter examines classroom pedagogies that focus on affect and the regulation of emotion as necessary parts of the professionalization of nurses. Nursing is a form of intimate labor (Boris and Parreñas 2010)—work that involves intimacy and the body. Combining both emotion and physical touch, intimate labor can include familiarity, sexual contact, bathing another, or being party to intimate information about another. It is important not to conflate intimate with emotional labor, though nurses perform both. Emotional labor instead concerns the face-to-face work in which "one displays certain emotions to induce particular feelings in the client or customer" (Hochschild, cited in Boris and Parreñas 2010: 6). Emotional labor can be performed, for instance, by prostitutes who project love to make clients feel good, domestic workers who suppress frustration or anger in order for their employers to feel comfortable (Boris and Parreñas 2010), or nurses displaying empathy to make a client cooperative. While the intimate has historically been positioned within the private sphere, and labor within the public, intimate labor such as nursing or domestic work crosses these realms and forces a reconsideration of what intimate work in the public sphere looks like. What Nurture teaches is the way that the intimate dirty work of affect and affective labor is made public, so that in order to become a nurse, one's affect—or performance of a particular kind of affect—is just as important as one's knowledge of biomedicine.

This chapter builds on the affective turn in anthropology. McElhinny (2010) asserts that the ways scholars differentiate between concepts such as affect, feeling, and emotion speak to their intellectual genealogies; thus, I locate my work in studies of gender, emotion, and labor. The feminist study of emotion was differently attuned to questions of gender from contemporary anthropological uses of affect, and that the recent turn in anthropology owes a great deal to this legacy—a debt that goes largely unacknowledged. The recent trend has mostly neglected the body of work by feminist theorists on the study of emotion and gender, which in anthropology appeared as early as the 1980s and 1990s. Studies by feminist scholars such as Catherine Lutz and Lila Abu-Lughod (1990) and Elinor Ochs and Bambi Schieffelin (1989) challenged the idea of emotions as biologically determinate and instead understood them to be culturally produced. As McElhinny (2010) argues, these studies also challenged the binary between reason and emotion, in which emotion was characterized as irrational in contrast with the rationality of reason; such irrationality was also associated with women, racialized groups, and the poor (311).

Here, I focus on the *social work* that these affects do. I argue that these classroom sites and pedagogies of affect are critical in the making of global workers. Therefore, scholars must take seriously the fact that "frustration" or "guilt" have become emotions that need to be suppressed or trained away. Similarly, power and marketability lie in one's ability to smile in the face of humiliation, a strategy that teachers in the neoliberal state explicitly articulate in order to produce legible immigrant women workers. A number of studies on globalization and neoliberalism have investigated the production of new subjectivities in which emotion is "managed." In these accounts, under neoliberalism a subject must cultivate herself as responsible, self-sufficient, entrepreneurial, and the idealized Western masculine self (Kingfisher 2002 and Rose 1996a, cited in McElhinny 2010), as women were encouraged to do in many of the workshops I attended. What I want to bring attention to, however, is how in contrast to this idealized, masculinized, neoliberal subject of the state, immigrant women learning to be professionals in the global market must conform to a contrasting gendered self. Thus, as this chapter demonstrates, race and gender importantly figure in the making of subjects under neoliberalism.

In this chapter I examine the notion of "care work" in a global perspective and analyze the colonization of the intimate labor that women do. The term *colonization* draws attention both to the assimilatory process by which a nurse must make herself into a legible worker in the Canadian context, but also to the ways that the state regulates and manages such intimate labor. The focus on intimacy and affect in the training of foreign nurses provides an excellent example of this interpellation and management. Further, these classes employ what I call "pedagogies of affect," which reproduce racialized notions of femininity deemed appropriate for immigrant women in Western settings. By pedagogies of affect, I refer to the educational imperatives surrounding the management of affect, emotion, feeling, and ways of being. These pedagogies serve the sanitized sensorium as they concern the explicit training of the interiority as well as the exteriority of the body.

In contrast to many studies of immigrant women that address their exploitation in low-wage work, here I examine the experience of displaced professionals. I focus on the training of particular forms of affect—especially conciliation, cooperativeness, and deference—at Nurture, which was a program designed to educate foreign-trained nurses to succeed on a national exam. Understanding the meaning and underlying logics of such classroom interactions reveals how ideas of race and gender are understood and inscribed on the bodies of immigrant women. Women, particularly those of color, are expected to perform Westernized notions of docility and deference in order to be marketable on the global stage. Despite the popular stereotype of the passive Asian woman (Guevarra 2010; Rodriguez 2010; Stiell and England 1999), in the context of training classes, nurses had to learn to suppress anger, resolve conflict, and become subservient—suggesting a fear that the immigrant woman is anything but an obedient subject. Rather than draw out some innate passivity, these classroom encounters suggest that Asian immigrant women need to mold themselves to fit this cultural notion of natural passivity to be legible workers. In these sites the neoliberal, entrepreneurial nurse-to-be must perform an alternate version of the self that counters the masculinized neoliberal subject. Pedagogies of affect render migrant nurses legible not only in the micro context of the training sessions but also in the macro context of neoliberal capitalism.

Nursing in Multicultural, Neoliberal Canada

Nurses occupy an ambivalent position in the world of care work, being both professionalized in the Canadian context and devalued as a gendered and racialized worker. Nursing provides an excellent example of the intersectional convergence of the practice of raced and gendered performance. These kinds of performances are not inconsequential, but critical to one's ability to make a living. Several authors have examined the racialization of nursing in Canada (Bakan and Stasiulis 1997; Calliste 1993; Damasco 2012; Das Gupta 1996 and 2009; Das Gupta, Hagey, and Turritin 2007; Flynn 2009). Among the most prominent, Tania Das Gupta (2009) details how in 1990, seven Black nurses and one Filipino nurse who worked at Northwestern General Hospital in Toronto filed complaints with the Ontario Human Rights Commission claiming they had been subject to racial harassment, and some had been fired or forced to resign. After four years, they received a landmark settlement in which the hospital paid each nurse $10,000–$100,000 for mental anguish. In addition, the hospital created a position for a vice-president of Ethno-Racial Equality. Das Gupta suggests that public cases such as this demonstrate the need for examining not only gender, sexism, and class, but also questions of race and racism within the nursing profession.

The kinds of racialized and gendered performances nurses are called upon to act out put them in the precarious position of being subject to race-based discrimination, but identifying race-based discrimination is not easy. Identifying gendered forms of racism in intimate interactions is complicated when one is responsible for a sick or dying person, a situation predicated on different forms of vulnerability. In Das Gupta's (2009) study of race discrimination for Canadian nurses, she found it was difficult for nurses to establish harassment on the basis of race because they had little evidence beyond their own descriptions of their experiences. As I demonstrate below, in the classes run by Nurture, there was no explicit mention of race or race-based discrimination, as the pedagogy was geared toward the management of one's own affect and the suppression of anger in the face of mistreatment. Given the important role of race and racism in hospital encounters, it is critical to examine this in light of the failures of multiculturalism and the failure to recognize explicit issues of race.

In the examples we have already seen, classes for foreign professionals do not focus on anti-racism training, but rather on making oneself into someone who will not be discriminated against. Indeed, as others have shown (Calliste 1993; Flynn 2009), throughout history Canadian immigration policies have discriminated against and created hurdles for women-of-color, migrant nurses. Agnes Calliste (1993) argues that between 1950 and 1962, immigration control created a context in which Caribbean nurses who wanted to enter as permanent settlers had to demonstrate they were of "exceptional merit," in contrast to white nurses who were admitted on more general qualifications (85). While this is no longer the case in terms of immigration policies, the state's legislation and management of the nursing profession has set up other significant hurdles that immigrant women of color must learn to scale.

Foreign-educated nurses are required to get accreditation according to the dictates of the College of Nurses of Ontario (CNO), the regulatory body for all nursing in the province. While not an academic institution, CNO is responsible for ensuring safe and ethical nursing practices for the public, as well as determining the criteria for becoming a nurse or practical nurse. It establishes the standards of practice, develops a framework for ongoing learning for nurses, and provides a complaint process for those in need. In order to practice as a nurse in Ontario and to use the titles "nurse," "registered nurse (RN)," or "registered practical nurse (RPN)," one must have a current certificate of registration from CNO.

According to CNO, there are seven requirements to register as a nurse in Ontario: "complete an acceptable nurse or practical nursing program; provide evidence of recent safe nursing practice within the past five years; pass the national nursing examination; be fluent in English or French; be registered in the jurisdiction where the program was completed; have proof of Canadian citizenship or landed immigrant status; and be of "good character and suitable for practice."[2] Foreign-educated nurses must also provide evidence of any convictions of a criminal offense or any offense; previous proceedings having to do with professional misconduct; incompetence; any physical or mental condition or illness; and any suspension or denial of a nursing license. Fees for this process total approximately $800.

In an interview with Linda, the executive director of Nurture, I learned that the organization arose from the realization that there is a contradiction in the current state of nursing: while there is a shortage of nurses in Ontario, there are a large number of nurses with foreign credentials who are unable to work. Recent healthcare reforms in Ontario have had a dramatic impact on nursing, as the provincial government has struggled to slash deficits by freezing or cutting nursing jobs—work that continues in the context of a severe nursing shortage. According to Judith Shamian, president of the Canadian Nurses Association, "Many nurses work part-time because they find it so exhausting when they get into the workplace . . . we are currently short of around 22,000 nurses. We compensate for that by having a lot of nurses doing a lot of overtime, which leads to other concerns" (cited by Winston 2011: para. 4). Citing a recent study of fatigue levels among nurses conducted by the Canadian Nurses Association, she says, "Nurses end up being far sicker than the rest of the population, so that absentee days in comparison with the general public are much higher. That's what happens when you keep working very long shifts and come to a point of exhaustion" (Winston 2011: para. 5). In 2008, Statistics Canada conducted a study of nurses' working conditions and found links between "medication error and both work organization and workplace environment, including working overtime, role overload, perceived staff shortages, or inadequate resources, poor working relations with physicians, lack of support from co-workers and low job security'" (Winston 2011: para. 6). Thus, rather than improve working conditions for all nurses, including addressing race-based discrimination, the government sees foreign nurses as a partial solution to the shortage.

In 2001, the provincial government, through the Ministry of Training Colleges and Universities, announced that it would provide funding to launch Nurture as a pilot program. Nurture was organized specifically to assist with the national nursing exam, which had been a major barrier for foreign-educated nurses. Linda suggested that many immigrant women fail the exam because they are "not aware of the legal and ethical framework of nursing," or what she also termed the "psychosocial" aspects of the profession, which is what they attempt to teach in the space of their classrooms.

What the nurses are preparing for is the Canadian Registered Nurse Examination (CRNE) and the Canadian Practical Nurse Registration Examination (CPNRE). The CRNE includes approximately 200 multiple-choice questions and takes four hours, while the CPNRE consists of 180–200 multiple-choice questions and also takes four hours. The exams are designed to test the basic competency expected of a beginning nurse in Canada. The passing score is 59–68 percent. While all applicants to Nurture must be fluent English speakers, the curriculum includes three levels of language instruction: "Intermediate Assessing, Reporting, and Explaining"; "High Intermediate Telephone, Documentation, and Intercultural Communication"; and "Advanced Communication Strategies for Working/Workplace-Ready IENs."

Nurture has worked in tandem with a number of settlement services in addition to local hospitals and palliative care centers. The program has been wildly successful and is now in its twelfth year. By the end of 2003, over two hundred nurses had signed up for the program and successfully passed the exam. Before its implementation, foreign-trained nurses had a passing rate of 33 percent; graduates from Nurture now have a 65–80 percent passing rate. According to CNO, the pass rate for RNs trained in Ontario in 2011 was 75 percent, while only 37 percent of those trained outside of Ontario succeeded; for RPNs, the pass rate for those trained in Ontario was 82 percent, but only 52 percent for those trained outside the province. Since 2001, Nurture has expanded beyond Toronto and served over a thousand foreign-educated nurses.

Participants in the Nurture program must take two mandatory courses: Competency Skills Assessment and Introduction to Nursing in Ontario. In addition, each participant spends 200 hours of practicum in a hospital setting. Students also receive mentoring and guidance in applying for government funding (in the form of loans to immigrants and bursaries) to pay for their Nurture program. Once they pass the nursing exam, participants are assisted in their search for work. At the time of my research, no other profession had this kind of mentorship and guidance for immigrant practitioners.

Entry into Nurture is highly competitive. To qualify, potential candidates must have a letter from the College of Nurses saying they are eligible to write the exam, they must be permanent residents in Canada, they need intermediate English skills, and they must voluntarily agree to join the program and to commit their time and money. In terms of costs, participants pay $700 for the two mandatory courses, or $4,000 for the complete package. In addition, participants must pay for books, transportation, and childcare, as well as specialized items such as lab coats. More than 50 percent of participants held bachelor's degrees; 90 percent of the participants were female, aged thirty to forty-five; more than 50 percent had a minimum of ten years of experience; and more than 70 percent spoke more than one language. Participants largely originate from Asian countries including the Philippines, China, India, and Pakistan, followed by Eastern Europe, the former Yugoslavia, Russia, and Latin America. Half were unemployed and the rest were working at survival jobs as cashiers or service workers. The maximum income for those participating was $20,000, and participants were largely from two-parent families with two children.

While in both global and Canadian national contexts foreign-trained nurses are very successful at finding work, foreign-trained immigrants from professions that are considered masculinized are much less successful, even within the field of medicine. Consider Basheera, a woman in her thirties who was trained as a doctor in Karachi, Pakistan. Basheera had migrated to Toronto alone, and was living in a government housing project in Scarborough, to the east of the city; at the time of our meeting she had been in Toronto for six months. I met her during fieldwork with a women's nonprofit center in the context of a job-search workshop. She had been learning the intricacies of what it means to have a firm handshake, but had grown increasingly frustrated with the process. Basheera never worked as a doctor again, eventually giving up the retraining and re-accreditation process. At the time of our last interview, she was working as a cashier at a food court in a local mall. Among those employed in 2006, 62 percent of Canadian-born professionals were working in the regulated professions, in contrast to the

24 percent of foreign-educated immigrant professionals who did (Zietsma 2006: 15).

The context that sets the scene for Nurture's practices is the idea that nursing itself is understood as a feminized profession. Several authors have examined in great detail the history of nursing and how it has come to be considered "women's work" (D'Antonio 1993; Flynn 2009; Gordon 2002, 2009; Sexton 1982). D'Antonio (1993) has written that since the responsibility for caring for the sick has historically rested on women, this laid the domestic roots of the practice of modern nursing. Building on the perceived idea that women were innately loving and caring, nursing became unquestionably something they could do. However, in the first half of the nineteenth century that "duty" became the actual profession of nursing, transforming with ideas of "expert knowledge, correct social order, viable occupational options, and the centrality of therapeutic alliances in the caring process" (34). Gordon (2002) has suggested that while nursing is the largest female profession in the United States, it was the first secular profession for respectable women and a feminist achievement; thus, nurses played a key role in developing the American hospital system in which nursing is devalued.

If nursing has historically been understood as women's work, it is perplexing that the education at Nurture focuses on the training of affect and feeling, a realm that has also been naturalized as the domain of women. Yet the existence of these trainings seems to denaturalize the presumed link between women, affect, and emotion. This contradiction also exists in the context of training around race and what kinds of bodily and affective performances are demanded of nonwhite women. It is important to understand that gendered and racialized performances of deference or docility are not endemic to Asian culture (I use Asian here because the bulk of Nurture's nurses-to-be are from Asian countries), but rather are part of a pedagogical training strategy that produces Otherness for immigrant women.

Nurture's orientation session for new students imparts much of the information I detailed above concerning "women's work," which gets complicated in the context of the multicultural state. At the one I attended, Linda, the executive director, assured participants they would receive excellent mentoring, but that they would need to learn the standards in Ontario and they would need to "assimilate." Linda's use of the word "assimilate" in the context of Nurture was seamless, but to my ethnographic ear it was painful. In the context of multicultural Toronto, a city that prides itself on "equality based on a model of difference," assimilation was central to much of the rhetoric I had heard in government training classes; if we are to take the success of Nurture's graduates seriously, assimilation seems to be the order of the day. Here, the emphasis is on affect as a governing and governable quality, or what I see as the colonization of the intimate labors of immigrant women. Linda assured the women that tutoring in how to assimilate would be available.

Another aspect of orientation that day was Linda's discussion of professional partnerships, in which immigrant women would have time to shadow other professional nurses. "The standards are different in Canada than in other countries; there are things that are difficult to quantify," Linda assumed. Job shadowing usually happened in the space of a hospital, in order for potential nurses to understand the protocol. If the classroom space is any indicator, what they are to learn in terms of protocol is how to suitably display the affect of a Canadian nurse. To end the orientation, Linda left the participants with five tips: be punctual, do not bring friends, be confidential, go early and stay later, and do not speak a language other than English because it is considered rude.

Teaching Gendered and Raced Affect

This disjuncture between training at the Center versus training at, for instance, Nurture demonstrates that on the global market, there is no singular gendered and racialized performance one must carry out to gain access to legibility. That is, acting like the masculinized white subject endemic to neoliberalism—through actions that include firm handshakes, strong eye contact, and the use of first names when referring to each other and superiors—only works in certain situations. In other chapters I consider the ways immigrant women trying to gain entry into masculinized labor (e.g., as a doctor, engineer, or lawyer) must learn to reproduce these very actions. Here, however, the focus is different and these nurses must act according to what is culturally appropriate for their gender at the time. For instance, in the 1940s Black women had a difficult time entering the field of nursing because nursing was defined around the Victorian ideal of "true womanhood," and that ideal excluded Black women (Flynn 2009). This concern about Black women in nursing and how it would affect the profession carried on into the 1960s and was only overturned by Black women's performances of femininity (Flynn 2009), to the point where today, Nurture's classes concerning the appropriate and correct affective and bodily performance for a nurse can be taught by Black nurses, and thus are central to the training in the field. The experiences of today's woman-of-color nurse contrasts with those of Black women in the 1940s. Then, "a true woman" was a white woman; in an irony of racial hierarchy, the nurse today is still a "true woman," but because that requires docility and subservience, Asian women can now perform this work as well. In both cases, the whiteness of multiculturalism is unspoken.

Prevailing constructs of gender and women are still ideologically linked with ideas of proper behavior that transcend the space of nursing. Women are imagined to be half of a heterosexual pairing, ideally responsible for domestic labor, including cooking and childcare. Thus, when women seek help in finding work outside the home they face a kind of perverse sociality that guides women away from professional fields and back toward their imagined place. In contexts such as these, an individual's identity as a "foreign immigrant woman" eclipses her professional qualifications and thus becomes a defining factor in her professional life. Notions of "appropriate modern womanhood" are intimately connected to the body and its regulation, the meaning of which has transformed historically but is still deeply wedded to racial and cultural ideals of hygiene and dress associated with an imagined West. Sherene Razack (1998) has suggested that images of the oppressed third-world woman, "the passive downtrodden Indian woman," and the veiled Muslim woman are "recurring and familiar images in Canadian public discourse" (100). The highly skilled third-world woman fails to have a subjective niche in the public consciousness, and so a skilled professional woman must mold herself to fit the culturally available tropes in order to become legible. She still carries the markers of difference, of Otherness, in which she is understood contextually as a "third-world woman," and she must perform that difference through Westernized notions of docility and deference.

The popular stereotypes of Asian women and docility circulate globally and set expectations for these women as workers—and thus have disabling effects. These portrayals of docile Asian women occur in television, film, and newspaper accounts and include representations as diverse as *Madame Butterfly*, *The World of Suzie Wong*, the women of *The Joy Luck Club*, and news accounts of South Asian Muslim women in need of rescue from their husbands—or representations, as Gayatri Spivak (1988) argues, that "white men are saving brown women from brown men" (297). These images of Asian women circulate globally and seem to insist on an inherent docility and deference to men and their elders, all of which works together to make the women seemingly ideal on the global care market.

Despite the assumption that immigrant women, particularly Asians, possess these qualities, these classes, and by extension the government, realize that these characteristics, behaviors, and affects actually must be taught. There are both ontological and methodological dimensions to how these pedagogies of affect are racialized, so that it is not just a matter of to whom docility and deference are taught, but *how* they are. In this context, the emphasis is on the governing of affect and the colonization of the intimate labors of immigrant women. In other words, there are racialized mechanisms through which pedagogies of affect train the entrepreneurial nurse-to-be to perform an alternative version of the self, in order to be legible and to counter the masculinized neoliberal subject of Western states.

Two representative sessions of Nurture's classes revealed to me how immigrant nurses are produced. The first class, "Nursing in Ontario," was located in a large office building in downtown Toronto. The classroom had the familiar institutional lighting and furniture of any government office. According to the course catalog, this class "provides the graduate nurse with an overview of nursing in Ontario in preparation for registration in Ontario or a return to active nursing for RNs who have been out of nursing practice for some time. [It addresses] issues such as trends in health care, the nursing educational process in Ontario, the role of the multidiscipline health care team, legislation and professionalism."

The twenty-two participants were mostly Asian women from the Philippines, China, India, and Pakistan. In addition there were seven Eastern European women, and one man. Libby, the middle-aged Black Canadian nurse I introduced earlier, taught the course. A few minutes into the class I noticed that I was sitting behind a woman from Pakistan who, during an earlier visit I had made to Nurture, refused to let me interview her unless I could find her a job. The topic for the day was "Disagreeing with Your Team," specifically in reference to medical directives, which are orders from doctors or other nurses. As Libby described, "Medical directives must be written in advance; the time frame varies, but they are always written. The order is written or oral and is taken within a specific time frame, and most importantly you must always listen to the doctor." Libby carefully outlined the division of labor between doctors and nurses, repeatedly asserting that doctors are more knowledgeable and must be deferred to in all circumstances. "However," she said, "if you are going to disagree with your team you must believe (1) that the plan of care is inappropriate, and (2) that the client has not given informed consent." If a nurse is to follow through with her disagreement, "she must follow the chain of command," which moves as follows:

> Disagreement with MD → talk with MD → situation is unresolved → supervisor (RN) → supervisor supports your concern → talk to MD → MD refuses → MD supervisor.

This chain of command demonstrates just how heavily policed nurses are in contrast to registered nurses and doctors, who effectively are left to their own devices. Libby reiterated several times that it was highly unusual to disagree with a doctor, who had much more training than a registered nurse did. "The doctor is typically in charge, and knows what is called for."

After the break, the topic for the rest of the class was "Restraint and Resuscitation," referring to the literal use of restraints on patients. Restraints, Libby suggested, provide an ethical dilemma for nurses because they literally control other people's bodies and restrict their movement. "Compared to your home countries," Libby said, "you must get used to restraining less." Her implicit assumption was that archaic practices of restraint were dominant in Asian countries. I, myself, was shocked to learn that in addition to physical restraints, there are both chemical restraints (tranquilizers and sedatives) and environmental restraints (seclusion and being locked in one's room). Throughout the lesson Libby differentiated between the participants' presumed "home" and the experience in Canada; home was described as a site of barbarism, while Canada was described as progressive.

The crux of the restraint lesson plan seemed to be the question of permission. "The nurse's responsibilities are to assess the client's behavior, consider alternatives, collaborate with the health team, and, most importantly, get consent." Libby emphasized, "Restraint is a treatment—you must get the doctor's permission and details of administering, and you must defer to his judgment." Not only were nurses expected to defer to the judgment of the doctor, but also to the family: "It is the family's decision whether or not to restrain; you must respect that." Indeed, many students expressed surprise that they would have to get a family's permission to use restraints, which they did not have to do in their home countries. Libby answered this by expressing that restraining a patient can lead to increased injury, skin breakdown, confusion, incontinence, constipation, loss of appetite, and bone loss, so they were to take this very seriously.

During the second class with the same participants the theme was "Conflict Resolution" and what Libby called "techniques to manage yourself." The first technique, deep breathing, was emphasized as a productive strategy to clear one's thoughts, which could later be followed by leaving the situation or distracting oneself by going for a walk, shopping, or taking a hot bath. Thus, in this government class to prepare nurses for taking the national nursing exam, part of the lesson was to suppress one's emotions. Alongside the previous lesson on deferring to doctors and registered nurses instead of disagreeing with them, this begins to paint a picture of the ideal nurse-worker.

Implicit in these "techniques to manage yourself" is the training of patience, as part of the affective training for flexible nurses. Libby's instructions centered on controlling one's temper in the face of mistreatment, to breathe deeply instead of yelling, to go for a walk or shop to take a hot bath. Nurses were taught to do anything other than face mistreatment directly; they had to be patient. Procupez (2012) has theorized the role of patience, suggesting, "The need for patience emerges when time no longer seems to stand still, where there is the sense of something else coming. Thus, far from an attitude of conformation or passivity, patience here involves the collective acceptance to work toward an objective in the long term despite the uncertainty entailed in the processes of negotiation with other sectors. In this sense, patience effectively entails a disposition of openness toward the unknown" (173). For the nurses, patience signifies two things. First it contains a temporal orientation that departs from what Procupez (2012) describes in her study of urban squatters. Instead of containing an inherent orientation toward the future (If I am patient now, there will be a payoff later), nurses are seemingly trapped in time, for they must always be patient while working. Second, patience is a learned practice that must be trained and cultivated, something to work toward.

Libby continued her lesson by insisting that the nurses think before they talk to other colleagues, because it is unprofessional to "gossip." "First," she illustrated, "stop being angry, be aware of your body language and tone of voice—you don't want to seem aggressive. You need to develop an approach or compromise; for instance, say you need a minute, then come back." Libby continued, "If you have trouble controlling your anger, you may want to consider counseling in the form of anger management. If others notice your anger is a problem, you may be sent to anger-management training. You're not being penalized; it's about patient care." Libby's instructions demonstrate several things. First, a nurse must always work to suppress her emotions. Second, if she is unsuccessful, she may be sent to anger management, which, despite Libby's denial of it, is no doubt a penalty. Third, and importantly, her lesson demonstrates that women are the ones who need to work at conflict resolution. The doctor in Libby's lessons was always a "he," a masculinized hegemonic force that needed to be managed and dealt with, but also deferred to as the authority in the room.

These techniques also assume that rage is a part of the job, and that these women will be expected to control it at the hands of doctors, patients, and other nurses who will mistreat them. Thus, being treated badly seems to be intrinsic to the profession. One is expected to become violently angry at some point, and Nurture offers instruction concerning how to act when that happens. What this counterintuitively suggests is that women are understood to *not* be "naturally docile," but rather to need to cultivate a certain affect in order to be successful as a professional nurse in Canada. In Libby's lesson, the two major barriers to conflict resolution are low self-esteem and a lack of experience with resolving disputes, which "must be achieved without violence." Her statement comes with an implicit idea that perhaps in "their home countries" these women are violent, savage, and in her words "lack experience with conflict resolution," yet at the same time have low self-esteem. These kinds of instructions and assumptions again suggest that these women must be disciplined for the market. Finally, Libby illustrated two models of conflict resolution: negotiation or compromise—in which both parties reach "an agreed concession by converging ideas and opinions"—and a mutual-gains model in which "each side profits from mutual work performed toward a common goal." The class ended with us all doing a behavior survey, and with Libby telling us that "through our lives we move between assertive, aggressive, and passive," and thus that these are not static but rather dynamic states of being. "You are in control of how you act." Class dismissed.

Learning Affect

I later had the opportunity to speak with Habiba about her experience with Nurture. She was a foreign-trained nurse who had migrated to Toronto six years before our interview. In Pakistan she had worked as a nurse for sixteen years; when I met her, she was working at a Coffee Time donut shop, which is a local chain. When I asked her about the classes, she happily expressed to me that they were "very helpful" and gave her information she would not have thought of otherwise. Habiba had already completed her practicum, so when I asked her about the differences between nursing in Pakistan and nursing in Canada, she said the biggest difference was the clients' attitudes toward nurses. "They're so hostile here, and they don't think we know anything." She said that clients regularly yelled at her in the hospital or told her to "get out and get the doctor." Here, Habiba does not suggest that her lack of authority is linked with race, but it is likely a factor. Part of pedagogies of affect consists of preparing workers for interactions in which they experience racism. In the face of it, they cannot yell or fight back, but must remain docile and deferent. Thus success in the context of Nurture, and indeed in the field of nursing, consists of managing one's own emotions.

Though I have been very critical of these teachings concerning affect so far, it is important to consider the fact that Nurture is very successful. Remember that the success rate for their students is between 65 and 80 percent, compared to 33 percent before the program was implemented. Considering this, it would seem that these trainings do work on some level. Consider Habiba's assertion that the biggest difference in nursing in Canada is that the patients are openly hostile toward her. It would seem in this context that a nurse would need to know how to control her feelings to keep her job. If this is the case, it seems to say more about the nature of feminized labor and racism, in which racialized women are paid to do the kind of care work not done by anyone else, than about classroom instruction. yeah

In addition to nursing, other forms of gendered labor also reveal a racialized performance of servility necessary for the global market. For instance, Mirchandani (2012) examines the experiences of Indian call-center workers who must perform what she calls "authenticity work" to refashion themselves into what Western clients expect of them. In these exchanges between call-center workers and clients, Indian workers must demonstrate contrasting qualities ranging from servility to assertiveness, performing a kind of affective labor for legibility. Her study demonstrates that "the exchange of labor and capital occurs in the context of national histories and power inequities that make negotiation of authenticity a central part of transnational service work" (1). Mirchandani rightly demonstrates that a performance of authenticity is central to doing one's job, when the workers themselves (and their sensorial and affective markers) signal their ability to do certain kinds of work.

In certain contexts, such as working as a doctor, being a masculinized, neoliberal entrepreneur gains one access to employment and social inclusion. However, in others, different kinds of gendered and racialized performances are called for in order to be read not only as appropriate citizen-workers but as gendered immigrant women workers. Tara Goldstein (1995) for example, has written on the need to rethink English as a Second Language curriculum for immigrant workers in Canada, which often assume it is necessary to learn English above all other languages in order to function in the workplace. In her ethnographic research, Goldstein demonstrates that in one factory workspace in Toronto, immigrant women had to learn Portuguese because the bulk of immigrants in this particular community were from Portugal and thus set the lingua franca of the factory. As Goldstein suggests, it is not always a singular form of language or even performance that makes someone legible. In the case of nursing, docility, deference, and reserve are all affects that make a foreign woman recognizable as a nurse.

Pedagogies of affect provide an entry into understanding the changing nature of gender and race in neoliberal societies. Neoliberalism has been cast as a macroeconomic series and set of practices and discourses that have had dramatic impact on the functioning of society. Scholars have been attentive to the ways such practices translate into ideologies of the local and everyday life. What I am signaling here is the way that gender and labor, including the intimate performances of what it means to be particular kinds of workers, have been transformed through processes of neoliberalism. In contrast to representations of an ideal masculine, neoliberal subject of the state, what I found was a distinct gendered performance that Asian women workers are expected to act out on the global stage. The required affects were understood as needing to be taught and learned; they were not seen as qualities intrinsic to Asian women, but as a set of strategies they must absorb to be legible as workers. These nurses are taught how to be neoliberal, entrepreneurial workers who must learn to suppress their anger and frustration in their racist and sexist encounters with doctors, patients, and even sometimes their peers. It is also worth noting the assumption that the mistreatment of nurses is acceptable, and that nurses need to learn how to deal with it, instead of indicating a necessary shift in attitude and treatment on the part of the profession and larger society. This stance is in itself neoliberal, in that it becomes the nurse's responsibility to manage her feelings when treated badly.

My fieldwork on classroom interactions and narrative accounts by professionals does not encompass the workplace contexts themselves, so I cannot speak to the ways this affective sensibility was or was not negotiated in hospitals or the ways nurses who get jobs experience their work. In the space of the classrooms I visited, the nurses were ultimately disempowered by their unemployment. However, many understood that this was a game they needed to play, focusing on their instruction rather than on activism to change an oppressive system. Agency in this context was exercised within the constraints of a system of neoliberal capitalism that kept them underemployed. These migrants, like all of us, need a paycheck at the end of the day, but they have to perform a foreign set of affects to obtain one. Affective sensibilities and attachments linger in larger-scale economic transformations, the very transformations that are responsible for situating these women as precarious workers.

Post-Fordist Affect

Questions of affect and labor transcend the space of Nurture's classrooms and have larger implications in the post-Fordist context. Pedagogies of affect describe the process by which affective performances are mapped onto particular kinds of laboring bodies, but there are also affective sensibilities that are endemic to the post-Fordist era and that emerge in the context of conditions for belonging. "Post-Fordist" here refers to the transformations in labor and governance I outlined in detail in chapter 1, which through rhetorics of flexibility have led to the increasing precarity of workers. Berlant (2007) argues that there is a "porous domain of hyperexploitative entrepreneurial atomism that has been variously dubbed globalization, liberal sovereignty, late capitalism, post-Fordism, or neoliberalism" (280). These terms have been used to describe a collection of phenomena impacting social life at multiple scales and in multiple domains. Throughout this ethnography, I use most of these terms to focus on different areas of social life in the contemporary moment. Here I use "post-Fordist affect" to draw particular attention to the relationship between affects and labor following transformations in the way humans understand work.

According to Hardt and Negri (2004):

Unlike emotions, which are mental phenomena, affects refer equally to body and mind. In fact, affects, such as joy and sadness reveal the present state of life in the entire organism, expressing a certain state of the body along with a certain mode of thinking. Affective labor, then, is labor that produces or manipulates affects such as a feeling of ease, well-being, satisfaction, excitement, or passion. ... One indication of the rising importance of affective labor, at least in the dominant countries, is the tendency for employers to highlight education, attitude, character, and "prosocial" behavior as the primary skills employees need. (108)

While the rise in the service sector created the contemporary articulation of intimate and affective labor in the post-Fordist moment (Boris and Parreñas 2010; Hardt and Negri 2004; Hochschild 1983), Ford and Fordism were also deeply invested in the production of particular laboring selves.

Henry Ford believed that workers who lived well were better workers. In 1914, he tasked the Sociological Department of the Ford Motor Company to oversee a range of social benefits for Ford employees under the leadership of Reverend Samuel S. Marquis. Employees received monetary incentives for living according to Ford's values of "living right," which included a range of standards from sobriety to proper hygiene. Investigators in the Sociological Department would appear at workers' homes to look for evidence of cleanliness and hygiene, sobriety, family values, thriftiness, sanitary conditions, and good morals (Palumbo-Liu 1999). Ford linked living well to a $5-a-day plan to give monetary incentives to workers who lived according to Ford's values. A Ford worker made a standard wage of $2.34 for an eight-hour day, but he could receive an additional $2.66 if Ford determined the worker was living well. The Sociological Department was responsible for determining if employees' personal lives and personal habits made them eligible for the full wage. In Henry Ford's value system, living correctly—or in a particular moral way based on hygiene, sobriety, and family values, among others—was directly linked to one's wage.

Ford's Sociological Department illustrates his investment in producing morally right workers through the control of their bodies and behavior. These mechanisms of control extended beyond the body and included correct affects as well as bodily dispositions. The Reverend Samuel Marquis wrote, "The Impression has somehow got around that Henry Ford is in the automobile business. It isn't true. Mr. Ford shoots about fifteen hundred cars out of the back door of his factory every day just to get rid of them. They are the by-product of his real business, which is the making of men" (Grandin 2009: 34). This is to say that while the articulation of post-Fordist affect is particular to the contemporary moment, it does have historical precedents in which bodies, affects, and sensibilities were tied to one's suitability and ability to perform work. These two historical moments demonstrate the ways that the management and control of affects is critical to the capitalist enterprise.

In the post-Fordist context, there is a kind of collective mourning for a promise of a better life that never materialized, of middle-class aspirations, or the promise of safety and security (Berlant 2007; Muehlebach and Shoshan 2012). Muehlebach and Shoshan (2012) write: "The variegated modes of re-membering, forgetting, grieving, and longing for these past horizons show multiple shades of ambivalence. On the one hand, we find a whole range of ways—some clamorous, others all-but-untraceable—in which people across the globe mourn, or struggle to resuscitate, certain moments of the Fordist dream. At the same time, to paraphrase Freud's (1953) com-ments on melancholia, it all-too-often appears as if we know *what* we have lost but not what we have lost *in* Fordism" (318). In other words, the affects produced in the wake of the post-Fordist era generate a kind of longing or melancholia for a bygone time and an attempt to recover a kind of stability or social belonging, a theme I take up further in chapter 5. Berlant (2007) describes post-Fordist affect as "a scene of constant bargaining with nor-malcy in the face of conditions that can barely support even the memory of the fantasy" (278). This kind of melancholia was reflected in the ways women spoke about work and unemployment.

This post-Fordist affect, a kind of nostalgia or desire for a past that included work stability, is importantly gendered and racialized. Nursing, because of its requirements of care and perhaps its physicality, has been gendered female. There is a systemic persistence in the post-Fordist era of devaluing work that women do and the feminization of particular kinds of wage labor. Saskia Sassen (1998) examines two instances of the incorpora-tion of women into wage labor and its subsequent feminization: the re-cruitment of women into new manufacturing and service work generated by export-led manufacturing in several Caribbean and Asian countries; and the employment of immigrant women in highly industrialized countries, particularly in major cities that have undergone basic economic restructur-ing. The feminization of the job supply and the need to secure a politically adequate labor force combine to create the conditions for precarious work. Thus, in the context of nursing, there is a labor shortage in Canada and a surplus of foreign-educated nurses, but the presumed solution to their difficulty in entering the field does not consist of reevaluating the ways foreign credentials are evaluated and counted, but in trying to change the bodily practice and affective performances of foreign workers in ways that are deeply wedded to racialized and gendered ideologies. Thus, these questions of affect are not bound to the classroom, but to larger articulations of what it means to try to live and work in the post-Fordist era with increasing job insecurity and precarity. This precarity is exacerbated for immigrant workers who find questioned not only their credentials and training, but their very bodily movements and affective displays that now mark them as fit or unfit for work.

Yet despite this alienation surrounding their bodies, affects, and suitability for work, there is still an "intense attachment" to Fordist labor (Muehlebach and Shoshan 2012), so that women seek out assistance in how to perform these appropriate affective displays for work, evidenced by the waitlists for such programs and my daily experience of volunteering at the Center. I was sometimes taken aback by the women I was meeting, some at their most desperate, their savings diminishing, their livelihoods unable to sustain them, and their children not living in a manner they had hoped. There was a moment at the Center that will forever be etched in my memory. I was in the habit of reporting to Zubeidah upon arrival at the Center. One day, shorthanded, she gave me the new job postings to affix to the bulletin board, and so I diligently tried to find a place to staple the listings between advertisements for local restaurants and movie nights. Suddenly a woman tapped on my shoulder. I turned, and was startled by how frantic she seemed. She started to speak quickly and passionately. She had lived in Canada for fifteen years and had happily worked in the healthcare industry, but recently she lost her job because she was never made full-time or permanent. As a precarious worker, she had few rights. She tried to go back home but it didn't work out; she had returned four months before and was desperate for work. She thought I was the employment expert because of the flyer I was holding. She begged me to help her.

This mourning, and desire, for steady full-time labor is an affective sensibility that the women in this study feel as they attempt to fulfill the promise of the good life that was not only a generational promise, but a transnational one. I explore this longing further in chapter 5, but what is important for this discussion of pedagogies of affect here is the ways affective attachments fuel the everyday encounters within and outside of the classroom.

As Molé (2012) argues, "In order to understand post-Fordist affect, we must take its paradoxes seriously: worker's near-totalizing investment in labor yet attending displacement from it" (377). Both within and outside their classroom, there was a deep investment in work despite their inability to find it. In Nurture classrooms as well as other settlement-services programs, there was a strong desire on the part of participants to gain entrance into a system that maintained their economic and social exclusion. Workers' investments in projects that contribute to their social exclusion may seem paradoxical in theory, but in practice they make perfect sense because women must succumb to these economic projects in order to survive. One cannot simply opt out of economic life. These women were subjected to the disciplining of their bodies and affects in order to be legible as good and modern workers, which was presented to them as necessary to support themselves.

Thus, affective and bodily performance is central to the making and practice of a modern worker. Flynn (2009) notes, "As with the category woman, there is nothing inherent or essential about the category nurse. The nurse is an invention, or a social creation, 'a role being played, not an essentialized nurturing identity being expressed.' In the complex web of the medical hierarchy, practitioners in training, like actors, learn how to play their roles, not only by gaining the required skills, but also through learning mannerisms and behavior that they are expected to display" (94). Within the sanitized sensorium, there are contrasting kinds of bodily performances, affects, and sensibilities required for entry into work. Nursing provides a special kind of case in the context of this study, in which performing a racialized femininity is central to one's presumed ability to work.

Expectations around affect transform, however, when women transition from intimate labor such as nursing to the cultural labor of performing difference. In intimate labor a woman performs a certain kind of feminized and racialized affect, while in cultural labor she performs a kind of sanctioned difference. The next chapter moves between the space of the classroom and the public stage of multicultural Toronto to look at the double bind that multicultural practice exerts on immigrant women, calling for the erasure of difference in certain contexts and the display of it in others. In the context of the cultural festival, for example, women must perform a kind of radical alterity embodied in the smells and sights of food, music, and clothing. Performances of cultural Otherness are crucial to the state's multicultural claims of liberalism and inclusivity, yet it continues to exclude immigrant women economically and materially.

CHAPTER THREE

SANITIZING CITIZENSHIP

In the 1910s the material link between being a "good worker" and being a "good citizen" was specifically highlighted in a festival sponsored by Henry Ford: "A giant pot was built outside the gates of his factory. Into this pot danced groups of gaily-dressed immigrants dancing and singing their native songs. From the other side of the pot emerged a single stream of Americans dressed alike in the contemporary standard dress and singing the national anthem. As the tarantellas and the polkas at last faded away only the rising strains of the national anthem could be heard as all the immigrants finally emerged. The enormous pressures which created this vast transformation amounted almost to forced conversion" (Gelderman, cited in Palumbo-Liu 1999: 27). Ford's festival took the multicultural metaphor of the melting pot as theater, demonstrating elite desire for the eradication of markers of cultural difference and celebrating the emergence of new Americans. We could interpret this festival as a historical precedent to the kind of cultural celebrations that are prevalent in Toronto today, though they employ a different metaphor: the salad bowl. This multicultural reworking of the melting pot is meant to celebrate cultural differences as a mix of distinct ingredients that complement each other but are not required to merge. The salad bowl comparison is more insidious because it suggests cultural acceptance, while in practice only sanctioning (and even producing) certain forms of cultural difference, a point discussed by authors such as Bhattacharjee (1992) and further explored in chapter 4. In contemporary Toronto, a radical alterity becomes the order of the day.

Ford's hygiene regimes may appear an archaic vestige of the past, but such civilizing programs are alive and well in the contemporary lives of unemployed immigrants to Toronto. This has meant the production of an appropriate citizen-worker in which the body as perceived by others is deeply implicated in one's ability to work. If in the Fordist context a worker was subject to a particular moral code, in the context of post-Fordist Toronto, a working body should be erased of all markers of Otherness: bodily odors, ethnic clothing (including the hijab), and foreign names. However, as the sanitized sensorium indicates, this reality exists in conjunction with ever-present public cultural festivals that purport to celebrate difference, which demonstrates that smells and ethnic clothes that are incommensurable on the job market are only contextually offensive. This contextual acceptance demonstrates two different sides of multicultural practice in Toronto.

This chapter explores how this practice of multiculturalism operates as a process of racialization, producing bodies as irrevocably Other through sensorial regimes. Jodi Melamed (2011) describes racialization as "a process that constitutes differential relations of human value and valuelessness according to specific material circumstances and geopolitical conditions while appearing to be (and being) a rationally inevitable normative system that merely sorts human beings into categories of difference" (2). Thus, racialization, or multiculturalism in this context, ascribes different levels of value to certain bodies and, further, "naturalizes the privileges of those who benefit from present socioeconomic arrangements and makes the dispossessions of those cut off from wealth and institutional power appear fair" (2). Thus, the process of racialization naturalizes power.

Within multiculturalism, race logics are embedded with liberal practices and thus include the recognition, toleration, and celebration of contextual sensorial difference as well as its marginalization and even expulsion from the labor market. The two sites explored in this chapter demonstrate a state-sanctioned sensorial form of governance, illustrating how the sanitized sensorium operates as a disciplinary tool. The sanitized sensorium reveals the ways that, in contrast to the rhetoric of "a nation built on difference," multicultural practice in Canada denies difference with regard to immigrant bodies while simultaneously recognizing that very difference in contextually specific sites. Both government and popular discussions in Canada on multiculturalism (through sources ranging from media accounts to government policy) describe a relinquishing of cultural imperialism and a celebration of "multi-ness," as demonstrated by cultural festivals or other public celebrations. This rhetoric is betrayed by the fact that neoliberal governance (in the form of government-funded, privately run settlement agencies) institutes certain ideals of bodily comportment on immigrants by attempting to teach them how to dress and act. This is an imposition of Canadian dominant culture; it is cultural imperialism in practice, and results in a form of racialization that has wide-ranging effects. Returning to the classroom for the last time, this chapter focuses on the sensorial aspects of these encounters between instructors and students. Sensorial regimes contained within the sanitized sensorium dictate bodily comportment and practice that are critical not only to belonging in the multicultural nation-state, but also to survival. Failure to present one's body appropriately results in exclusion from economic and late capitalist projects, leading to partial inclusion at best and at worst economic exploitation.

Sensorial regimes are a critical component of modernizing projects, as modernity itself produces racial knowledge. Rather than simply disciplining the alien Other, or eradicating racialized differences, critically important is the fact that modern projects also work to produce selective forms of racialized, sensorial alterity, disciplining Other subjects into a minoritized space. As Edward Said famously argues in *Orientalism*, these Westernized notions of self and Other produce not only ideas of the Other as savage and wild, but also simultaneously ideas of the self as civilized. Thus these contradictory strains of multicultural practice have dual effects, marking the racialized Other while simultaneously positioning the West as enlightened and civilized. When racialized women are compelled to perform different kinds of sensorial practices in dual contexts conditional to their belonging, these performances themselves become a constant reminder of their partial inclusion.

Taken together, these scenes of abjection and the threat of radical alterity provide the backdrop for a kind of empire of the senses in which the politics of smells, sights, and sounds have become not only a means of Othering, but of colonial expansion and nation-building. Paying attention to the daily affective attachments people have to sensorial phenomena and to the perceived affront to the senses, this chapter weaves together these contradictory state practices—the simultaneous erasure and recognition (or production) of differences as inscribed on the bodies of immigrant women—in order to analyze multicultural practice as a form of racialization. The multicultural project as experienced in urban Toronto—a city of tremendous racial, ethnic, and religious difference—calls for a particular set of expectations, demands, and negotiations regarding citizenship. There are multiple actors involved in the making of multicultural praxis: state workers, nonprofit workers, the public, the media, immigrant women of color, and self-described immigrant community leaders. Here I focus on the interweaving of these categories of people, publics, and representations.

Complicating Multiculturalism

Multiculturalism in Canada is a contentious thing. In October 2015, leading up to an election that would overturn Stephen Harper's conservative government, then immigration minister Chris Alexander and Minister for the Status of Women Kellie Leitch proposed measures to stop "Barbaric Cultural Practices Against Women and Girls," saying that Canada should have a "Zero Tolerance for Barbaric Practices Act" and that if re-elected, the government would institute an RCMP (Royal Canadian Mounted Police) task force and tip line for those wanting to report barbaric acts. In practice, the Barbaric Practices Act, as the public is calling it, consists of amendments to the Immigration Act and Criminal Code that already made such acts illegal, including polygamy, forced child marriage, and so-called honor killings. So what this new act would do is effectively link for the public these crimes with some essentialized notion of Muslim culture.[1]

These concerns around barbaric Muslim acts are linked to recent comments by former Prime Minister Stephen Harper, who used the phrase "old stock Canadians" in discussing refugee policy in a public debate. He said he would offer to bring more refugees than Canada has historically, but that there are limits: "We do not offer them a better health-care plan than the ordinary Canadian can receive. . . . I think that's something that new and old stock Canadians can agree with." When later asked about what he meant, he said, "It's supported by Canadians who are themselves immigrants, it's supported by the rest of us—by Canadians who have been the descendants of immigrants for one or more generations."[2] For Harper, an old-stock Canadian is one who was born in Canada and whose parents were born in Canada, effectively producing an essentialized notion of citizenship and of who belongs. The language of "Barbaric Acts" and "Old-Stock Canadians" echoes (and not too subtly) Orientalist constructions of the Other defined in contrast to an enlightened old-stock Canadian.

These kinds of debates signal the challenges posed to the practice of multiculturalism in Canada, a practice that has been subject to critique since its implementation as federal policy.[3] Its early supporters and canonical writers in the field, such as Charles Taylor (1994) and Will Kymlicka (1995), describe multiculturalism as a progressive form of liberalism in the Canadian context. Others have addressed whether or not liberalism as a doctrine is compatible with multiculturalism, leading some to argue whether multiculturalism is the problem, or if the real issue is in essentialist understandings of cultural diversity (Abu-Laban 2002). Vered Amit-Talai (1996) argues that the symbolic effectiveness of multiculturalism in Canada arises from its ambiguity, in which "vague ideas" of ethnic and cultural pluralism are conflated with civil rights, social justice, and government policy to create a symbolic bundle that is "as politically charged as it is indeterminate" (90). In October 2010, an editorial in the Canadian national newspaper the *Globe and Mail* (2010) argued that national discourse around minority culture should eliminate mention of multiculturalism and focus instead on "the concept of citizenship."[4] Rather than promote a multicultural society, they suggested that national discourse should promote individual membership as a Canadian citizen. Thus, multiculturalism in Canada and elsewhere has already been under scrutiny as the most effective means of dealing with racial and ethnic diversity. Indeed, I found that contradictions between the state's rhetoric of multiculturalism and the impact of its practices emerge in moments of friction among state bodies, civil society, and aspiring citizens. Looking closely at these points of conflict can reveal how multicultural policy arises through concrete social practices, and how aspiring citizens translate these policies into their everyday lives. The range of conflicts and interactions among governmental agency workers, immigration counselors, and immigrant women in Toronto demonstrates the changing nature of multiculturalism and citizenship in contemporary Canada.

Within Canadian multicultural policy there is an implicit approach to race that both produces and enacts racial hierarchies.[5] If all Canadian cultures are equal to one another except one, then what remains at the core of Canadian multiculturalism is an English (or white) subject. As Talal Asad (1993) argues, what becomes "crucial for [multicultural] government is not homogeneity versus difference as such but its authority to define crucial homogeneities *and* differences" (111). Slavoj Žižek (1997) takes up this question of multiculturalism and racism when he writes, "Multiculturalism is a disavowed, inverted, self-referential form of racism, a 'racism with a distance'—it 'respects' the Other's identity, conceiving the Other as a self-enclosed 'authentic' community toward which he, the multiculturalist, maintains a distance rendered possible by his privileged universal position" (44). This equation of multiculturalism with racism critically draws attention to the issue of proximity so that cultural difference is to be respected, even tolerated, but from a distance. This toleration, this form of respect serves to mask racism and race-based discrimination. Race matters, and any national project must use race even if it disavows it (Balibar and Wallerstein 1991). These theoretical discussions have taken on real-world significance in Canada, where the terms and context of multiculturalism have been hotly contested.[6]

The presumption that Canada is post-racial because of its commitment to multiculturalism was recently challenged by a report released from the United Nations Committee on the Elimination of Racial Discrimination, which examined the Canadian state's compliance with international law concerning racial equality. While it acknowledged positive measures in place, the committee highlighted a number of concerns impacting racial and ethnic communities in Canada: increasing socioeconomic gaps determined by race; racial profiling, including that of Black Canadians by police; the overrepresentation of Black and Indigenous people in the prison system; and the discrimination Black and Indigenous people encounter in the criminal justice system. In fact, Black men in Toronto are three times more likely to be stopped by police.[7] These facts were most recently supported by a *Maclean's* article that suggested, "Canada's race problem? It's even worse than America's," comparing the material conditions of the Black community in the United States to that of the Indigenous population in Canada.[8] The author argues, "Our Fergusons are hidden deep in the bush, accessible only by chartered float plane," given that 49 percent of Indigenous people live on reserves in remote parts of the country and make up less than 1 percent of the total population of the Greater Toronto area.[9] Further, half of Canada's Indigenous children live in states of poverty, 64 percent of them in Manitoba and Saskatchewan. Indigenous youth suffer at greater rates than nonindigenous youth; they are seven times more likely to be murdered and five times more likely to die of suicide. One in three young people in police custody is Indigenous.[10] While multicultural rhetoric denies social inequality, it is evident in the treatment of those considered Other.

The challenges to multiculturalism in these varied cultural contexts signal a kind of "crisis of multiculturalism," one that is often blamed in the contemporary era on what has come to be considered the "Muslim problem,"[11] a term used to describe a perceived radicalization of homegrown Muslim youth, those of the second generation who have participated in a range of events including the "Toronto 18," caught in 2006,[12] and the 2015 joining of ISIS by three British Pakistani girls.[13] The problem has been described as one of unassimilated minorities, and so these discussions are often accompanied by a call for a return to assimilation. This crisis of multiculturalism is not due to the presence of unassimilated minorities, but rather to the ways that difference is controlled, managed, and contained through liberal multicultural practices that create competing narratives of citizenship, which further alienate already marginalized aspiring citizens. So in this case, the widespread unemployment of skilled immigrant workers is not a multicultural problem of unincorporated immigrants; it is not a problem of the "savage," uncontainable Other. It is, in fact, a crisis of whiteness.

In conjunction with these theories, anthropologists have studied the politics of recognition in diverse societies. Elizabeth Povinelli (2002) has written extensively on late liberalism in the Australian context, focusing on the impasse of liberal conventions of law and policy revealed in the interface with indigenous worlds, what she has called "liberal settler multiculturalism." This articulation of the management and control of populations is distinct from postcolonialism (as in the work of Franz Fanon or the Subaltern Studies Collective): "Colonial domination worked by inspiring in colonized subjects a desire to identify with their colonizers," while, in contrast, "multicultural domination seems to work . . . by inspiring subaltern and minority subjects to identify with the impossible object of an authentic self-identity" (Povinelli 2002: 6). Instead of recognition, this has led to calls for a radical form of difference.

These questions of recognition have also been explored in the Canadian context in reference to Indigenous communities. Glen Coulthard (2007) has written about how self-determination efforts by Indigenous people in Canada have been recast as questions of "recognition," a process that, he asserts, simply reifies colonial power. Audra Simpson (2014) has provocatively recast this question of recognition in her study of the Mohawks of Kahnawà:ke, an Indigenous community that insists on self-governance and refuses Canadian or American citizenship. Her work explores this as a politics of refusal, instead of a politics of recognition. These theories of settler colonialism, which describe the displacement of Indigenous people by a colonial occupation, are conceptually and politically critical for comprehending racial and ethnic difference because they acknowledge that ongoing immigration results in the continued settlement of occupied land and the colonization of Indigenous people. At the same time, however, the scholarship simultaneously marks points of shared experiences and possibilities for coalition building between marginalized immigrants and colonized Indigenous peoples. But it is important to not equate these two phenomena, which would lead to rendering Indigenous populations as simply another ethnic group.

Finally, critical in this discussion is the fact that multiculturalism is a gendered phenomenon.[14] This chapter draws explicit attention to the violence inflicted by the multicultural state in the name of civilizing immigrant women. Such a civilizing mission seeks to eradicate not only cultural difference, but also markers of Otherness inscribed on immigrant women's bodies. The state emphasizes culture and cultural explanations to rationalize the foreign-trained worker problem, thus obscuring the racial and gendered nature of capitalist exploitation. Exploring the gendered logics of institutional structures demonstrates how culturally inscribed ideas about the Muslim woman are translated in the intimate interface between immigrant women and the state. This work thus reveals how these ideas and practices attempt to make Muslim immigrant women's bodies legible to the neoliberal, multicultural state, which ultimately does violence to them.

Sanitizing the Other

One of the settlement-services centers I worked with in downtown Toronto conducted a project called "No Hijab Is Permitted Here." In discussing the project with Amal, a member of the organization from Somalia whose expertise was in helping Muslim women find work, she told me they found that having a Muslim name had become a real barrier. "While professional organizations are gatekeepers," she said, "there is a real difference between visible Muslim women [meaning those who wore a hijab] and non-visible Muslim women." As part of the project, they had done focus groups in which Muslim women shared their difficulties in accessing the job market: "We felt we needed to document these problems." She admitted that even for her, the results were shocking. In the experiment they attempted to control for everything except the hijab, so they sent pairs of women of similar nationality, age, and height out with comparable résumés to see what would happen. Participants in the study attempted to seek employment in manufacturing, sales, and service sectors because these were considered common employment opportunities for women whose skills and education are not accredited. Experiences ranged from those wearing the hijab not being given application forms, to those without the hijab being given extra application forms for their friends. This study highlights the failure of the practice of multiculturalism in Toronto, signaling that racialized difference continues to result in economic exclusion. Rather than addressing this issue directly, settlement-services agencies govern new immigrants, domesticating their bodies for legibility in Canada.

Also crucial in this discussion are understandings of the relationship between the ideology of the state (here, multiculturalism) and the kinds of affect produced and regulated in its name. Ann Stoler (2002) has examined the connection between the "broad-scale dynamics" of colonial rule and the intimate spaces in which such forms of governance are enacted. Drawing on the work of Foucault, she suggests that these intimate spaces demonstrate what might be called the "microphysics of colonial rule," within which she locates the "affective grid of colonial politics" (7). Elizabeth Povinelli (2002) has examined Australian liberal multiculturalism as an ideology and practice of governance and a form of "everyday affective association and identification" (6) to explore the corporeal politics of Australian multiculturalism. Following Stoler and Povinelli, I examine the practice of multicultural governance in which intimate forms of embodiment are subject to regulation and control.

Settlement services in Toronto govern through a range of techniques—including affect, which is significant both politically and epistemologically. Stoler (2002) has written about the range of bodily affects implicated in colonial rule, from Javanese nursemaids being instructed to "hold their charges away from their bodies so that the infants would not smell of their sweat" (6), to Dutch children being forbidden to play with the children of servants for fear that they would begin "babbling and thinking in Javanese" (6). These instances were part of the project of rule in the colonies and were part of the colonial state's investment in "the education of desire." In the case of multiculturalism and the body, and the immigrant body in particular, the question of smell is of particular import. Smells express concepts of Oneness and Otherness and contribute to establishing bipolarities of smell, such as the evil odors of evil spirits versus the good odors of good spirits, or how men should smell strong while women should smell gentle (Classen 1993; Synnott 1991; both as cited in Low 2005). Discussions of immigration and smell have focused on the ways that smells have marginalized immigrant bodies; indeed, the smell of cooking on the body is a mark of Otherness.

In the context of the contemporary multicultural state, the immigrant body is constructed as the carrier of all that is undesirable and thus must be cleansed in the name of modern citizenship, which is crucial in the project of rule. Contrary to the notion that multicultural paradigms do not require particular modes of embodiment and self-presentation, in Toronto bodily praxis was predicated on a racialized ideal of what it means to participate in the public sphere. Citizenship is based on embodied practice in which certain bodies are subject to particular kinds of regulation and control. As Povinelli (2002) argues, "Liberalism is harmful not only when it fails to live up to its ideals, but when it approaches them" (13). Thus, in settlement-services classrooms, it is by enacting a form of care, through sensorial pedagogies, that liberal practice does harm to immigrant women.

Women's unemployment is managed at the level of the everyday through instructions on training their bodies and affects for legibility. As discussed in chapter 1, settlement-services workshops assumed a particular kind of unemployed subjectivity that, as I will elaborate on more here, needs to be erased of its sensorial difference. These intimate modes of governance demonstrate deeply held assumptions or conditions within the practice of multiculturalism in Canada in which sight and smell shape the limits of acceptability. The following classroom encounter exemplifies this limit. Dana, the instructor, was from a large, well-established international association that conducts nonprofit work. She was a white woman in her mid-forties, with short, white hair and a tall, lanky frame. She introduced herself to us, but did not ask the same of her audience. When I later interviewed Dana about how she came to give these trainings, she described a trajectory that was common among all but one of the workshop coordinators I spoke with: she was born and raised in Canada and had entered the workforce after her children had gone away to college. When I asked her about the instruction and how she decided on the content of the workshops, she said she would gauge her audience's needs after meeting them. While she had a uniform syllabus for all the workshops, she made changes depending on who was in attendance, which is a significant detail. Although smell was highlighted when teaching women from the subcontinent, the instructions were markedly different when participants were primarily from Europe. With non–South Asian audiences, facilitators did focus on bodily comportment involving gestures, but never on smell or ethnic dress.

The theme for that day's class was "Business Etiquette," and the room was packed with twenty women. Dana began with a remark that signaled her assumptions about class and education. She recommended that all participants at some point go to another local agency that offers English as a

Second Language classes, as well as academic tutoring up to grade-twelve level. One audience member, indignant and upset, said, "Literate women here work alongside the illiterate women." Dana had not realized that her audience was composed mainly of fluent English speakers who were highly skilled in specialized professions in Pakistan.

Dana emphasized, "It doesn't matter what you did in your home country. You're in Canada now." When thinking about clothing, she suggested, job seekers should consider their surroundings; she focused particularly on advising the participants—none of whom was wearing a headscarf at the workshop—not to dress "traditionally." "You need to consider how they perceive you. You need to fit," she said, adding, "10 percent of what interviewers consider is 'fit' in the workplace," effectively suggesting, if you wear a headscarf, you are never going to get work. Dana stressed, "You always need to look good, even if you're just dropping off a résumé." She suggested, "Don't wear too much make-up, don't wear too much perfume, and make sure your clothes are clean and don't have any distinctive smell. . . ." But her voice trailed off as she considered the implications of her suggestion—that these professional women would attend job interviews smelling "distinctive," and that such marked difference would become a hindrance to their employment. She further suggested, "Dress plainly, so you don't distract the employer from what we're saying, yet dress formally, don't wear sunglasses, and do not take your children to your job interview." Of note here is Dana's use of "we," referencing a racial and national community that excluded her audience.

She continued by saying about job applications, "We can't always understand your names, so please print clearly, or if you can, change your name, get a nickname if it's hard to pronounce." When questioned about dressing formally, she suggested participants "go out and see what people are wearing, dress plainly, be up-to-date, but dress modern." This directive necessarily puts the supposedly traditional practices these immigrant women held in Pakistan in direct opposition to constructed modern practices required of them in Toronto. This configuration not only renders Pakistani norms (in this case, what they wear) as archaic, but also creates a temporal relationship between traditional practices "in the past" and modern practices "in the future," reproducing a teleology of progress that marches toward the West. She reiterated, "Always be sure to shower first—you want to smell clean and not like Indian food, or masala, or foods that are foreign to us. You want to present yourself as clean and professional." Her emphases suggested to her audience that, at present, they were neither clean nor professional.

Dana then played a ubiquitous video called "First Impressions," which I had to watch in many of these workshops. A smiling man appears, dressed in a business suit headed for his first interview. A voiceover explains, "Success in an interview is 45 percent packaging, 35 percent responsiveness, and 10 percent experience. Interviewers will know whether they like you in the first seven seconds." Cut to a Latina woman named Rita, wearing bright makeup and revealing clothing, arriving for an office interview with her children. The receptionist looks at her with distaste. The voiceover reminds the viewer, "Be nice to gatekeepers, such as secretaries and administrators. They have a lot of control." Rita is rude. In another scene, a Chinese businessman named Chang has also paid too little attention to his appearance. He reaches out to shake the hand of his interviewer, who responds with a frown at Chang's limp handshake. Chang then bows, and offers his business card by holding two different corners with both his hands. Chang fails at his efforts to produce small talk and he sits on the edge of his chair, rather than in the middle. He also takes coffee, which he immediately spills. The voiceover says never to take coffee. Ultimately, Rita fails to find work. Chang, however, is considered successful, according to the video's narrator, because he managed to find a six-month contract. Next, a large animated face appears on the screen, detailing the mechanics of vocalization, including where to place one's tongue in one's mouth, as it is markedly different for native speakers of different languages (in these instances, Mandarin and Spanish). The voiceover suggests, "Focus on hearing the correct number of syllables and sounds in order to learn which ones to stress the way a native speaker would." The faceless narrator advises, "Choose a Canadian nickname, like Mike, or Mary. It'll make it easier."

When the video was over, Dana reviewed some key elements, emphasizing behavior: "During an interview you need to be confident, make eye contact, [but] don't be too over-confident—you need to have a good attitude, don't be too pushy." Many of the participants expressed shock and horror when the video revealed that interviewers will decide whether they like you within the first seven seconds of meeting. But the video's message was clear: Chang and Rita struggled in their job search because they do not have the appropriate bodily comportment to make it past the first seven seconds, not to mention the first interview. The video provides a highly gendered account of what the two did wrong, with Rita's mistakes emphasizing her role as a mother, her clothing, and her sexuality, and Chang's focusing on his inability to perform masculinized American business culture with his limp handshake and deferent bow. Both are illustrated as haphazard and clumsy. The entire class burst into laughter when the video described Chang as "successful" after he managed to acquire a short-term contract, rather than a full-time job.

At the end of the lecture, the participants loudly discussed the fact that Dana's "business etiquette" consisted of instructions on how to dress, speak, and act. This emphasis on comportment provoked indignation from many. One participant, Naseem, said to me that she had come across many workshop participants who were not working in their fields. "They learn how to shake hands, but nothing else!" she said. Many voiced their concerns about the specificity of body language and clothing over job placement. When I later had the opportunity to speak to Zeba about her experience in the workshop, she highlighted the issue of smell. "Why do they think I smell bad? It is just food. They eat Indian food at the shopping center!" Zeba immediately homed in on the hypocrisy of the workshop leaders, and indeed the larger Canadian public, which accepts the smells of an exotic South Asia and participates in its consumption in one context but not in another. As the workshop illuminated, smell is particularly significant in the moral construction of self and Other, and part of the process of racialization. It functions as a medium through which judgments are made concerning raced, classed, and gendered Others. As a process of Othering, the act of perceiving the odor or smell of an individual defines *both* the self and the Other through difference (Low 2005).

Smell is implicated in a social and moral order tied to the prevailing ideology of multiculturalism in Toronto and is an important part of the process of racialization. Or, put another way, smells can racialize. Classen, Howes, and Synnott (1994) have argued that the sense of smell has been excluded from the realm of reason, associated instead with savagery. Rinaldo Walcott (2003) has examined the ways that the "food odors" of Somali residents in a primarily white condominium in Toronto were imagined to be an "affront to 'Canadian ways of living'" and were used to mark them as outsiders (126). This is a civilizing mission of a particular sort, distinct from colonial projects that aimed to turn natives into white gentlemen (and -women). The similarities lie in the production of a national, or even global, professional worker whose sanitized body is interchangeable and universal, and is intimately tied to social class and upward mobility. Workers in the global market are called upon to demonstrate, to borrow a phrase from Koichi Iwabuchi (2002), the sweet scent of Asian modernity—which in this case is no scent at all.

That Dana instructed the women not to smell like South Asian *food* points to how smell is also particularly gendered in this context. The smell of food reminds people that these "foreign-trained professionals" also cook, invoking images of the domestic arena and women's unpaid work. As in this and nearly all of the workshops I attended, instruction was directed toward their "South Asian–ness," such that smell and appearance become intertwined with cultural and bodily difference. While mediated by the senses, the inclusion and exclusion of Pakistani women in Canada's public sphere is about being, in the words of Mary Douglas (2002), out of place. It is not only about "smelly bodies," but about the *idea* of smelly bodies. The issue of smell defines how a Canadian (or national) body should be: the national body does not smell—or, more accurately, smells in such a way that the very odor disappears. It is not an issue of not smelling, but of smelling "like us," with the attending assumption that "we" have no smell. "We" are neutral.

Scholarly work has explored the role of the senses, and smell in particular, in the making of the social body. Low (2006) highlights the connections between smell and morality, whereby "smell as a social medium is intertwined with issues of olfactory acceptance and hence social and moral approval" (608). Rather than focusing on the body as such, I am interested in the body as a social medium by which sensory phenomena are affectively registered and translated into social ideas not only of belonging but also of morality and good citizenship. Smells have also been representative of immigrant communities' inability to assimilate. Manalansan (2006) has described a tension in the interpretation of immigrant odors, in which the smells are either conditional (i.e., they can be removed) or they adhere to the body, thus justifying the removal of the bodies themselves. Employing Kristeva's notion of abjection, Hyde (2006) has further argued that the expulsion of "odorous Others" is a means by which polities maintain their status. What I seek to contribute to these important works is an examination of the ways that the "smell" of South Asia is a means of both *exclusion* and *inclusion*, and the ways the liberal multicultural state manages such sensorial phenomena as an important part of the process of "immigrant integration."[15]

Bodily smell has been intimately tied to class and modernity. As Classen, Howes, and Synnott (1994) write, "Smell has been marginalized because it is felt to threaten the abstract and impersonal regime of modernity by virtue of its radical interiority, its boundary-transgressing propensities and its emotional potency" (5). George Orwell claimed the " 'real secret' of class distinctions in the West could be summed up in four frightful words . . .

The Lower classes smell," further suggesting that "race hatred, religious hatred, differences of education, of temperament, can all be overcome, 'but physical repulsion cannot,' whence the persistence of class distinctions" (Orwell quoted in Classen et al. 1994: 8). Orwell astutely draws a connection between olfaction and the symbolic representation of socioeconomic status, real or perceived. However, it is not something intrinsic to smell itself that codifies meaning; rather, these meanings are socially and culturally produced. Thus, any food smell, even a distinctly North American one like that of hamburgers for instance, if detected on the body of a South Asian may signal Otherness because of the perception that they already represent alterity, that they already and always, smell bad.

In the contemporary era, the whole body, not just its smell, becomes a site of engagement with the production of citizenship and modern subjectivity. Nayan Shah (2001) has written eloquently on the centrality of the relationship between immigration, citizenship, and the body to symbolic practices of inclusion and exclusion. Shah traces the ways that concerns about the Chinese were central to "the social classifications of racial danger, difference, and subordination" (5). The idea of cleanliness, or the uncleanliness of immigrant bodies, has been imagined not only to be a threat to social cohesion, but also in fact a literal threat to the health of (white) citizens. State practices of instituting order on seemingly disorderly subjects are central to the modern project.

The marking of immigrant bodies was made particularly evident in the case of Razia, who participated in a workshop geared toward foreign-trained professionals from diverse fields. Razia had been living in Toronto for a year and a half, and had been a practicing lawyer in Pakistan for five years before immigrating. In order to be re-accredited as a lawyer, she learned she would have to begin her education again. While holding several survival jobs, such as making kebabs at an Indian restaurant and cashiering at Walmart, she attended a range of unemployment workshops that did not teach her how to become employed as a lawyer. She regularly wore a scarf around her neck, and while some employers in various survival jobs were accepting of it, unemployment workshop leaders suggested she stop wearing it. Razia was not wearing anything resembling Pakistani clothing or representing "the Muslim veil." With a tone of disgust, she told me, "I got it at the Dufferin mall. Why do they think it's Pakistani? Because I'm Pakistani?" The scarf she wore was marked as a "Pakistani scarf" because a Pakistani was wearing it; smells and bodily adornments became marked as different because of the wearer, which points to the ways that this process is always doomed to fail. Even though she did what was required of her and attempted to erase traces of minority culture from her body, what she wears and how she smells will always be marked Other because of the color of her skin.

Another leader of an unemployment workshop for South Asian women went one step further by describing the hijab as dangerous. She illustrated this point by using the example of a woman who was encouraged not to wear her hijab for an interview at a home for the developmentally disabled, since one of the patients could pull at the scarf and strangle her. She did not, however, identify necklaces or dangling earrings as similarly dangerous; the hijab became emblematic not only of tradition and the past, but of something that could now choke or strangle them. This workshop leader inadvertently provided a materialist explanation for a metaphorical problem. The wearer of the hijab presents a kind of cultural Other that injures its wearer through the perception that she is inassimilable, dangerous, and threatening—all at once. Such Otherness is uncontainable and irreconcilable with the modern project of producing model citizen-workers.

Being directed not to wear the hijab was repeated in every workshop I attended in which Pakistani women were present—regardless of whether any were wearing one. It is important to note that at least in Toronto, it is not typical for Pakistani women to wear the hijab; however, the hijab and shalwar cameeze suits are popularly understood as traditional forms of bodily adornment in contrast to the modern dress associated with appropriate secular womanhood. These kinds of moments illustrate the ways secular modes of governance explicitly direct Pakistani women on how to move and how to dress. While it is true that the hijab has a particularly contentious position as not only a cultural, but also a contested religious signifier, for my purposes here the point is simply about the marking of Otherness in all its varied semiotic forms, and the equation of such marks of Otherness with unemployment. There is a large body of scholarly work concerning Muslim women and dress, in particular veiling and bodily comportment as well as the relationship of veiling to inhabiting an appropriately pious subject (e.g., Fernando 2010; Mahmood 2001). Here I include practices such as wearing the hijab as a form of racialized difference (particularly after 9/11), and so when nonprofit workers suggest the limiting of such clothing practices, they invoke the refashioning of immigrant bodies and promote a particular kind of racialized secular body.

As authors such as Miriam Ticktin (2008) have described, the state ultimately decides what national and religious performances entail; so, for instance, wearing the hijab is fixed "as a coerced act from which [Muslim] women must be saved" (84). As Sherene Razack (2001) has argued in the case of South Asian women in Canada, women are given the choice of either attending to cultural differences and being stereotyped as Other, or of ignoring cultural differences and reifying the idea of the universal, liberal, individual subject. As the example of settlement services demonstrates, modernizing projects aimed at immigrant integration relocate systemic issues of unemployment to a problem of the body: "Don't wear the hijab if you want to get a job."

Through the training workshops, immigrants are taught a kind of cultural habitus for legibility in the public sphere (here, the working world) in Toronto; but these practices reveal the ways multicultural claims of universality are in fact conditional. In this sense, it is a process that is doomed to failure since these women will never overcome the obstacle of their raced and racialized bodies. These unemployment workshops present a white Canadian subject who is invisible and who participants are supposed to strive to embody—the other markers (clothing, comportment, bodily smells) are simply ways of not naming the actual fact of their foreignness. This kind of Othering cannot be explicitly articulated as such and instead becomes a question of food, music, and clothing.

Although Dana was a well-meaning presenter, an attempt to erase difference seeps into her account—not despite her helping immigrant women, but because of it. Beyond the immediate intentions of the workshop leaders, however, it is indeed possible that if women showed up to a job interview smelling like foreign foods, they would never achieve inclusion in the formal economy. The problem thus transcends the space of the workshop.

This phenomenon illuminates multiple publics, among them the job market and the cultural festival, in which the smell of food on the body of a woman, for example, is understood in two diametrically opposing ways. In the context of the job market, the smell of South Asian food on the body suggests that these foreign women cook foreign food at home; but during cultural festivals, the smell of generic South Asian food reminds Canadian consumers of the exotic lands where these foods originate. This distinction suggests that in its embodied form, South Asian food smells repugnant; yet in a disembodied form, it is appealing. The smell of food on an immigrant body can be described or understood as private, and therefore dangerous and threatening to the multicultural nation in one respect, and alternately treated as a public, commodified, accessible form of pleasure for white Canadian consumption of the other. Thus, the meanings of different smells do not only vary cross-culturally but also contextually. Sara Ahmed (2000) argues, "Ethnicity becomes a spice or taste that can be consumed, that can be incorporated in the life of the one who moves between (eating) places. Differences that can be consumed are the ones that are valued: difference is valued insofar as it can be incorporated into, not only the nation space, but also the individual body.... By implication, *differences that cannot be assimilated into the nation or body through the process of consumption have no value*" (117–18, emphasis in original). Between these different contexts, the look and smell of citizenship change.

Sensing Citizenship

The senses convey meaning. "They [the senses] are operators, which make it possible to convey the isomorphic character of all binary systems of contrasts connected with the senses, and therefore to express, as a totality, a set of equivalences connecting life and death, vegetable foods and cannibalism, putrefaction and imputrescibility, softness and hardness, silence and noise" (Levi-Strauss 1964 quoted in Sutton 2010: 210). Here Lévi-Strauss conveys the contradictions the senses can embody and project. To his list, I would add "the self and other." The senses, then, convey messages about the social world. Turning to the sanitized sensorium, competing social meanings can then be ascribed to the same sensorial phenomena to signify belonging and non-belonging depending on context. Between the site of the classroom and the cultural festival, the conditions of belonging shift. For instance, rendered in terms of the sensory pleasures of an exotic South Asia, foreign smells become part of an acceptable model of difference: "I am tolerant; that food smells really good." In the cultural festival, such smells become cultural commodities, rather than liabilities. The broader implication here pertains to the contradiction at the heart of multiculturalism: Be different, but only in certain contexts. Multicultural practice in this context specifically *calls for* foreignness, exoticness, and smelling "different." Foods that are "foreign," marked "bad" in the context of job searches where difference is to be mitigated, are now marked delicious when difference is to be embraced. Such "ethnic" identifiers like food, music, and clothing inform the sanitized sensorium and help to construct people's perceptions of what it means to be South Asian, and by extension, just how "South Asian" one can be and still qualify for inclusion into Canadian society. The management of difference does not go undisputed, however. In the next chapter I will focus on the agency of the Pakistani women I interviewed as they fashion alternative models of the self by resisting norms, values, and constructions of appropriate citizenship around the category "South Asian." But first, it is important to highlight the contradictions between the sanitization that happens in the space of the workshops and the public face of multiculturalism because of the distinct roles immigrant women have in these different contexts: as flexible workers in one and as displays of multicultural Canada's inclusivity in the other.

In 2001, the space for a South Asian cultural festival was created by the demise of Desh Pardesh (DP), a multidisciplinary arts festival that functioned as a venue for underrepresented and marginalized groups within Toronto's South Asian diasporic community to participate in public culture. DP was a lesbian- and gay-positive, feminist, anti-racist, anti-imperialist, and anti-caste organization that operated from 1989 to 2001. It was originally conceived as "Salaam Toronto!" and was administered by Khush (a collective of South Asian gay men in Toronto) as an alternative space for South Asian diasporics. The DP festival was funded by academic institutions, media and film boards, and government-sponsored grants for LGBTQ organizations; however, the festival and its administrative body closed due to a financial crisis in 2001 (Desh Pardesh, 2007). Its demise left a vacuum, leading other segments of the South Asian community to turn to the government for more formalized recognition of the community.

On December 14, 2001, the government of Ontario declared May South Asian Heritage Month under the South Asian Heritage Act of 2001.[16] Throughout that year, parts of the Ontario community had agitated to establish an Indian Arrival and Heritage Month, but the government rejected the name to avoid confusion with laws pertaining to Indigenous populations—a point I take up in more detail in chapter 4. Since then, the federal government in Ottawa has hosted celebrations throughout the country, the largest of which is on Parliament Hill. Members of all levels of government participate in South Asian Heritage Month, making public appearances and giving speeches that encourage "diversity." For instance, in recent years, representatives such as then Minister of Citizenship, Immigration, and Multiculturalism Jason Kenney,[17] have attended. In a speech at

DesiFest, the event that closed the South Asian Heritage Month activities in 2008, Kenney said:

> Our core Canadian values are democracy, freedom, human rights, and the rule of law. The more than 200,000 people who come to Canada annually from every corner of the world embrace these values, adding an often indefinable element to our sense of who we are. . . . It's great to witness such a committed and dedicated group of people who clearly see links between their Canadian citizenship, their civic participation, and their commitment to maintaining a connection with their cultural heritage. . . . Canada has an enviable record of integrating newcomers by encouraging their full participation in our society. One of the cornerstones of our pluralistic society is that all citizens benefit from equality under the law, regardless of their cultural or religious background.

As this quote demonstrates, the government is deeply invested—not only financially but also ideologically—in the promotion of "diversity," and more specifically to South Asian Heritage Month.[18]

Many people consider this monthlong celebration to be part of the success story of Canadian multiculturalism because of the recognition it provides minority subjects. However, while political philosophers Charles Taylor (1994) and Will Kymlicka (1995) have written that multiculturalism in the Canadian context is a progressive kind of liberalism, critics such as Yasmeen Abu-Laban (2002) have argued that the central problem with it lies in the essentialist understandings of cultural diversity it promotes. Talal Asad (1993) asserts that while "difference is certainly a crucial issue at the level of the law's treatment of individual citizens (the bearers of rights and duties), it is also relevant to the individual's desire to have and to maintain a collective identity" (262). Further, David Theo Goldberg (2002) has argued that the multicultural state is inherently a racial state, writing that the "apparatuses and technologies employed by modern states have served variously to fashion, modify, and reify the terms of racial expression, as well as racist exclusions and subjugation" (4). Multicultural policy was designed with the central concern of managing racial and ethnic difference by creating categories (census and legislative), thus becoming a population-based management tool that controls and contains the bodies of citizens and subjects.

As a census category for both a visible minority group and an ethnic origin, "South Asian" signifies a unified community, despite the actual diversity of its "members" in diaspora. For example, in a report titled "South Asians in Canada: Unity through Diversity," a study developed by Statistics Canada in partnership with the Department of Canadian Heritage, the authors claim: "The South Asian community is one of the most diverse visible minority groups.... And yet, the South Asian community is one of the most unified when it comes to the value they attach to family interaction, the maintenance of social networks within their cultural group, and the preservation of ethnic customs, traditions and heritage languages" (Tran, Kaddatz, and Allard 2005). Interestingly, all of these characteristics are always used to define and describe the impossibility of their full incorporation (refusal to shed ethnic customs, language, and group-based identification).

The flagship event of the South Asian community in Toronto takes place in August in the form of a cultural festival called "Masala! Mehndi! Masti!" (MMM), which official materials translate as "Spices, Hennah, and Fun." (A number of my interviewees stressed that they thought it was peculiar to use the term "Masti," as they understood it as a derogatory term for girls who do "bad things.")[19] As I walked through MMM one year, I noticed that the small section of tables for nonprofit groups were eclipsed by stages of South Asian dance performances, Indian food stands, and stalls selling jewelry.

Abhishek Mathur and Jyoti Rana created MMM in 2001 in the wake of the death of Desh Pardesh. In an interview with Meena, a member of a nonprofit organization involved with MMM, she said that while DP dealt with political issues, she felt that MMM represented "status quo Bollywood." Local community activists miss DP, believing that it was more a political venue than one for entertainment. Despite resistance from members of the activist community, MMM has been a tremendous success. Attendance between 2001 and 2008 grew from 25,000 to 100,000. The event is held at Harbourfront every year and typically consists of a three-day summer festival with dance performances, comedy, art, photography, mehndi parlors, food stalls, and cooking demonstrations.[20] There was also a midnight yoga session by an organization called Yogapalooza.

This particular year MMM was very well attended, with approximately 60,000 people participating. It prominently featured two commoditized elements always associated with South Asia in these festivals—food and clothing. The food section was under a tent away from the main building and adjacent to the outdoor marketplace. Many popular restaurants from "Little India" had set up stalls to sell food. Mango lassi was sold everywhere as a popular, imagined authentic South Asian drink, alongside butter chicken and samosas. Of significance is not just the fact that Indian food was being sold, but also the type, with each stand specializing in generic fare that could be purchased at any food-court restaurant in any mall. Similarly, the garments for sale represented a popular notion of South Asia—one that arises out of film, television, and media representations of the country. There were numerous stalls that featured Indian sari fabrics, heavy gold and silver jewelry, lighter cotton fabric tunics, and leather slippers. In conversations with the vendors, I learned that the buyers here were most often tourists who wanted to purchase an authentic piece of India, thus revealing that these particular commodities also signify very different meanings depending on who wears them.

Another area of clothing sales differed greatly from that understood to be traditional dress, including silk-screened T-shirts and "Canadian" clothing fashioned by Indian designers. The T-shirts had Indian-themed patterns printed on them, with the intended market being young, hip South Asian women who attend the festival. These clothing stalls, fashioned by local young Indian women designers, enable a similar type of commodity purchase. In this case, the fashionable, often second-generation South Asian woman, although she may feel more entitled, is also purchasing a piece of culture in the way the tourist might.

Cultural festivals emerge as a type of sensorium in which subjects are supposed to distinguish between appropriate and inappropriate moments to display their Otherness. In the context of the cultural festival, particular kinds of differences are admired and appreciated as signs of an authentic South Asia. During South Asian Heritage Month, dance performances, arts exhibits, and food stalls (predominantly Indian) take the celebration of culture out into the city streets. The local Little India on Gerard Street closes down several times during the month for food fairs. At every event I attended, long lines of South Asians and non–South Asians alike would form around the food stalls. Because the goal of these festivals is outreach to the larger community, there is often a large percentage of non–South Asians in attendance. Over the years as I waited patiently in line at various South Asian festivals for my mango lassi, I overheard a number of conversations between non–South Asians remarking on how delicious the food smelled and how exotic it all was.

The focus on South Asian food also draws attention to another aspect of the sensorium, that of taste. In this sense, taste takes on a double meaning, signaling the sensation of food on the tongue, but also appropriateness and cultural capital. The sensorium is a sensuous experience taking into account tastes and culture. As Bourdieu (1984) has argued, cultural capital denotes social distinction, which mediates belonging and non-belonging. "Taste," then, translates the literal smells of South Asian food into the metaphorical realm of cultural capital and social distinction. Taste becomes an aesthetic, such that social class and belonging are mediated by one's cultural practices, habits, and performances.

These markers of taste are not only experienced and performed by immigrant women, but also by non–South Asian Canadian visitors to these festivals and by extension by the multicultural state itself. That is, non–South Asians gain cultural capital and distinction in the context of a multicultural state by their participation in authentic performances of minority culture. Demonstrating not only tolerance for cultural difference, but also contextualized pleasure, becomes a kind of social distinction and cultural capital for non–South Asians. By extension, the multicultural state also gains cultural capital by permitting these kinds of performances of minority culture, as a sensuous experience of difference. For instance, the United Nations Alliance of Civilizations praised Canada for this practice, stating: "Every summer, Canada celebrates its multicultural reality with numerous festivals. These festivals bring together a rich diversity of cultural heritages, represented by ethnic and community groups living together in Canada."[21] These cultural performances benefit the state on the international stage, as they directly contribute to Canada's reputation as multicultural and inclusive. Therefore, acceptable difference and cultural capital for both the producer of difference (here, South Asian women) and the consumer (multicultural Canada) are intimately connected.

The smells of South Asian food signal the consumption of South Asian commodities and culture, which themselves are fine for local food courts and cultural festivals, but inappropriate in the context of work. These kinds of phenomena signal the ways the smells of an imagined South Asia are only situationally repugnant. There is the "quotidian dilemma" of cooking smells representing both cultural heritage and the means through which minorities are "Othered" (Manalansan 2006). Smells, unlike offensive bodies, cannot be contained; as such, the focus on offensive odors highlights an anxiety over managing refugee bodies in public space (Ong 2003). The Toronto example contributes to these important works in illustrating how South Asian food smells and forms of embodied difference also become a means of inclusion and beneficial cultural commodification. Here, I build on a long critique of liberal multiculturalism that the only forms of acceptable difference consist of "food, music, and language" (e.g., Fish 1997; Žižek 1997).

There is an inherent power differential in multiculturalism, with some having the power to determine inclusion and exclusion and others who must remain subject to such judgments. Žižek (1997) critiques the rhetoric of multiculturalism by arguing that respect for the Other is merely illusory. "Liberal tolerance" merely condones some practices of "the Other," such as celebrating ethnic cuisine, while denouncing divergent cultural practices under the umbrella of "fundamentalism." He writes, "The 'real Other' is by definition 'patriarchal,' 'violent,' never the Other of ethereal wisdom and charming customs" (37), further suggesting that multicultural logic is an inherently classed discourse in which global elites are favored; their superiority is maintained through their claims to respecting different cultures, thus creating a patronizing Eurocentrism. While critics of multiculturalism are correct in the context of the multicultural festival, multiculturalism does something different when it comes to demands on the body to qualify for work. Immigrants must perform these differing forms of embodied citizenship— the sensory, the visceral—to become legible, but these two contexts do not exist in isolation, but rather are intrinsically interwoven and central to the practice of multiculturalism.

One secondary example of a cultural festival that illustrates this contradiction in multicultural practice is the Canadian National Exhibition (CNE) public Eid prayer. While not the only Eid celebration in Toronto, every year on the Muslim holiday, the Muslim Association of Canada hosts a prayer meeting at a CNE convention center in which close to 15,000 Toronto-area Muslims participate. It is advertised as an invitation to "join this grand celebration that has become a fabric of Ontario's heritage and Toronto's multicultural mosaic."[22] A large, plain building, the CNE is normally deserted during the winter, but on that day, the streets are filled with people. Little girls wearing patent-leather shoes and frilly dresses run around together in groups. Families struggle to stay together amidst the crowds trying to enter the buildings. There is a point just before the entrance where families divide, men entering one door and women another. Small children, especially boys, throw tantrums at the audacity of being separated from their fathers and the indignity of having to sit in the women's section. Women pray in the second half of the hall, while men pray in the first. People carefully lay out large cloths, or small prayer mats, and try to stay shoulder to shoulder, lest the devil get in between them, as I was told over and over and which resonated with my own religious upbringing in Toronto. At the back of the prayer hall, in the spirit of a festival, there are small carnival rides for children: a Ferris wheel, a carousel, and games. Along the right side, tables are set up to sell all manner of desserts, as well as prayer books, Islamic educational tools, and Muslim baby-name books.

One year, former Toronto mayor Mel Lastman was there to give a speech. Everyone was excited. Lastman is a small man with a large head of silver-grey hair, short in stature, and very loud. His speech was concise, focusing on how well-adjusted and hard-working "you" and "your" children are, the "you" referring to the Toronto Muslim community. "You should be proud." I looked around, expecting to find expressions of horror or distaste, but was met instead with pleased expressions at his characterizations of Muslims in Toronto. The former mayor's speech, with its hearkening to the "model minority," is indicative of the core contradiction in Canadian multiculturalism. While multicultural practice in Canada allows for the erasure of certain types of difference, it is also invested in recognizing (even producing) other kinds of difference in the name of creating a Canadian national identity imagined to be predicated on inclusion. The same markers of bodily difference celebrated in multicultural sites, however, are denigrated in the context of the job search. This is indicative of another way that immigrant bodies have become central to the making—not undermining—of national identity, and how they are a crucial site to witness the implementation of the sanitized sensorium.

Through the example of Toronto's settlement services, I have sought to examine emergent contradictions in Canadian multicultural policies and new forms of governance, to examine how social inequalities are managed in liberal democratic contexts. Neoliberal forms of governance aimed at South Asian immigrant integration result in the disciplining of immigrant bodies by illustrating obstacles to their successful transition to full participation via the formal economy. However, as the example of the South Asian festival suggests, other practices within the Canadian regime of multiculturalism tend to reinforce those same differences. Thus, these various attempts at "inclusion" produced by different modalities of state governance have unintended, contradictory effects. Here, these contradictory forms of interpellation—the attempts to simultaneously erase and celebrate (read produce) differences—result in the further marginalization and alienation of immigrant subjects.

As I have argued in this chapter, the look and smell of South Asia are markers of both inclusion and exclusion. This is evidenced by the different contextual value of the smell of an exotic South Asian festival versus a repugnant South Asian body on the job market, or the wearing of what is understood to be traditional dress in a cultural festival versus on a job interview. Smell serves as a marker of Otherness, but its meaning varies contextually. The practice of multiculturalism reveals an implicit process of moralizing that takes place through the politics of multiculturalism in Canada and is enacted through the senses. This moralizing process simultaneously attempts to celebrate, produce, and erase differences inscribed on the bodies of immigrant women through what I have suggested is a sensorial regime. The partial inclusion of immigrant bodies into public national life has been widely discussed by social theorists. Here, I have drawn attention to the sensory dimension of multicultural politics, and to a terrain of multicultural practice, in order to understand the conditions of citizenship enabled by this model. This pedagogical tendency in the settlement-services sector is not coincidental or to be chalked up to a few bad instructors. The sheer number of times I heard highly skilled women instructed to take off their headscarves, change their names, and bathe indicates this is a systemic problem of the modernist project in which there is only one way to be a model citizen-worker—and that is to be "like us."

The sanitized sensorium primes both the greater Canadian public and Pakistani immigrant women themselves to engage a multicultural public through sensorial regimes. In Toronto the sights, sounds, and smells of immigrant bodies produce in different contexts contrasting narratives of citizenship and multicultural belonging. These sensory conditions contain the possibility of inclusion, and yet the constant reminder of their Otherness. However, performing within the sanitized sensorium has the capacity for subversion, as well. For instance, eye contact takes on new meaning from within the sanitized sensorium. Rather than only signifying masculinized business culture, eye contact signals both facing white culture and being seen by it. The moment of contact generates an affective encounter between self and Other that produces both in that moment. That is, through a colonialist lens, or from the perspective of the colonizer, the Other is viewed and categorized as more and less aberrant for inclusion. Through a subversive lens, or from the perspective of the racialized, the Other views back, bearing witness to the trial it is subjected to, similarly gauging what is necessary for not only inclusion, but also survival. The next two chapters explore how women react to these sensorial regimes and conditions for cultural citizenship—how they look back. Taking on the affective and sensorial experiences of racialization, the next chapter examines the consequences of the creation of the multicultural category "South Asian."

CHAPTER FOUR

RACIALIZING SOUTH ASIA

The extended face-off with conservatism has had a deforming effect, encouraging multiculturalism to know what it is against but not what it is for.—HENRY LOUIS GATES JR., "Beyond the Culture Wars"

"Who are they, the South Asians?" Madiha asked as she looked around the annual incarnation of Masala! Mehndi! Masti! (MMM). Madiha had migrated to Toronto from Pakistan and was a frequent visitor to the local immigrant women's settlement-services organization where we met. She had volunteered to sit at a table at MMM to represent the organization and distribute information on their services. To Madiha, "South Asian" was "just a Canadian thing," and she did not categorize herself in that way. To her, South Asians were Indians, and this event, like all of South Asian Heritage Month, had been created for Indians, not Pakistanis. During the numerous planning activities leading up to South Asian Heritage Month events in Toronto, conversations always inevitably turned to the meaning of "South Asian," which many Pakistani women rejected because of its cultural homogenization. During one such conversation, Naseem, originally from Karachi, said, "South Asians here are brought under the same umbrella. Canada does it because we look the same." Echoing Madiha's question, she asked, "Who are they, 'South Asians'? . . . I never heard 'South Asian' before coming here."

This self-distancing from "South Asian" was a narrative I heard repeatedly during fieldwork, and yet another example of how multicultural state practices can end up excluding subjects and citizens through practices aimed at inclusion. But, as I also learned, identity is complicated. When explicitly asked about the categorization, most I spoke with rejected it. Yet many of those same respondents were women I had met through South Asian organizations, and many of them also participated in South Asian Heritage Month, indicating that they did engage strategically with the category when necessary. Nadiya's statements represent this perspective well. She was a receptionist for a financial firm. Born in Karachi and a practicing Muslim, Nadiya had migrated for marriage under family reunification. In Pakistan she had been working as an elementary school teacher, which she had planned to do in Toronto. However, upon arriving she found out it would be impossible due to barriers to accreditation, so she never tried. She had been working for eighteen months as a receptionist after being trained for six months in computer science, but expressed gratitude for being able to work at all. She lived in a government housing project in Scarborough.

When our conversation turned to the category of South Asian, she said, "South Asian is a newly coined, politically correct term. I have been in this part of the world for six years now and only very recently have I come across it when filling out a form. Previously I have always referred to myself as a Pakistani due to lack of another word." Her remark that she only recently came across "South Asian" when filling out paperwork is indicative of her understanding of it as a governmental category of difference, and one that she might alternately accept or reject depending on the context. Social theorists have written about the complex negotiation racial, national, and sexual Others must engage as they navigate majority culture (e.g., Kurien 2003; Muñoz 1999, Spivak 1988)[1]. This chapter charts that negotiation with multicultural categories of inclusion as part of the back and forth that happens in the process of racialization and the making of multiculturalism, asking how women react to these sensorial regimes and demands for citizenship.

Multicultural state ideologies of citizenship try to force Pakistani women into liberal constructions of a "South Asia" that they often do not identify with, both racializing them and leaving them further excluded from acceptable and knowable forms of difference. In this context, the sanitized sensorium creates a demand for recognizable difference, a radical alterity, which renders them invisible as Pakistani and hyper-visible as South Asian. As the previous chapter detailed, Pan-Indian food, music, and clothing invoke a sensorial register that triggers acceptance—a kind of self-congratulatory multiculturalism that allows the greater Canadian public to feel morally good. In response, Pakistani women talk back to the state, often resisting, but sometimes accepting or even subverting the category "South Asian."

In taking up this racialized subject category in multicultural Canada, this chapter builds on the rich anthropology of citizenship. Moving beyond its formulation as an identity imbued with legal rights and affiliation to a particular nation-state, anthropologists have theorized cultural citizenship to understand a belonging that moves beyond legal papers (Blackburn 2009; Koll 2010; Ong 1999; Rosaldo 1997; Siu 2005). The concept of cultural citizenship refers to the right to be different in terms of ethnicity, religion, or language with respect to a national community, without compromising one's right to belong in the sense of participating in a nation-state's democratic processes (Rosaldo 1997). While Rosaldo focuses on group rights, Aihwa Ong (1999) examines individual agency. Ong suggests that citizenship is a process and a disciplining tool the state uses to distinguish between "ideal" and "unfit" citizens. More recently, anthropologists have theorized cultural citizenship as an analytic frame to understand the social and political exclusion of citizens despite their formal entitlement to legal rights.[2] In contrast to these important works that describe a call for recognition, Pakistani Muslim women's self-distancing from the category of "South Asian" happens in *response* to the state's attempts at multicultural inclusion and recognition. That is, women react to the marginalization they experience when the state tries to interpellate them as citizens and subjects. What happens, then, when a form of recognition imposed by the state does not resonate with one's identity? I argue that these state policies and practices of multiculturalism create divisions just as communities are striving for inclusion and attempting to define their identities in the context of migration and transnationalism.[3]

In recent years discussions surrounding questions of state recognition have focused on Muslim minority culture in an imagined West and on a few key debates, including the wearing of the Islamic headscarf in France and the "reasonable accommodation" debate in Québec. These issues have largely focused on the relationship between an ostensibly coherent group identified as "Muslims" and an equally imagined "West." Ethnographic work concerning Muslim groups in racially and ethnically diverse societies has focused on the politics of inclusion in a colonial regime, or a settler society, calling into question ideologies of secularism and multiculturalism, as well as conceptions of citizenship and national belonging.[4] Such important studies have demonstrated the cultivation of a particular kind of Muslim selfhood and its relationship to state practices. However, what has been less examined is the effect of state practices of recognition (or misrecognition) on the relationships between Muslims and other Others in an imagined West. Writing on the problem of recognition in the Australian context, Elizabeth Povinelli (2002) argues that state practices and policies create a form of identification that demands a radical alterity of its citizens and subjects. Charles Taylor (1994) also argues, "A person or group of people can suffer real damage, real distortion.... Nonrecognition or misrecognition can inflict harm, can be a form of oppression, imprisoning someone" (25). In the Canadian context, I argue that these forms of recognition or legible Otherness (radical alterity) produce a discomforting alienation among Pakistani subjects in Toronto, fomenting the conditions for communal tensions between Pakistanis and Indians. "South Asia," the state-sanctioned category of inclusion, becomes in practice a category of exclusion. Its meaning varies from state understandings of it as an inclusive category to individual understandings of it as "a gloss for India."

Within contemporary debates surrounding multiculturalism, in particular a rhetoric of "equality within a model of difference," struggles of identity are waged on immigrant bodies. These struggles remake ideas of citizenship and the nation in an era of global migrations and demonstrate a social order in which citizenship itself is based on embodied difference mediated by and through the senses. Throughout this book, but crucially here, the focus is on the intersection of two broad analytical areas regarding multiculturalism. First, multiculturalism is addressed as a set of legal and liberal practices, with particular focus on the politics surrounding the formation of a cohesive nation in the midst of a range of diverse practices and claims. Second, I look at the lived experience of multiculturalism through moments of friction between state bodies, civil society, and aspiring citizens to examine the ways multicultural policy arises through practices and how aspiring citizens translate these policies into their everyday lives. What does it mean to become a citizen of the liberal settler multicultural state when there are limited and proscribed subject positions for inclusion?

This chapter begins by examining narratives that women continually invoked surrounding the category "South Asian." Their perspectives are representative of the damage governmental attitudes, narratives, and rhetorics around multiculturalism, difference, and minority culture can do to the affective attachments of community members. I then turn to an examination of the origins and politics surrounding South Asian Heritage Month to understand the ways particular kinds of cultural differences become encoded in law and policy, and then how they get implemented in practice. Finally and importantly, throughout this chapter I hope to demonstrate ethnographically how these categories are produced in conjunction with a range of actors as a process of racialization. State classificatory systems often become a means through which the state governs, rather than an accurate reflection of how citizens identify themselves (Bernard Cohn 1987). While the state's system of classification can never fully reflect self-understandings of citizenship and belonging because of the contradictory and complex nature of subjectivity and personhood, it is a crucial factor in the ways resources are allocated and census categories are produced, and thus form one (important) part of the process of racialization. This happens at multiple scales: state-produced categories of inclusion, grassroots organizing by certain segments of the community, and racism itself (both in the era of "paki-bashing" in 1970s and 1980s, and in the post-9/11 period).

Engaging "South Asia"

The question "Do you identify as South Asian?" was one that I asked in more and less obvious ways throughout fieldwork. The overwhelming majority of the women I spoke with rejected the term South Asian, saying that it conflated the interests of Indians and Pakistanis. Of those who did not like the term, many felt that in lumping all Pakistanis, Indians, Bangladeshis, Nepalese, and Bhutanese together many interests are lost, and sometimes that gesture simply becomes a gloss for India. Yasmin illustrated this perspective. I had met her while working with a settlement-services agency that handles unemployment issues. She had been an engineer in Lahore before migrating with her husband and children, and at the time of our interview she was unemployed. One day she said to me, "I feel South Asian somehow caters more towards Indians, rather than everyone of South Asian origin." Responses to whether or not someone considered herself South Asian ranged from, "I refer to myself as Pakistani Canadian," to "Definitely not South Asian, it's just Indian," to "Canadian of Pakistani origin." Many also felt that the category was not defined from within, but was simply imposed by the Canadian state because, according to one Pakistani woman, "we all look the same."

Mariam's situation elucidates the relationship between multicultural constructions of South Asia and the complexities of identification in diaspora.

I first met Mariam by accident. I had been searching for Pakistani women's organizations and found just one in an old copy of the *Blue Book*, a directory of social services in Toronto. I called the number listed for the president of the National Guild of Pakistani Women, and Mariam answered. Shocked by my interest in her, she revealed that the organization was in a state of disarray because there was little interest from second-generation Pakistani women to take up the leadership. "The only reason you found me," she confessed, "is because I haven't changed my number in twenty years." We often spoke about her own experiences of migration and her perceptions of community-building efforts. Our first meeting occurred at her workplace, a public elementary school in the West End of Toronto where she was doing social work. Mariam told me that she moved with her young daughter from Karachi to Canada in 1966, one year after her husband had immigrated to study engineering at the University of Toronto; she joined him as a part-time student in sociology, eventually earning her master's degree. "Until 1969," she told me, "there were only twenty Pakistani families in Toronto," a small but cohesive group. In the mid-1960s there was "no discrimination," she told me. "By 1969, though, there was a recession, and so came discrimination." Pakistanis worked with Indian organizations to address issues of racism and human rights violations. The derogatory term "Paki" was introduced, but, according to Mariam, "Pakistanis didn't really understand it—the *Toronto Star* explained it to us."

The history of "paki-bashing" in Toronto is important for understanding the stakes of political naming and self-identification. "Paki" is a racial slur used to denigrate people from Pakistan. The term dates back to the mid-1960s, and is thought to have originated in Britain. Though discussed extensively in the context of Britain, and to a lesser extent in the United States, paki-bashing also happened in Toronto. In a study on racism in Toronto conducted in the 1970s, researchers found images of Pakistanis circulating that they deemed racist: "Indians (including Pakistanis) coming from the subcontinent are not wanted anywhere. They are [depicted as] the wretched of the earth, unable to feed, clothe, or house themselves. They are lazy and slothful and come to live here on welfare" (Khan 2012: 159). Some members of the Pakistani community of Toronto felt the *Toronto Star* was to blame because of an article published on May 10, 1975, titled "Racism: Is Metro Turning Sour?" In the article, a nineteen-year-old housewife was quoted as saying, "Everyone I know is against Pakistanis. They are dirty, physically dirty—you can see it on them. And they smell.

Their houses are dirty too. That's what my friends tell me" (quoted in Khan 2012: 161). This was the first time the term appeared in a Canadian media source. In a response to the piece, Khalid Hasan, a member of the community, wrote: "That you chose to quote a mindless nineteen-year-old Scarborough housewife who in turn quoted 'friends' to the effect that all Pakistanis live uncleanly, is unfortunate. Surely there are less provocative ways of highlighting the irrationality that lies at the heart of all racism. You unwittingly succeeded in stamping on the mind of your average reader an image of the average Pakistani which he may continue to nourish despite its total unreality" (quoted in Khan 2012: 161). These responses led to a protest by the Pakistan Canada Association in which 300 people marched on Nathan Phillips Square (Khan 2012: 162).

By the 1970s, "Paki" was used widely in Canada—in addition to "dothead" or "curryhead." A Sikh temple that was built in the new Little India in the early 1970s was vandalized, with swastikas and "Paki Go Home" painted on its doors (McCaskell 2005: 6). Raghu Krishnan (2003) writes of his own experience with Paki-bashing in Toronto in the 1970s. He reveals that those of South Asian origin, first- or second-generation Pakistani immigrants to Toronto, suffered in an atmosphere of violence and constant taunting. This memory of racism, he writes, contributed to his own radicalization in high school, which later led him in 1989 to found the United Coalition Against Racism at the University of Toronto. He also founded the Toronto Coalition Against Racism after a skinhead attack on Sivarajah Vinasithamby, a Sri Lankan Tamil refugee who was working in a restaurant (Krishnan 2003). The former head of the Council of Agencies Serving South Asians told me that this widespread violence, which cut across South Asian community lines, led to coalition building within the Toronto South Asian community.

Paki-bashing led to popular Indian-born novelist Bharati Mukherjee to leave Canada for the United States. In a 1981 *Saturday Night* magazine article she wrote: "I was frequently taken for a prostitute or shoplifter, frequently assumed to be a domestic. The society, or important elements of it, routinely made crippling assumptions about me and about my 'kind.' ... I quickly learned that the country is hostile to its citizens who had been born in hot, moist continents like Asia."[5] Toronto-based filmmaker Deepa Mehta has similarly commented, "I've been called a Paki bitch many times; I've had tomatoes thrown at me."[6] In May 1980, Amir Din, a Pakistani resident of the government housing project on Tandridge Crescent in Rexdale, was beaten in front of his wife and children when they returned home with groceries. A group of ten white youths hanging out in the lobby of the building started calling them names. One of them tried to kick Mrs. Din. Then one of the kids held the elevator door open while two others kicked and punched Mr. Din, using a broken soda bottle to cut him.[7] "I feel angry; I feel scared—helpless, I guess," he said in an article in the national newspaper, the *Globe and Mail*, asserting that "being called a Paki happens every day," but this kind of violence was new. Decades later, in a 2007 article in the *Globe and Mail* called "Do ethnic enclaves impede integration?" Amrita Kumar-Ratta, the Canadian daughter of Indian immigrants, was quoted as saying, "I have been called Paki. People say things like 'Go bathe so you don't smell like curry anymore.'"[8]

That afternoon at her school, Mariam revealed her own experiences of discrimination. She told me that she had worked as a sociologist in Pakistan, and after getting her master's degree at the University of Toronto she managed to get work as a contract sociologist in Toronto: "It was the most difficult time to get work." In job interviews they would say, "My God, you speak English!" Asked where she learned it, she would reply sarcastically, "I learned it on the plane," which, according to her, they always believed. Eventually she got a job working for the Canadian government and then for the school board, handling cases of racism and violence involving Indians in particular—but at the time, she told me, the term "Indian" included Pakistanis.

Racial and ethnic categories are historically and culturally produced and continue to be reconstructed over time by both individuals and society, as shown by analyses of the malleability of South Asian identity formation in the United States (George 1997; Koshy 1998; Leonard 1992). George (1997) argues that nearly all upper- and middle-class South Asians in Southern California refuse to be raced: "[Rejecting a] racial identity for themselves [is] a response to the multiracial world they inhabit and . . . a response to the current mode of immigrant-bashing rampant in California" (32). In fact, processes of classification in the United States have been particularly fraught. In the 1950s, Indian immigrants to the United States were categorized as "Hindu," though most were Sikh; in the 1970 U.S. census, South Asians were listed for the first and last time as "white"; in 1977, they lobbied for and won reclassification as "Asian Pacific Americans"; and they eventually won the category "Asian Indian" in the 1980 census. Koshy's (1998) work effectively demonstrates the ways in which ethnicity is historically constructed. She writes, "Asian in the United States and Britain is not merely a geographical referent but a metaphor shaped by particular geopolitical relations" (25). The construction of the category of South Asian, while similarly malleable, has been very different in Canada.

Nadiya, who highlighted experiences of discrimination, particularly around work, echoed Mariam's stories. She once told me, "I now would use the term South Asian specifically when applying for a job, to avoid negative stereotyping." This appeal to avoid stereotyping as Pakistani and/or Muslim is indicative of the discrimination Nadiya had experienced on the job market. While she uses the category in that realm to help her, it points to the discrimination that Pakistanis still feel they are subject to, and the ways that "South Asia," which she believes is "a newly coined politically correct term," erases religious differences, thus making that discrimination invisible.

Identifying Religious Difference

In the Canadian context, the state's imposition of the South Asian category of inclusion has two interrelated effects. First, it conjures the specter of the historical struggle for a national identity based on an independent Pakistan;[9] second, it elides religious identity, and therefore renders invisible the discrimination Muslim immigrants feel they are subjected to. Thus, when everyone becomes simply "South Asian," particular histories, contexts, and experiences, such as Muslim marginalization, are lost in diaspora. Communal tensions between diasporic South Asians do not stem from primordial differences between Pakistanis and Indians, as they have been described through the language of ethnic conflict, but as I demonstrate here, are an effect of a "liberal settler multiculturalism" (Povinelli 2002) that heightens differences between groups.

Mariam had very strong feelings against the category "South Asian," which surprised me given that she had spent much of her career working with Indian as well as Pakistani organizations. "Indians are in the forefront of South Asian Canada," Mariam told me. "For example, there are two Pakistani dancers not identified as Pakistani in a famous Indian dance group." Mariam also felt very strongly that Pakistanis were not included in South Asian Heritage Month. In speaking with a number of members of other organizations with "South Asian" in their names, including the organizers of the Heritage Month festivities, I was told that Pakistani participation was encouraged, but it was difficult to find any who wanted to take part. Drawing on her experience within the Pakistani community, Mariam told me, "Pakistanis don't dance or sing [despite the fact that she had just complained that Pakistani dancers were not identified in a famous dance group], and they think that these festivities are un-Islamic, so they don't go." I did in fact speak to a number of Pakistani women who did not want to participate in "South Asian" events because they considered them un-Islamic for serving alcohol or having dance performances. Mariam also felt that Pakistanis are not represented because there is not a lot of leadership within the community. "Pakistanis need something like an organized voice. . . . We've gone more into religion—Islam has replaced country." She believed that for Pakistanis in particular, the religious differences seemed the most difficult to overcome.

The assertion of a Canadian identity over a Pakistani or Muslim identity can also be contextualized in a post-9/11 world in which such allegiances may be suspect. Sunaina Maira (2009) argues that cultural citizenship is of particular import for South Asian Americans because "legal citizenship is not enough to guarantee protection under the law with the state's War on Terror, as is clear from the profiling, surveillance, and even detention of Muslim Americans who are U.S. citizens" (82). These contemporary exclusions from cultural citizenship, she writes, have historical precedents in the cultural exclusion of nonwhite groups, including Asian Americans, as "perpetual foreigners" (Tuan 1998, cited in Maira 2009). One of the issues with cultural citizenship Maira articulates is that, while movements for cultural citizenship are critical of state practices, they are still embedded within a framework of inclusion. In talking with Mariam, discussing post-9/11 hate crimes against the community took place alongside our discussion of cultural festivals; cultural citizenship, violence, and state action are fused for Arabs/Muslims/Others in the post-9/11 world.

After 9/11, Mariam said, "there was a major shift in the Canadian community and my students were traumatized. There were more Muslim students being harassed." She described speaking at two conferences in the aftermath of 9/11 and working with the Canadian Muslim Liberty Association: "Assaults against Muslims have gone up ten times! And the police know this, but there's no help for students. There's trauma, there's fear, people don't believe the students." She offered the example of a ten-year-old Iranian boy who was traumatized, dreaming night after night that a plane would hit his apartment building. "Teachers and the principal felt he was fine, but his mother called the school many times over the course of two months. Eventually the principal called me; I had to explain it to him [the principal]. I found a Farsi-speaking therapist to help the boy." She went on to say, "But women have it the worst. When I go to mosques, I tell women to stop wearing the hijab. Safety first, but the mullahs don't like it."

Some, who chose not to align themselves with South Asians, have felt that they have had to compromise their Islamic beliefs, which they consider to be a key part of their culture, and further, that the grouping of all South Asians is a homogenizing gesture that will impact the identity of the next generation. The former president of the National Federation of Pakistani Canadians, Noordin, expressed this set of ideas. Noordin had been in Canada since 1968. Once in Toronto, he met and married a Pakistani woman with whom he had four children; at the time they were both attending the University of Toronto. He had been educated in Pakistan in electrical engineering before moving to London to do a two-year diploma in computer science. He was from Sialkot in the Punjab and decided to move to Canada for economic reasons. When he first arrived in Canada, he worked in a factory for a year doing labor before finding work in IT. For the past twenty years he had been working in investments involving real estate. He has been active in community building, forming organizations and building connections.

He cited a major issue facing the Pakistani community: how governmental categories hindered larger community building for Pakistanis. "Our entity as Pakistanis is challenged by the provincial and federal government. . . . We are all grouped [into] South Asian as one. I'm not South Asian. I want my Pakistani heritage to be recognized. I don't want my children to lose their identity as Pakistani. Our children have an assimilation problem. We want them to assimilate, but also to keep within our religion and cultural circles." Noordin points to two issues in this narrative. First, Pakistani community building is hindered by governmental categories and rhetoric that insist on melding those from diverse countries into one cultural group. Second, this categorization hinders assimilatory efforts on the part of the next generation (because, I suspected, for him assimilation for his children was not intended to be as South Asian, but as Canadian). That is, the desired assimilation into the majority group rather than into another minority group.

Noordin was very resistant to the formation of South Asian Heritage Month:

> The Pakistani community feels it should not be called South Asian Heritage Month; it's Indian Heritage Month because there was not consultation with the Pakistani community or the consulate. We

should not be taken up as one group. There are many countries in South Asia, Pakistan, Sri Lanka, Bangladesh, etc. They all have different cultures. People don't have that much in common; the religion, social, culture, economics are entirely different. India is a larger country, a bigger community. I worked with Indian groups; they try to monopolize the situation, acting like a big brother. Each country should be given their own identity.

Noordin was very resistant to sharing an event with the Indian community, but he later told me that he was very comfortable working with the Sikh community. "I have noticed that I feel more comfortable with Sikhs than Hindu—maybe it's the language of the Punjab; we have some culture in common with the Punjab." For Noordin, it seemed that national divides between Pakistanis and Indians were insurmountable, while religious differences between himself and his Sikh friends were overcome by a common history in the Punjab. Many considered the categorization "South Asian" to be a façade for hegemonic Indian nationalism, which would erase Islam as a part of one's identity. Furthermore, despite a history of racialization and violence against Pakistanis, people still choose that identifier over South Asian to affirm a post-Partition identity that was hard-won.

Embracing Coalition Building

However, not everyone agrees about the use or rejection of the term. Some Pakistani community members I spoke with had an economic interest in coalition building. Faisal, for example, was a well-established Pakistani businessman who had moved to Canada in 1969 as a student. He was president of both the Canada-Pakistan Business Council and SOS, a charitable organization that exists in thirty-one countries. He worked extensively with Indian and Pakistani businessmen in Toronto and told me, "We get along well, but there isn't much integration because of religious differences, which restrict [Hindus from participating in Muslim] religious activities." However, he told me that at cultural events, such as festivals, "we all come under the same platform." He went on to say, "People do get along well because Canada is tolerant. In general there is a good understanding between India and Pakistan. There is respect for each other. People become colorblind." It is interesting to consider his last comment, which seems to suggest that Indians and Pakistanis are racially different. Importantly, it also demonstrates the power of the language of the multicultural state and the influence of the concept of color blindness in Faisal's understandings of diversity and minority culture, which are aligned with the multicultural state's desire to imagine itself as color blind and inclusive.

Like Faisal, Aisha referred to herself as South Asian. I first met her through her role as an organizer of Toronto's second annual Basant Festival, a kite-flying celebration that also takes place in Pakistan. Like Mariam, Aisha was in her sixties. One day we met in the coffee shop of a large bookstore in downtown Toronto in advance of Basant. She and I had met through mutual acquaintances, and she was trying to recruit me to volunteer at the festival. Aisha had moved to Toronto four years before our interview. She was born in Karachi, and her husband was from Lahore. Many of her family members from her mother's side had moved to Canada and the United States. In the aftermath of Partition, her family lived in East Pakistan (now Bangladesh). Her story was unusual among the ones I collected during fieldwork, as it was one of upward mobility that continued into the diaspora.

During our conversation at that bookstore, she revealed: "We have no common clubs. Some Indians or Pakistani are reluctant to come to [South Asian] events. People say they don't want to go. They say it's an Indian event. We've tried Pakistani food in Indian venues, but it doesn't work; everyone wants butter chicken." She went on: "There isn't enough communication between Pakistanis and Indians here—they live in small pockets. We should band together here." In reference to South Asian Heritage Month she said:

> The Pakistani aspect was very small this year. It will be different next year. Pakistani dancers exist; there is singing and dancing, but it's not culturally approved. They think the only women involved would be prostitutes. It's because of the fundamentalists, they think everything is wrong. It's not true for the new generation. They [the parents] live here and go see Bollywood films, but they don't want kids participating. In Bengal, you are supposed to entertain guests in the domain of dance ... and singing. Indian culture is at a higher level because dancing and singing is part of their culture.

While organizing the Basant Festival in Toronto, she experienced resistance and was repeatedly and angrily told, "Basant is a Hindu festival." While she uses the term "South Asian," she still marks religious divides within the community, as Faisal did. There may be a temptation here to conclude that the poor tend to communal tension while the rich do not, but that would be a simplistic understanding of the dynamics within the community. Rather, there are ways that class and economic interests (of capitalism) override seeming differences in the interest of making money. Both Faisal and Aisha were businesspeople who wanted to make contacts and develop connections; even so, both their narratives were haunted by Partition-era religious divides, and both asserted that those are the most difficult divisions to overcome.

Prema Kurien (2003) has written on the concept of "South Asian" and how meaningful it is to Indian, Pakistani, Sri Lankan, and Bangladeshi immigrants in the United States. The debate is roughly divided between those interested in coalition building to address common concerns versus those who want to maintain individual group identities. The former claim that there are numerous cultural similarities, and policymakers do not see differences between South Asian groups anyway, while the latter argue that the cultural and political differences between groups are too great. She argues that in diaspora, religious differences and tensions have exacerbated. Mariam's and Aisha's perspectives reveal contrasting attitudes toward "South Asia" in the diaspora. Both felt the need for community building, but while Aisha embraced it, Mariam did not.

Mariam's perspectives reflect some of the ways the state-sanctioned version of South Asia does not resonate with the majority of the Pakistani community in Toronto. Asking Pakistanis to identify as South Asian—that is, with a group to which they feel little belonging—results in their marginalization by the very form of recognition meant to give them political voice. Multiculturalism in Canada is predicated on notions of inclusion that cut across ethnic and racial categories, as well as religion and national affiliation. Ironically, such attempts at state inclusion have served to exclude Pakistani women from civic participation as South Asians because they do not see themselves represented in such government-sponsored cultural events like national heritage days and ethnic festivals.[10] These perceptions of the meaning of South Asia are particularly revealing in the context of the development and origins of South Asian Heritage Month and the government's involvement in imposing the category.

The Origins of South Asian Heritage Month

In 1988, the Ontario Society for Services to Indo-Caribbean Canadians celebrated the 150-year anniversary of the arrival of Indians to Guyana.

In April 1997, the Indo Trinidad Canadian Association (ITCA) began commemorating what it referred to as Indian Arrival Day. In 1998 the name was changed to Indian Arrival and Heritage Day, and in 1999 the ITCA began celebrating May as Indian Arrival and Heritage Month. In 2001, Raminder Gill, the only Indian Member of Parliament, introduced Bill 98 in the Ontario legislature, which was passed on the condition that the name be changed from Indian Heritage Month to South Asian Heritage Month over concerns that there would be confusion with Indigenous groups. Thus, in Ontario, May is South Asian Heritage Month and May 5 is South Asian Arrival Day. According to the Canadian government, the South Asian Heritage Act was passed to celebrate the presence of people from India, Pakistan, Bangladesh, Sri Lanka, Nepal, and the Caribbean.

While South Asian Heritage Month and South Asian Arrival Day are widely celebrated, many are not aware of the latter's direct tie to Indian indentured labor. May 5, 1838, actually marks the formal end of slavery and the beginning of the system of indentured labor in the British West Indies. That was the day that 396 Indian immigrants, referred to as the "Gladstone Coolies," landed in Guyana from Calcutta. According to Moon-Ho Jung (2006), "The word *coolie* was largely a product of European expansion into Asia and the Americas, embodying the contradictory imperial imperatives of enslavement and emancipation" (13). They were lured with false promises and coercion by professional traffickers, who also used practices such as forced detention and kidnapping. John Gladstone, a plantation owner in British Guiana, turned to Indian indentured labor as the solution to the "emancipation problem." After complaints were filed with the British Anti-Slavery Society, there was an investigation of the working conditions of the "Gladstone coolies," revealing beatings and extortion. A quarter of the laborers died by the time their contracts ended in 1843; the majority of those who survived returned to India, despite their option to remain in British Guiana (Jung 2006: 14). Between 1835 and 1918, 341,600 indentured laborers were relocated from India to Guyana.

Despite these grim origins, in Canada, Indian Arrival Day is not a time of critical reflection on the dark history of indentured labor and exploitation, but a celebration of transnational migration and arrival. In this way, South Asian Heritage Month itself is haunted by the specter not only of Partition-era communal tension, but also the violence and exploitation at the heart of Indian emigration. Celebrating the first boatload of indentured laborers to the Americas is indicative of a kind of historical blindness. It erases the history of violence at the heart of this kind of migration in the name of claiming national belonging in a place that condoned labor exploitation. Erasing this history also allows the state and immigrant communities to turn a blind eye to the damage caused by multiculturalism. This act is reminiscent of what Ananya Bhattacharjee (1992) calls the "habit of ex-nomination," referring to the way some South Asians in the United States attempt to recapture their middle-class status in diaspora by ignoring real social issues such as violence against women in the intimate spaces of family life. Similarly, Bhattacharjee's insights apply to the examples above of Faisal and Aisha, who demonstrate through their interest in the financial benefits of coalition building a desire to regain status lost during migration. As I argued in the previous chapter, South Asian Heritage Month is considered a success story of Canadian multiculturalism because it gives recognition to minority subjects. "South Asians" are also another kind of success story of multicultural inclusion, in contrast to the marginalized racialized category of "Muslim" and "those who look that way."

South Asian in Practice

South Asian Heritage Month consists largely of cultural festivals occurring throughout the country with the help of the federal government in Ottawa. Masala! Mehndi! Masti! is the premier event of the South Asian community in Toronto. While it typically happens in the summer, and outside of the official South Asian Heritage Month, conversations around MMM and other festivals held in May concerned questions of who was "South Asian." I also reference them again here because attending cultural festivals like MMM and listening to Pakistani women talk about them demonstrated that their relationship to the South Asian category is also importantly gendered. As many writers have argued, the performance of culture and nationalism has been understood in the intimate spaces of family life and cultural practice as the purview of women (e.g., Chatterjee 1993; Kaplan, Alarcon, and Moallem 1999). In these contexts, women are understood to be the bearers of tradition, culture, and language, handing them down to the next generations. The dependency on women's bodies becomes both representative of Pakistani nationalism and acceptable multiculturalism, which also relies on women's bodies and labor. The category of South Asia is already gendered because, in representing the nation through cultural identifications and allegiances, women do symbolic and material labor but are not included in the exercise of power. Thus, we can perhaps read Pakistani women's rejection of being categorized as South Asian as a rejection of multicultural practice that only includes them in symbolic (and not material) domains. While these women may be invisible in certain cultural contexts, they are hyper-visible in the context of cultural celebration.

When viewed through the lens of patriarchy, South Asian Heritage Month festivals occupy an uncomfortable space in liberal settler multicultural politics, as well as in practices of recognition and belonging. Women's performances are central to South Asian Heritage Month festivities, in the form of more obvious Indian classical dance, but also in cooking authentic Indian foods and performing in heteronormative (and patriarchal) family structures, including providing childcare. These particular calls for the recognition of difference by multicultural state practices not only normalize certain categories of identification (as South Asian) but also recognize and regularize only particular forms of gendered performance (cooking and dancing). In the cultural festival, women are expected to perform intimate cultural labor while at the same time the state devalues that kind of work. Within the sanitized sensorium, the labor of the cultural festival is co-opted, controlled, and contained by the state and its commitment to multicultural policy, practice, and performance. While women's performances in these contexts are integral to the representation of culture, they happen within constraints of acceptable difference; they are heterosexual, heteronormative, patriarchal, and South Asian. The production of radical alterity in the making of South Asia is therefore also gendered. Thus, when women reject the label South Asian they are rejecting state discourse and the state's power to produce their bodies.

All the South Asian organizations I worked with played a role at MMM through activities ranging from staging workshops to staffing an informational table, which targeted its flyers to what the organization called "a more mainstream family-oriented" audience, toning down its leftist inclinations. A notable exception, perhaps proving why this was necessary, was a table for a South Asian organization that promotes safe-sex practices and family planning. That day they were distributing condoms with wrappers that had attractive images of Indian goddesses on them. As I traveled down the path between tables, I noticed that many of the condoms had been tossed on the ground once participants who perhaps condemned the idea of premarital sex realized what they were. Engaging with the realities of premarital sex and birth control, real issues facing the community, were not part of the celebration of South Asian Canadian culture.

During the last day of MMM I had volunteered to sit at one of the tables with Lubna, a forty-year-old single woman who was originally from Karachi. I had met Lubna at an unemployment workshop at a local immigrant women's organization. It had been raining all day, but that did not deter the hundreds still in attendance. As Lubna and I sat waiting for someone to ask us a question, she told me that she felt the entire festival suggested a "mainstream *Indian* population" that was very different from the Pakistani population: "We're poorer, not well organized and don't do Bollywood or dancing. So who is this for?" These divisions within the community were highlighted and exacerbated during these festivals. Comments such as Lubna's demonstrate that subjectivity is central to the lived experience of immigration and citizenship in Toronto, as is the role of the sanitized sensorium in constructing multicultural citizenship. The immigrant body becomes a site of discipline and illuminates how ideals of normative citizenship, and thus national identity, are constructed as well. Taking this into consideration, we can see the ways that whiteness is naturalized as the center and subject of liberal multicultural discourse. Examining the everyday experiences of immigrants as partially included subjects demonstrates the challenges and fractures in notions of citizenship.

Cultural Producers

Pakistani artists are considered central to the making of South Asian public culture, and some have been central to South Asian cultural festivals. For the group of Pakistani artists I met, cultural production, employment, and social inclusion were intertwined. I found that it was impossible to discuss identity and self-referencing without addressing larger social issues pertaining to belonging, such as work and stable employment. Exploring their feelings not only toward art and South Asian Heritage Month, but also migration and citizenship, including their own problems with securing a livelihood, draws together questions of identity (and self-naming), belonging, and marginalization in the public culture of Toronto and the multicultural state.

While in Toronto I became friends with Rhea, who was the executive director of the South Asian Visual Arts Centre (SAVAC) at the time. SAVAC was established in 1993–94 by a group of visual artists who were curating the visual arts of Desh Pardesh; in 1994 it was incorporated as a nonprofit organization along with the Alliance for South Asian AIDS Prevention. In 2008, they changed their name to the South Asian Visual Arts Center and became federally incorporated. In 2013, they were awarded a multiyear Ontario Trillium Foundation grant for a project that traces SAVAC's origins as part of Toronto's history. Through my relationship with her and other artists I met, I was able to organize a roundtable discussion with eight Pakistanis artists (three men and five women) about issues they had faced living in multicultural Canada. Most had gone to the National College of Art in Lahore and were trying to establish themselves as artists in Canada. At the time, SAVAC was the only artist collective in Toronto organized along ethnic lines. During our roundtable, I asked if anyone ever thought about returning to Pakistan. Zafir, a Pakistani artist, said, "There are Kashmir issues, Afghani issues. There was intellectual stiflement in Pakistan. I was either going to stay and fight or pack up and go." Saad added, "I don't know if people come here for economic betterment. Most people from art schools will find a more comfortable situation at home, so most come for access in the intellectual sense." Zakiya added, "I expected it to be more open, more friendly, more open intellectually. In the first year I found it to be very difficult. It's very limiting here, the Pakistani community in Toronto is limiting. To them, I'm eccentric. It's hard to connect with other people. In Peshawar, people are very open." Tabina interjected, "I disagree, people from Peshawar are very male oriented. I didn't find it so open."

When I asked about their participation in cultural festivals, Zakiya said, "I've been to an Eid function that was like a cultural festival. Food, music mostly. It's nice to feel like it's Eid; it's nice to take the kids there, then go home." Sarish said she went to MMM, but "didn't like it. The performer we went to see wasn't good. The food was good, though." Rhea added, "The mission of Masala is to bring South Asian art out in the mainstream. It's family-oriented art. Not like Desh Pardesh. Masala does a good job of getting the community together. It's a weekend to have artists present their work. It's a very limited expression of art, it's a community or commercial event. It's a promotional event, rather than a grassroots event." Zakiya added, "It's more like Bollywood art." Rhea pointed out, "Its strength is its huge audience." Zakiya explained, "The art shows in Pakistan have religious limits. Defense and Clifton [neighborhoods in Lahore] are fine, but elsewhere it's limited."

I asked about the term South Asian. Lila told me that she heard it in Toronto for the first time. Sarish said, "It's discriminatory, we want a different identity. Why the South Asian brand?" Saad questioned Sarish's statement, perhaps trying to defend Canadian state practice: "It could be racial. We're not white, we're not Chinese, we're South Asian?" Sarish responded, "Why do we need to identify?" Both Sarish and Saad struggled to make sense of the South Asian category; Sarish marked it as a branding strategy by the government, while Saad tried to understand its origins.

It was getting late and several members had to leave. Making their apologies, they headed out the door. Rhea turned to me, "It's hard for people like Saad because he worked for twenty-five years as an architect." Sarish added, "There's lots of frustration, it shatters your confidence." Lila added, "Doctors are facing this too. Doctors are not at all accepted. No matter how much you know before you come, it's a different picture here. You have to do your résumé again. My Uncle was a banker in Pakistan, top-level management. He was told he needs to work on his résumé. It feels strange and it makes him angry." For Saad and others in his position, cultural production, earning a living, and belonging were inseparable. Discussing their identities was about discussing multiculturalism, their art, and having a source of income.

I later had the opportunity to meet with Lila and her husband at their home, where we discussed these issues further. I had been wandering around the Etobicoke neighborhood looking for the address I had been given when I ran directly into Lila. She had wet hair and was running outside to pick up a tea towel that had fallen out the window. In her thirties, she wore dark-framed glasses, had long black hair, and seemed really cool and interesting, so I immediately wanted her to like me. We took the elevator up to her apartment to meet her husband, Tahir. Both artists, they had been in Canada for five months at the time, having migrated from Islamabad. They were originally from Karachi, but had studied in Lahore. They moved to Canada because they wanted to explore the world. They were happy with their decision. Lila told me, "I didn't expect Canada to be the way it is. I expected to stand out, but here there are more Pakistanis than in Pakistan." She also elaborated, "I prefer not to use the word South Asian. Here people are put into cultural groups. I never used it before and I'm not going to now." In Pakistan, they had their own gallery, which they ran for two-and-a-half years before closing it. They both attended settlement-services workshops on arrival and said the classes "felt useless . . . telling everyone the same thing, doing the same thing." She elaborated, "People come here with years of work experience. Why erase what they know and begin again?" She continued, "odd jobs are degrading. They degrade your dignity. It's frustrating because you're not even good at odd jobs. People think the West is money, but no one can prepare anybody unless they're physically here." While Tahir was still unemployed, Lila had begun working as an assistant at SAVAC.

I did not get a chance to speak with Maha at the SAVAC roundtable, so we arranged to meet later at her workplace in the graphic services department for one of Canada's major banks. She went to the National College of Art in Lahore and graduated with a Bachelor of Design. Her father was a civil engineer who moved the family. Maha was born in Lahore, moved to Saudi Arabia when she was three, then back to Pakistan when she was seven. After she graduated from college she worked for an ad agency in Lahore as a graphic designer for two years. She decided to leave Pakistan because the social and economic system was terrible. "The economy was going down the drain," Maha said, "people who can get out are getting out. In Pakistan, the religious fanatics won't let the country progress. I wish Partition hadn't happened, India is ahead of us, more stable." Her grandparents were in the Indian part of the Punjab, but moved to Lahore after Partition.

Maha was married in Pakistan, but moved on her own ahead of her husband. The plan was that she would stay and sponsor him, but ultimately she decided to end the marriage instead. She had no friends or family and stayed with acquaintances in Mississauga for two weeks, but became uncomfortable because she felt she should be paying them rent. At first she wasn't sure if she should stay in Canada, but ultimately she decided that she would. She initially found work as a waitress in a Pakistani restaurant. The owner, a Pakistani immigrant himself, understood her situation and gave her a salary advance so she could get her own apartment in Mississauga. She saved up and bought a computer so she could begin trying to find work as a designer. She put her portfolio online, sent out résumés to two thousand organizations she said, and had ten interviews. While I am not sure if Maha really sent her résumé to two thousand businesses, her reaching for a number that large suggests that her search was broad and intense. She found work in a restaurant for ten to eleven months, then started doing freelance work for the company she is now with. She explained, "My manager took a chance when he hired me. He hired me in a senior position," which she felt was based on her strong portfolio. She had been at the job for three years and found herself happy and secure, although the job itself was not creative because her work had to succumb to corporate standards.

When I asked Maha how she felt about the term South Asian, she said she did not use it. "I say Pakistan, or a place near India. People don't use it in Pakistan. A country gives someone an identity." Her remarks here signal the relationship between her identity and her national affiliation. Maha did not want to identify as South Asian, perhaps because of what she told me next: "Once, three or four white teenagers stopped me and asked if I was Muslim. I could see the hate and anger in their eyes so I kept walking. They ran and yelled at me." She decided not to go on walks alone anymore. Being identified as South Asian erases the discrimination she experienced, and the hate crime she escaped. Identifying as Pakistani demonstrates a form of resistance to that erasure and it allowed her to assert a part of character that was important to her. Despite the fact that Maha does not like the term for herself, she has lots of Indian friends. "The tensions between the countries are because fanatic extremists are running the countries, giving people the notion that people don't get along." In Maha's case, her dislike of the term South Asian has nothing to do with tensions between Pakistanis and Indians, but rather is about her desire to maintain an identity as Pakistani.

A few years later, on a return trip to Toronto, I was having lunch with a friend at a restaurant in Little Italy. After sitting down, I looked up and recognized the artwork on the walls: a series of paintings by Zakiya. I had told her about venues like this over coffee one day when she asked me about the art scene in Toronto. I had mentioned this restaurant in particular, which was known for having a rotating art exhibit featuring local artists. I was so happy to see that she was able to make her art present in the Toronto scene. But being visible, even for artists, can be a double-edged sword, as public and state discourses have the power not only to recognize but also to circumscribe the terms of belonging.

These artists and cultural producers want to be seen for what they are, not how the multicultural state might project them. Their stories and perspectives help paint a broader picture of the Pakistani Muslim immigrant community in Toronto. Exploring individual experiences regarding their art, South Asian Heritage Month, and making a living demonstrates the ways identity and belonging are intertwined in individual experiences of marginalization in a range of social spheres. And while their migration trajectories or experiences finding work may be different from some of the other foreign-trained professionals I spoke with, there were also important similarities in terms of how they felt about being interpellated.

Imagining Citizenship

In planning sessions for these kinds of South Asian festivals, there was often tension regarding the construction of the category South Asian. I repeatedly heard the sentiment that Amina expressed to me: "I refer to myself as Pakistani and don't agree that all Indians, Pakistanis, et cetera can be called South Asians. We might come from similar geographic regions but have individual characteristics." As Naseem said earlier, "South Asians here are brought under the same umbrella. Canada does it because we look the same. Who are they, 'South Asians' . . . I never heard 'South Asian' before coming here." I had met both of these women while conducting fieldwork at a nonprofit for South Asian women, so I was surprised by their reluctance to call themselves "South Asian." But I realized that it points to the material necessity behind certain kinds of coalition building.

Despite its contention, the category was also mobilized by nonprofits that drew on what Gayatri Spivak has called "strategic essentialism" in order to obtain funding for activities and programming having to do with cultural celebrations, employment, and health issues—all related to the settlement-services encounter between nonprofit workers and immigrant women. The Canadian government most often gives funding to particular ethnic groups, thus creating conditions in which there is little inter-ethnic coalition building and smaller groups are lumped within larger ethnic categories. "South Asian" circulates widely and is understood as a means to gain government resources because it is a legible category of multicultural difference. Ironically, this category that celebrates the "multi-ness" of Canadian society serves to exclude members of those very communities it is meant to include. In private, these identifiers became fraught because they did not coincide with women's self-understanding of their citizenship and belonging in the multicultural state and in processes of migration. Through their disidentification with the term, Pakistani women actively redefine belonging by resisting and negotiating with available multicultural categories. Their own understandings of South Asia were haunted by their own personal experiences of migration and dislocation.

In *Feminist Genealogies, Colonial Legacies, Democratic Futures* (1997), Jacqui Alexander and Chandra Mohanty write, "We were not born women of color, but became women of color [in the United States]. From African American and U.S. women of color, we learned the peculiar brand of U.S. North American racism and its constructed boundaries of race" (xiv). Their insights speak not only to their own experiences, but also more broadly to the experiences of immigrants who are interpellated into North American racial formations, which demonstrates the constructedness of such categories of inclusion.

relate to Fanon

This chapter has examined women's experiences of multiculturalism and the politics of recognition to demonstrate how different segments of the South Asian immigrant community feel about and engage with multicultural governmental practice. I have sought to illustrate how the state-imposed category of "South Asian" can perpetuate and even naturalize divisions between Pakistanis and Indians in diasporic Toronto. By socially producing racialized difference, the Canadian state ultimately encourages Pakistanis to identify with a category that many feel champions the interests of Indian immigrants while marginalizing their own. Multicultural governance in this instance leads Pakistanis in diaspora to resist and reframe their conscription into the category of "South Asian," which has now become the dominant name for them in Toronto, institutionalized and enshrined in South Asian Heritage Month. Their resistance demonstrates that communal tensions are naturalized and sustained by (post)colonial, multicultural governance, which (like the colonial state) manages not only differences but acceptable categories of belonging as well.

As the relationship of Pakistani women to the state-supported category of South Asian attests, the liberal settler multicultural state has the power to name minorities and therefore circumscribe the limits of inclusion. But that power lies elsewhere, too, in the terms of scholarly debate on multiculturalism, which has similarly been colonized by liberal discourse. Descriptors such as "difference," "toleration," and "ethnicity" are still common terms in the scholarly writing on these issues. As Audre Lorde (1983) famously wrote, "The master's tools will never dismantle the master's house," and thus it is critical to engage the work on settler colonialism and bring it into conversation with the liberal discourse of multiculturalism.

In calling attention to the fact that Canada is a racial state (Goldberg 2002), I have attempted to show that, despite the presumed disavowal of race politics on the part of government policy makers, multiculturalism is a discourse of race. The framework of racialization emphasizes the ways racial and ethnic difference is both central to state practices and constantly produced through moments of friction between citizens and the state. In this context of race-making, Balibar and Wallerstein (2001) challenge the notion that racism is a relic of past histories and societies. Rather, they argue that it is a social relation that is embedded in contemporary social structures, including the nation-state and the relationship between the margin and the center. In their analysis, racism is a profoundly modern phenomenon tied to capitalism and class conflict. Taken together, discourses of settler colonialism and the racial state confront discourses of the state (both popular and scholarly) that move away from the liberal language of state multiculturalism and instead call attention to the underlying politics of racism, patriarchy, and heteronormativity that undergird late-liberal policies and practices.

These issues demonstrate the affective dimensions of the tension between visibility and invisibility in contemporary social life. Misrecognition is not the same as not being recognized. Misrecognition is being seen not as you are, but who you are assumed to be, and defining how you are going to be. This misrecognition has material effects in that it produces a kind of gendered precarity in which women struggle to survive and to maintain their dignity in the face of extreme marginalization.

CHAPTER FIVE

THE CATASTROPHIC PRESENT

I don't think of nation-states as land, it's where your people are. The Prophet Muhammad taught loyalty to whichever land you're living in, it's your moral duty.
—INTERVIEW WITH SAFIA

On one of my last visits to the Scarborough housing projects I visited a Pakistani woman I had come to know well during my fieldwork. In her sixties but unable to retire, she was working as a cashier, although she had been a teacher in Pakistan. I was horrified when I saw that she had become accustomed to the very large rat that was living in the apartment and even said she found it funny, calling it her "friend." After I gently suggested that she did not have to live like this, and that rats were dangerous disease carriers, it became apparent that she was afraid to complain for fear of eviction. I was incredibly moved by this incident, which stood in stark contrast to the ways the South Asian diaspora was understood in the Bay Area, where I had been living. Images of the successful Indian businessman or entrepreneurial dot-com worker were prevalent in Silicon Valley; emblematic of "flexible citizens," they were meant to represent the new global order. In Toronto, I was confronted again and again with the dark underside of global processes that produce both these figures. On one end of the spectrum of the South Asian diasporic experience is the Indian dot-com worker, seemingly secure in his upward mobility, while on another end of the spectrum exists the marginally employed Pakistani woman too afraid to complain about her living conditions for fear of ending up on the street.

This final chapter explores the anxiety, desperation, and lived experience of existing in a state of precarity, particularly when that precarity is gendered. Throughout this book I have largely focused on theories ranging from the anthropology of the state and neoliberalism, to critical studies of multiculturalism, to those of citizenship and belonging; this last chapter focuses on the embodied experience of precarity. Precarity invokes a moral and ethical register of individual responsibility that I have thus far attributed to neoliberal practice, but it is also important to consider the affects that accompany notions of individual responsibility such as anxiety, uncertainty, and desperation. Precarity is an affective register that itself signals a range of states. These precarious states exist in and through the sanitized sensorium, a consequence and an effect of the making of citizens and subjects. This chapter examines what it means to live in a state of precarity as a subject of globalization and late capitalism. It explores what living in precarity can say about the interface between the government, the market, and the social world in which we must live.

Accompanying neoliberal economic transformations that began in the 1970s in the global market which emphasized market competitiveness and labor-market flexibility was the rise of increasing insecurity for workers and the emergence of the "precariat," which refers to a worker without economic stability (Standing 2011). While the notion of precarity indexes a particular conception of work that is secure, it fixes a kind of identity and lifestyle (Allison 2013), "linking capitalism and intimacy in an affective desire for security itself" (Berlant 2011, cited in Allison 2013: 7). Thus, precarity refers not only to unstable work conditions but to the accompanying social world that feels uncertain or unstable. Throughout, this ethnography has sought to bring together the political economic with the intimate and affective, examining how bodies are gendered and racialized in the context of global capitalism—in other words, how it *feels* to be a problem (Du Bois 2008).

To examine ethnographically the lived experience of precarity, or more precisely in this case, the gender of precarity, is to think through the affective dimensions of living in a seemingly permanent state of insecurity, to ask again how women react to the sensorial regimes of belonging. Like resources, precarity is also distributed unevenly. Judith Butler (2009) suggests that some people are more vulnerable to precarity because of factors such as gender, class, or race, and urges us to think of precarity not as an existential condition, but rather a social relationship: "The differential distribution of precarity is at once a material and a perceptual issue, since those whose lives are not 'regarded' as potentially grievable, and hence valuable, are made to bear the burden of starvation, underemployment, legal disenfranchisement, and differential exposure to violence and death" (25). Thus, the precariousness of certain kinds of gendered and racialized bodies is mediated by and through social processes which render a hierarchy of value mapped onto individual lives.

There has been important work on the relationship between precarious labor and one's gender in different historical moments (e.g., Boris and Parreñas 2010; Ong 1987; Parreñas 2001). For instance, Ong (1987) demonstrates the ways Malaysian peasant women became cheap transnational labor in the late twentieth century, exploring the "deconstruction and reconstruction of gender in the shifting webs of agency and domination within the family, the labor system, Islam and the wider society" (219). The phenomenon of women becoming precarious workers is not a new one, and needs to be understood in a longer range of capitalist historical practices that have hindered women's economic security. The foreign-trained-professionals problem is a contemporary manifestation of this social phenomenon that produces precarious workers.

Reading women's life stories allows for an examination of the lived experience of precarity, which is not only an economic condition but a sensorial experience. These narratives demonstrate the sensorial and affective registers by which people come to understand their belonging or not belonging, and how they respond to the sensation, the incommensurability that marks them and attempts to interpellate them as second-class citizens. Despite a loss of prosperity after leaving Pakistan and in the face of this economic marginalization, I was surprised to find that the women I spoke with affirmed their desire to stay in Canada and rejected the idea of returning to Pakistan. Instead, they were actively invested and engaged in claiming citizenship as a Canadian subject. How do we understand this inherent paradox in which there is an affective attachment to a good life involving secure work and upward mobility, while being violently excluded from it? Women's understandings of citizenship, identity, place, and belonging are critical in understanding how these affective attachments to the good life are political. In their stories, women invoke discourses of a promising future in order to understand their liminal and marginal position; and in so doing, position themselves as good citizens deserving of full participation in the nation-state.

If inclusion in the state entails economic participation, then unemployment represents a kind of failed citizenship; therefore, the mobilization of Canadian citizenship (which emerged in conversations) is a form of agency that they reimagine in the face of economic marginalization. Embedded in the narratives presented here are strains of hope and optimism, which illuminate important features of the affective dimension of precarity. José Muñoz has theorized hope "as pointing from the past's unfinished business to a future beyond the present to sustain the (queer) subject within it—he explicitly frames the present as a prison" (Muñoz 2009, cited in Berlant 2011: 13). In Berlant's reading of Muñoz, "The present is more or less a problem to be solved by hope's temporal projection" (Berlant 2011: 13). Building on this, Berlant argues, "Optimism is not a map of pathology but a social relation involving attachments that organize the present" (13). In the examples provided in this chapter, hope or promises of a better life provide a means out of the catastrophic present—a present that includes unemployment, underemployment, misidentification, racism, and violence.

The Race and Gender of Precarity

Precarity has been theorized as a social condition arising from fluctuating market conditions and resulting in increasing instability, both economic and social; but it is also a gendered and racialized phenomenon. Understanding the explicit way these processes impact the lives of women is necessary for grasping the ways global processes are not only imagined, but configured and enacted. For instance, David Harvey's (1990) analysis of culture in the period of late capitalism has been extremely influential in understanding the shifts in the ways humans experience time and space. Geographer Dorinne Massey (1994) has effectively critiqued this work by drawing attention to the role of gender. Massey asks the critical question, who experiences time-space compression? In her analysis of social mobility, she counters the claim that capital is the only determinant of one's ability to move, and suggests ways that gender also becomes a powerful limitation. For example, women's mobility is limited not only by capital, but by threats of "physical violence, being ogled, or made to feel out of place" (2), thus suggesting a power differential in time-space compression. Therefore, the precarity that emerges through processes of globalization is also a gendered and racialized one.

One way to see this gendered and racialized precarity is through examining the relationship between globalization, transnationalism, and labor. There is a sizable literature on immigrant women, labor, and the global economy.[1] For instance, Rhacel Parreñas (2001) examines Filipina domestic workers in the global economy who must leave their own families to do care work for other families. These workers experience downward mobility to do menial labor in the global economy at the expense of caring for their own children and families at home, working in uncertain conditions for unfair wages and limited job security. Immigrant women's access to employment and work stability is circumscribed by their gender and race as their bodies, affects, and dispositions are coded on the global job market. Settlement-services workshops, as we have seen, produce normalizing discourses and behaviors around cultural and bodily difference that are marketed as the solution to unemployment and precarity.

Examining the work experiences of immigrant women of color highlights the need for an explicitly transnational or global frame in order to understand the feminization of certain kinds of labor and the accompanying affect required to make women workers legible on the global market. This is one way that processes of global labor migrations produce racialized and gendered national subjectivities. In "Is Local: Global as Feminine: Masculine? Rethinking the Gender of Globalization" (2001), Carla Freeman reimagines Catherine Lutz's (1995) question, "Does theory have a gender?" to ask about the gender of globalization. Freeman argues that not only has globalization theory been gendered masculine, but also the very processes defining globalization (e.g., the spatial reorganization of production across national borders) have been. She provocatively asks about the implications of a divide between "masculinist grand theories of globalization that ignore gender as an analytic lens and local empirical studies of globalization in which gender takes center stage" (1008). An account of the gender of globalization thus would take seriously the feminization or masculinization of particular processes, while not privileging grand-scale theories over localized examples as more serious social theory. Thus, an explicitly global framework would take seriously the ways that large-scale processes result in the feminization of labor and the systematic marginalization of women of color from participating in the global economy, and would not simply dismiss examples of women's experiences as localized, but as real evidence of the ways globalization operates. As such, gender is central to understanding elements of the global economy and cannot be considered in isolation of structural arrangements. A focus on highly skilled laboring women demonstrates the particular ways immigrant women's skills are devalued, forcing them into low-wage labor and unemployment.

Yet despite their downward mobility after leaving Pakistan and their economic marginalization, the majority of the Pakistani women I spoke with reaffirmed a desire to stay in Canada and did not want to return to Pakistan. They did not want to go back and were actively invested and engaged in claiming citizenship as a Canadian subject. Responses to my question, "What made you decide to move to Toronto?" ranged from "There were too many riots and killings at home" and "I was tired of the pollution and the violence" to "I heard the health and education system would be better for my daughter" and "I wanted to push for the future of my kids, and I'm uncertain about the political situation in Pakistan. I wanted a secure future." These narratives invoke a sense of security in which home is a site of violence and danger, and Canada is a place imbued with hope and possibility. Sacrifice then becomes a means to produce a hopeful outcome for the next generation, and thus living in a state of precarity in Canada is less precarious than living in a state of precarity in Pakistan.

Living in Precarity

Zainab and Parveen were both in their thirties. Of the stories I retell here, these two most closely represent the numerous narratives I heard in the field. Zainab was a thirty-nine-year-old Pakistani woman I met at the Center. Though she had worked as a doctor in Pakistan, she was unemployed in Toronto. She had migrated with a husband and young daughter, but the pressures of migration put undue stress on her marriage, which eventually ended. When she and her husband (both doctors) first moved to Toronto two years before I met her, they expected a different quality of life. After the first six months, they spent the $10,000 they were required to bring as part of their immigration process; most went toward paying for first- and last-months' rent on a small basement apartment in a low-income neighborhood in Scarborough, Ontario. Zainab went to all the relevant settlement-services agencies she qualified for, learning her rights as a new, permanent resident. She contacted the College of Physicians and Surgeons of Ontario (CPSO), the governing board that regulates the practice of medicine in Ontario. She was referred to "Career Transitions for International Medical Doctors," a government-funded resource for internationally trained doctors to find alternative careers in health care. She also learned that she effectively would have to begin her training again to work as a doctor, and even an alternate career in healthcare would require additional (and expensive) training. Eventually, she abandoned the idea because of the tremendous added financial cost. After Zainab separated from her husband, she moved into government housing with her child. This was a good alternative for her because the rent was contingent upon her salary; if she were to suddenly lose a job, they would not end up on the street.

In the contemporary moment there is a collective mourning for the promise of the good life—middle-class aspirations, including a nice place to live and stable work—that has failed to come to fruition (Berlant 2007). The affects that emerge signal a longing for a time in the past, or a frustration with the failure of a promise. Zainab was living on money she had borrowed from her brother, but was adamant that she did not want to go on welfare. She told me, "I came here because I wanted to work, not to live off the government. They need to recognize my credentials. I don't understand why they don't and why I have to go back to school. I'm a doctor."

Zainab had always had a lot of friends in Pakistan, but in Toronto she found herself socially isolated. She had tried making friends with other women she met at local settlement-services agencies and at the mosque she attended every Sunday, but she ended up having to spend all of her time either at settlement-services agencies or caring for her child—and in more recent months, dealing with the details of her divorce. She even found it increasingly difficult to speak with her relatives back home because she was embarrassed. The process of immigration had taken a psychological toll on her as well. "I wasn't this nervous before," she once told me. "I used to trust people, but now it's hard—you just don't know where you stand in this country." When I asked her what she meant, she said, "Everyone at the centers is competing for these small jobs, and you don't know who is going to sabotage you." These issues of trust in the workplace have lasting effects on one's psychological well-being, contributing to depression and anxiety.

In later conversations, when I asked her about why she stayed when she could go back to her life as a doctor in Pakistan, she asserted a discourse of future success—not for herself, but for her daughter. "I know it's not perfect here, but it's better for her here than in Pakistan. There are better opportunities. She's Canadian. We're both Canadian now." Later, when I asked her how she self-identified (as "Pakistani, South Asian, Pakistani-Canadian, Canadian, or something else"), she firmly said, "Canadian." This assertion never failed to surprise me, and so when I pushed further and asked her whether she thought of herself as Pakistani, she said that while it was her background, she was now Canadian. In Michèle Lamont's (2000) study of working-class American men, she asserts that they "dissociate socioeconomic status from moral worth. . . . They contradict the classical view that American workers are deprived of dignity because they are unable to live the American dream" (3). In Zainab's case, even though she, a trained doctor, was unemployed, her expectation was that this would not be the case forever. Either through her daughter, or her own future prospects, she believed she would eventually gain standing in the country to which she now claims national affiliation. Her ongoing criticism of the credentialing process for foreign-trained professionals served as a critique of the state's practices, suggesting that in order for this change to happen—for skilled immigrants like her to achieve full freedom—the entire state has to reform. Considered this way, her demand for a Canadian shift is not a modest one; it asserts a kind of identity-rights claim to resources that are not available to those living in Pakistan.

Parveen, a young woman in her thirties, had only just arrived in Toronto when we met. We met at the Center, where she seemed shy and nervous about speaking with me, but also eager to help. What I was doing was something of a mystery—kind of a student, kind of a volunteer, maybe someone who had access to resources—so I was also something of a curiosity at the Center. While her English skills were good, we conducted some of our conversation in Urdu, which seemed to make her more relaxed and speak with more ease. Parveen had moved to Toronto from Karachi three months earlier. She spent a lot of time telling me about her husband and his arrival in Toronto from Karachi via Sweden, where he stopped to complete his education in communications. It was not until we had been speaking for a while that she revealed that she had been a surgeon in Pakistan. When I asked what precipitated her migration to Toronto, she suggested it was her husband's choice and said that they both wanted to leave Karachi because of a climate riddled with "pollution and violence."

Parveen said, "I was initially bored here because I was busy there, and I miss my parents. Now I get two kinds of depression: home depression and snow depression," she told me with a laugh. O'Neill (2014) has written on the violence of boredom, and the fear that the unemployed have of boredom. Taking boredom as an everyday affect (Stewart 2007), O'Neill explores not only downward mobility but the ways that boredom "registers within the modality of time the newly homeless' expulsion to the margins of the city. In this sense, boredom is a persistent form of social suffering made possible by a crisis-generated shift in the global economy, one that has forced tens of millions of people the world over to come to terms with diminished economic capacities" (11). Boredom, then, is not something to be taken lightly, but rather an affective disposition that can do violence to one's sense of self. Also important is the second part of Parveen's statement about the transition from one climate to another, from the heat of Pakistan to the bleakness of a Canadian winter and everything that comes with it. A Toronto winter can be isolating for those unaccustomed to the rhythms of the city. The sociality of Toronto is predicated, for those raised there, on being outside regardless of the weather. Even now on trips home during the winter, no matter how far a destination, from half a mile to several, I simply wear my parka and submit to the weather. For Parveen, and indeed others at the Center, that kind of a walk would seem absurd in the winter. I lived what to me was walking distance from the Center, a walk I happily did no matter the weather, and yet the women I met saw it as strange, their incredulity often followed by a statement like, "You're a real Canadian." These kinds of moments illustrated the cultural distance between myself and the women I was supposed to be studying and the everyday ways that belonging is registered. I had that elusive cultural capital and those unmarked benefits because of my upbringing in Toronto, things they were reminded daily that they lacked.

Parveen learned that in order to become a doctor in Canada she would need to complete another internship following two to three years of study—in effect, completing medical school again. She expressed frustration at the process because the year before she had been a resident medical doctor in cardiac medicine, and working in a hospital's intensive care unit, but in Toronto she would have to begin again. She would have to be reeducated, take medical exams, and redo her residency, which would qualify her to work again in four years. After extensive online research and speaking to other practicing doctors, she found that even if she becomes accredited, it is likely that as a foreign-trained doctor, she will be sent to a relatively remote area of Canada to practice. She told me that if she cannot get her credentials recognized, or if she decides to give up, she has thought about pharmacy work or something else related to health. "As long as it's in health, I'm happy." I was always surprised at her level of optimism in the midst of such struggle. Parveen was relatively new to Toronto and was still weighing her options, but because her finances were limited, she was already experiencing downward mobility. It is quite likely she will not end up working as a doctor in Toronto. She, like most of the women I interviewed, was not financially stable; they found their lives completely disrupted, their savings obliterated, and their credentials ignored.

To grasp this experience of precarity, it is also crucial to understand the gendered dimension of unemployment. In the Fordist-Keynesian context, the assumption of a heteronormative, patriarchal family structure with a male breadwinner who is responsible for the family formed the foundation for state policy concerning employment and welfare (Fraser 2009). These persistent assumptions around masculinity seem to assume not only a heteronormative, but also reductionist model of familial relations in which economic stability rests entirely on the shoulders of an imagined husband. For instance, Collins (2003) has argued that these gender ideologies frame practices by U.S. corporate managers who oversee women factory workers in the Global South. She writes, "In the cruelest of ironies, gender ideologies permit managers to use the insufficiency of the maquiladora wage against women workers. Factory owners have pointed to the fact that household members pool their incomes to argue that women's earnings in the maquiladora are only 'supplemental'" (Collins 2003, cited in Tsing 2009: 162). Thus, women's earnings are imagined to be part of a whole, while men's earnings are imagined to support entire families, despite the realities of any given family structure.

These gender ideologies frame a variety of capitalist practices pertaining to women's wages. High rates of women's unemployment somehow do not seem to register in the cultural imaginary at all. This is despite the fact that in Canada, the unemployment rate for women and men in 2013 was almost equal (6.6 percent for women, 7.5 percent for men); however, these numbers change when race and ethnicity are factored in. For instance, in 2009, the unemployment rate for Indigenous women was 12.7 percent and 15.1 percent for Indigenous men.[2] In the United States, in 2013, the unemployment rate for adult women (over twenty years old) surpassed that of adult men. Recovering from the 2009 economic collapse, male-dominated industries (including construction and manufacturing) improved, while female-dominated industries (in the public sector) have been in decline.[3] Yet, in this context, there is simply no language to understand women's unemployment, as women are imagined to be able to rely on the economic fortunes of men. Women's economic burden is somehow now secondary to men's suffering, or this "crisis of masculinity." Yet, women continue to do a disproportionate amount of housework and childcare in addition to needing to supply a steady source of household income. As the case of Zainab demonstrates, after her divorce, she is also responsible for childcare and is the primary breadwinner in her home, performing what Hochschild (2012) calls "the second shift."

As already demonstrated, this process of transnationalism serves to gender these women as workers, funneling them into lower-paid, contingent labor; and thus, women have borne a particular burden in these global transformations. In the context of my research, while women and men were both underemployed or unemployed, the kinds of work opportunities afforded to women pay less. Thus, being "flexible" for women has economic consequences. For instance, while a Pakistani man and woman may both enter as highly skilled engineers, once they try to find work in Canada they are funneled into very different kinds of work, such that women typically earn substantially less. However, rather than an aberration, these differences according to gender are central to the functioning of late capitalism. For instance, Anna Tsing (2013) has argued that the performance of gender, ethnicity, nationality, religion, and citizenship is fundamental to supply-chain capitalism (subcontracting, outsourcing). She theorizes "super-exploitation" to understand a form of "exploitation that depends on so-called noneconomic factors such as gender, race, ethnicity, nationality, religion, sexuality, age and citizenship status" (158). Thus, in certain contexts "diversity" is central to the functioning of capitalism. While I have argued in this book that racialized Otherness is an impediment to be trained away in some circumstances, there are other forms of "diversity" that are central to the capitalist project, such as being able to pay women less for their labor.

Histories of Precarity: Bushra

Bushra's story illustrates a longer history of the foreign-trained-professionals problem; she was among the earliest migrants I interviewed, having moved to Toronto in 1975. The current state of unemployment for those with foreign credentials is sustained and naturalized at the intersection of competing forms of governance, which have turned toward neoliberal strategies since the 1990s. The current plight of unemployed, skilled workers has been further impacted by ever-growing numbers of immigrants from Asian countries, and the problem is particularly pressing since the numbers of the unemployed continue to grow. However, as Bushra's story demonstrates, the Canadian state has a long history of policing regulated professions, and the racism and discrimination that undergird this unemployment have much deeper roots.

I met Bushra while I was working with an organization for senior Muslim women, here called Dosti (which translates to female friend), whose acting executive director was a woman from Pakistan. It was a smaller section of a larger foundation that was established in 1999 as a nonprofit organization, with support from the Don Mills Foundation for Seniors Inc. and the Ontario Coalition of Senior Citizens Organizations. A 2012 study by Ryerson University found that a majority of Muslim seniors living in Scarborough felt "abused, neglected and angry." Among the 203 seniors interviewed (61 percent South Asian) at the North American Muslim Foundation and at four local mosques, most were living with family and thus were not socially isolated, but they did feel emotionally isolated. Sixty-eight percent felt appreciated and 79 percent felt respected; however, 87 percent felt neglected, 72 percent felt powerless, and 83 percent felt abused by their family or friends.[4] The concerns of Muslim seniors are often elided in discussions of citizenship and belonging. With particular concerns and needs, their experiences are often imagined as a special case, rather than as central to questions of migration.

The Dosti foundation worked to counter the isolation many Muslim seniors felt. It was not a nursing home, but a drop-in group where Muslim women could spend the day socializing and participating in volunteer work, such as raising money for Pakistani causes. One attendee told me that she used to go to the Croatian Islamic Centre regularly, but once she "heard men talking about women, saying they are like this . . ."—trailing off, not wanting to repeat what she had heard—she decided she was more comfortable praying at home. She gained her sense of a diasporic Muslim community through her activities at Dosti instead. It was a pleasure to attend their meetings, as they often involved storytelling; in these contexts I did not mind being configured and understood as "daughter" but rather embraced the sense of community produced in these encounters.

Bushra was in her sixties, and the most vocal member of Dosti. I met her at the recommendation of another member. I was sitting at one end of their large conference table, speaking with another woman about her experiences living in Toronto; embarrassed by her own story, the woman repeatedly told me that I should be speaking to Bushra instead. At the end of our conversation, she gently pushed my rolling chair toward Bushra and walked away. I rolled over to Bushra and the small group of women she was speaking with, a little embarrassed myself. I needn't have worried; I was immediately welcomed by the women. I waited quietly until they finished their meeting, at which point Bushra turned to me and smiled. Bushra was a small woman with big hair; I can only describe her as wonderfully sprightly and outgoing. She was known throughout Dosti for being completely outspoken and utterly charming. She was incredibly self-assured and confident despite the considerable challenges she had faced.

Bushra was trained as a doctor in 1959 at Fatima Jinnah College in Lahore. She moved to Karachi as a young doctor in order to establish her own hospital, and worked in the maternity ward. Not only was Bushra among the first women doctors in a major Karachi hospital, to her substantial credit she had also volunteered with underprivileged groups in Pakistan and worked primarily in clinics in the slums of Karachi. In 1967, she moved to Bahrain, where she worked as a doctor until 1971, at which point she moved to London. She had no problem getting her Pakistani degree recognized in Bahrain or the United Kingdom, where she specialized in obstetrics and pediatrics. In describing her experience in Bahrain, she said, "The patients [in the Bahrain hospital] who needed blood transfusions asked for British blood [instead of Arab], and I said you don't want it—it's full of alcohol. The nurses would tell the patients with a wink, 'Don't mess with this doctor.'"

It bears taking a moment to reflect on this desire for "white blood," a visceral and bodily manifestation of a racist politics that presumes contamination from a racialized Otherness. In this moment, racial discrimination does not end at the skin—the limit proposed by Sara Ahmed (2000) in her analysis of slime as the space between self and alien Other—but in this case permeates that barrier and the accompanying ideologies of difference and contamination. Bushra met this threat of contamination with humor; instead, she invoked another racialized and cultural stereotype to counter the patient's racism and discrimination, that of the drunk British. She turned the question around, effectively arguing that Arab blood was healthier and not contaminated. The ways one managed racism and sexism varied according to context. For instance, foreign nurses were taught to deal with disrespectful or angry patients by walking away and managing their own affects, as a move toward professionalism. In those workplaces the display of certain kinds of affects, such as anger in the face of outright racism and sexism, is considered unprofessional, forcing a kind of performance of politeness onto the subjects of discrimination. In a very different context (and speaking as a doctor, not as a nurse) faced with a request for "white blood," Bushra made a joke to sweep aside the patient's racism.

In 1973, Bushra moved to Nigeria and worked in a family health clinic sponsored by Johns Hopkins University. Two years later she left Nigeria for Toronto, and immediately thereafter her only son began experiencing seizures. He was diagnosed with cerebral palsy, which put a strain on her marriage and her day-to-day life. In Toronto, she discovered that it was unlikely she would be able to work as a doctor. She did begin the process, however, and in fact passed all the exams necessary to practice medicine, but there was no one to care for her son while she did her internships. She could not afford the expense of essentially being retrained without any social or financial support, and so ultimately made the decision to leave medicine. In order to provide for themselves, she and her husband opened a dollar store that eventually closed down due to financial difficulties. Her marriage could not last through the strain, and they separated. Her son now lives in a daily care facility since she is no longer able to care for him. Bushra said she "has a great regard for this country because everyone was so helpful in [her] worst times." She no longer worked but was by no means retired. She volunteered with the Red Cross, the Daily Bread Food Bank, Dosti, formerly with the Easter Seal committee, and was also learning Italian.

When asked about her feelings about Pakistan, Bushra revealed to me, "In Bombay, I grew up in violence. My father felt we Muslims were trapped because every few days there were riots between Hindus and Muslims. He thought we would get out of this with Partition. We had the British rule and the Hindus treated us like this—what would it be like when we were ruled by Hindus? But Pakistan is terrible now." Bushra was twelve years old during the Partition of India. Her father worked for the Muslim League, and she recalled fondly that as a child she would stand on a chair to tell people how to vote, an act which bonded her and her father. In January 1948, her family moved by ship to Karachi. She had not been to Pakistan in many years, and described it as "a carcass [from which] people are trying to get what they can." In Canada she felt that she was among her people, and she never thought about returning to Pakistan. "I decided to leave the day after the second war with India ended. I used to imagine retiring there, but not now.

After I'm home for a few days, I'm claustrophobic. I live in Canada now. I'm a Canadian."

Bushra's description of Pakistan as a "carcass" is telling. A carcass is the dead body of an animal, a corpse, the remains, the leftovers. A carcass is the discarded remains of something that has been used up. Her use of the word to describe Pakistan represents perhaps her own past disappointments with what she perceives as the failed project of Partition, the emptying out of the remains of the British Empire, and the failures of Pakistanis to take on the making of a new nation-state. She lived through it. Her experience of Partition was about her own experience of violence and abjection. The promise of a future and the failure of the project are mirrored in her own experiences of migration.

Narratives of diaspora have described a particular kind of temporal orientation in which those "living in diaspora" are inextricably tied to an imagined homeland located in the past. Brown (1999) contends that these kinds of approaches to diaspora tend to take the moment of dispersal as the starting point of analysis, "rather than examining how historically-positioned subjects identify both the relevant events in transnational community formation and the geographies implicated in that process" (293). Brian Axel (2002) has questioned the constitution of the South Asian diaspora as necessarily linked to a particular place, more specifically, a "place of origin." Using the example of the Sikh diaspora, he posits the notion of the "diasporic imaginary" to conceptualize the formation of diaspora through temporality, affect, and corporeality. For Bushra, in contrast to many narratives of diaspora in which home is a site of eventual return or is yearned for through nostalgic longing, Pakistan is a place best left in the past.

Bushra's story is compelling in its historical sweep: she lived through Partition, the post-1965 transformations in immigration law and practice, and helped transform the gendered dynamics of the field of medicine. In addition, she had to deal with day-to-day racism and violence throughout her life, such as having a white British patient ask for another doctor, or request "white blood." Despite her expertise and training, various forms of sensorial phenomena marked her belonging and nonbelonging in the eyes of patients, other professionals, and the Canadian state. Despite these accounts, multiple migrations, and downward mobility, the identity marker Bushra ultimately settled on was "Canadian." Bushra's case is different, however, from the others described here in one key way, which is that she migrated at a different historical moment and was able to access services that later migrants could not benefit from. Her story details and illustrates the long, historical roots of the devaluation of immigrant labor in Canada, while also demonstrating the everyday struggles people encounter in the process of global migration.

Like Zainab, Bushra also asserts a Canadian citizenship and identity in the face of economic marginalization. This assertion is a form of agency, but it manifests differently in the context of Bushra's life. Her story demonstrates a long-term commitment to resistance as a process. Having lived through so many historical contexts, events, crises, and ruptures, she is now older and revered by other women, held perhaps as a kind of elder of this community of immigrant women because she has a history and perspective on struggle. For Bushra, struggle is something that people do not experience only once, but something they live with. Even though she no longer wants to return there, she is not disconnected from what is happening in Pakistan. She has clearly performed her allegiance to the hurt and sick in Pakistan, just as she understands and articulates issues of trauma and justice in Canada. Her life struggles did not stop when she moved to Canada, because her life has always been about resistance, which also illuminates a commitment to resistance that is not particular, essentialist, or singular, but rather an ongoing process. She understands that being in Canada is not about retiring from struggle; rather, in Canada she continues to fight against oppression. Her ongoing commitment to resistance is not just about individualistic gains, but is always communal and based on the contingencies she experiences.

In understanding the production of precarity for these women workers, it is also important to examine the cultural meaning of the term security, and what it means to live in security. Bushra's story illuminates questions of safety and security during Partition, when mass migration was accompanied by mass violence. After the 9/11 attacks, the term security has been singularly equated with the cultural response to terrorism led by Homeland Security. This culturally inflected version of security has taken on international significance for instance in the Global War on Terror and the justification for the war in Iraq, events that have had material consequences for Pakistani migration. Security in this sense indicates national security from terrorist threat and has largely eclipsed the concept of human security, as described by the United Nations Development Program to mean "freedom from fear and want" (King and Murray 2001). "Freedom from fear" has infiltrated North American foreign and domestic policy, to the marginalization of "freedom from want." Michelle Lowry (2002) has argued that Canada's immigration system creates human insecurity for new immigrants. Security has been discursively constructed as a category that works against Muslim immigrant women, instead of a category that forwards their interests.

Bushra's story also demonstrates several ruptures that mark living in a state of precarity. For instance, her multiple migrations (post-Partition Pakistan, Bahrain, United Kingdom, Nigeria, Canada) illuminate the different ways history and cultural context shape migration experiences. In the 1970s, she had no trouble working as a doctor in Bahrain, the U.K., and Nigeria, but when she moved to Canada in 1975 she learned that she would not be able to do that work unless she went back to school. On the global market, at any given moment, one's skills and experience can be differentially valued or legitimated and despite qualifications, training, and experience, one's livelihood can be taken away.

Histories of Precarity: Abida

This section reveals Abida's experiences of precarity as manifested through her multiple migrations. Beginning with her experience of Partition, her migrations have had long-term effects on her self-understanding as South Asian and Muslim in diaspora. I met Abida through mutual acquaintances who first brought me to Dosti. Abida migrated to Canada in 1962, and had been active in the Canadian Council of Muslim Women, the All Pakistan Women's Association, and Dosti. After arriving in Canada she did her teacher's training and worked for over thirty years before retiring in 1998. She began the All Pakistan Women's Association (APWA) in 1995–96, and served as president of the Canadian Council of Muslim Women (CCMW). When we met, APWA was working on a project to fund Pakistani high school students who wanted to go on to higher education. "These are bright kids with unfortunate circumstances," she said. It was clear that for Abida, her nonprofit work was critical to her identity and self-understanding as a citizen.

Abida felt her job trajectory did not reflect those of others because she went to teacher's college in Canada. She described how she wore a sari to an early job interview, where she was asked, "Are you going to wear saris in class while teaching?" She said "Yes, when I open my mouth people will know I'm not from here," meaning that attempts to hide her perceived foreignness were futile because of her accent. They hired her anyway. She said being Muslim on the job did affect her. For instance, she did not mix socially with the other teachers since she did not drink alcohol and their sociality was predicted on social drinking at local bars. They were sensitive to her, she said, refraining from vulgar jokes if she was in the staff room.

She used the term South Asian or Muslim to describe her identity. "Sometimes people ask if I'm Italian, but I say I'm Pakistani. People from India, Pakistan, Sri Lanka, all those countries, Afghanistan, Iran, are genuine people." For Abida, her South Asian identity was deeply tied to her childhood experience of Partition. She moved to Pakistan in 1948, while in high school. Growing up she lived in a big house and had Hindu and Muslim friends.

> In 1947 there were riots and I was scared. I learned how to use swords and guns when I was ten to twelve years old. My brothers all got training. I was too young, I didn't really know about the problems. I wasn't really scared, but saw tanks and people with guns. Then trains came with refugees. We helped to bring people to their home who [had] lost everything. Girls drowned themselves so they wouldn't be taken by Hindus and Sikhs. There are examples of very good people who protected others. The masses went haywire, they didn't know what was right or wrong. It didn't matter who they were. The rapes... very unfortunate. Whenever there's war, there are not very civilized people doing things, even though religions teach differently.... My parents were in the movement and believed it was good for people to keep their identity in their own way. There was friendliness, but there still used to be communal riots.... People had motivation [for an independent Pakistan] to have an Islamic state to govern the way they wanted. There was lots of patriotism and spirit.

I later asked Abida about her personal experience of migration during Partition. She told me the following:

> We traveled in 1948 from Aurangabad to Bombay on train; from there we took a ship to Karachi. My two brothers came first, then relatives started coming, they stayed with us until we found places for them. The ladies and children used to live in two rooms, and a washroom and a kitchen and balcony, the men slept in the garden.

People thought it was better for the ladies to go into the house and for men to guard them. We did this for a few months. We didn't take much with us. I was told I could only bring a few things that were really important to me. I used to collect chocolate wrappers. I took the wrappers and a shirt I liked.

Abida laughed and said, "It's funny how beautiful I thought those wrappers were." The image of beautiful, shiny chocolate wrappers was to me a shining example of hope in the face of uncertainty, the emblems of a child who wanted to keep something familiar and beautiful with her.

In contrast to Bushra's experience, Abida was very fortunate financially. She was trained in Canada and therefore able to use her training to support a middle-class life in Canada. She originally studied in Karachi and London, eventually earning a master's degree in zoology and microbiology, before moving to Alberta in 1962 as a student. She moved to Toronto because of the larger Muslim community. She also remained married, which helped her financially and emotionally support herself and her family. Abida's story is interesting because of the ways precarious past migrations inform present circumstances and self-understandings. Her experience of Partition was of leaving home as a child with few belongings, and of being a refugee confronted with stories of rape, violence, and war. Her use of the self-identifier "South Asian" is interesting in this context because it represents her effectively undoing Partition, or putting the country back together. Identifying herself as Muslim represents her commitment to religious affiliation and meaning making. While Bushra described Pakistan as a "carcass," Abida told fond stories of Hindu aunties and uncles; thus her use of the term "South Asian" attempts to resolve the precarity produced by historical events.

Precarity as Loss

Manar was a young Pakistani woman working at a pro bono South Asian legal organization in Toronto, located in a large concrete building downtown. The institutional architecture was at odds with the warm and welcoming atmosphere in the building. We had corresponded over e-mail and she agreed to meet me at her office downtown. She was still busy working when I arrived, so I waited in the lounge. Manar was the project director for the Toronto region of this particular South Asian organization, and she consulted extensively with Pakistanis who were not able to work in their chosen professions. She also spoke to these issues from personal experience; although she had been a lawyer in Pakistan, she was not able to act as legal counsel in Toronto because she was not accredited to practice law in Canada. She could only advise and counsel informally. When we met, she was having trouble making ends meet. Manar spoke to me at length about her personal history.

> I grew up in a conservative environment in Pakistan. I was married at twenty-four and we lived in Karachi. In 1996, my son was diagnosed with a heart condition. It was for him that we wanted to move. I applied first for a visitor visa to England for his medical treatment because it would take so long to immigrate abroad permanently. I had been to England, but at customs, they said they didn't know why I wanted to take my son and my husband with me. It took so long, but finally they approved me. We were going to go on December 13, but my son died on December 12. If we lived in a developed country, my son would have had a better chance. On January 6, we were in a car accident and my husband died in my arms. I paid my taxes in Pakistan, but when we went to the hospital, we were not treated like human beings. I felt disappointed in the system.

Manar stayed with her mother-in-law in Pakistan while she waited for a visa to get in to the United States. She had practiced law in Pakistan, but in the United States she worked on and off at a gas station in North Carolina, which led her to feel like she was drifting through life. Consequently, she applied for and received a full scholarship to study in London for a master's degree. She had to fly back to Islamabad from the United States to obtain her British visa for school, as one has to go through the immigration interview in the country of application. Her visa process was slowed due to a coup in Pakistan, but eventually it was approved; she then had five or six days to move before her visa expired. She finally made her way to Britain to study, and later migrated to Toronto.

I really liked Manar. In fact, I looked up to her; I thought she was really cool. I had recently returned to Toronto for the first time after living in the United States, away from my family, and because of the nature of my fieldwork I was forced to confront my own feelings about my relationship to Islam. Manar and I would meet periodically throughout my time back. Once I was at an Ifthar party, which is a party to break fast during Ramadan. We were waiting patiently, watching the minutes pass on the clock. I wasn't fasting regularly, but I thought out of respect that I would fast on that day. Unaccustomed to not eating, I was starving and having trouble paying attention to anything but the time. As we were comparing watches, Manar said, "Look, I don't think God's going to begrudge us a few minutes." It was the first time I had heard someone talk like that. In my family, there were aspects of my religious upbringing that had been very strict. Breaking the fast was one of them. This moment was meaningful to me because it revealed that Manar would not take herself or her religious practice so seriously that it was removed from the practicalities of life. God wouldn't begrudge a few minutes.

When I first met her, Manar had been in Toronto for two-and-a-half years. When I asked if she liked living in Toronto, she told me she loved it because of her independence. When Manar arrived in Canada, she immediately began attending job-search workshops. Every day she aggressively sent résumés, thirty to forty applications she said. It took her a year and a half to find a law-related job, and she was still not able to work as a lawyer. Her personal life had been going well. Manar had been dating someone and was thinking about getting married. I asked her if she ever thought about moving back. "Pakistan feels so distant," she replied. "I don't want to. Maybe I'll go back when I'm older. Right now, I have no desire to visit Pakistan. I can't be a lawyer here per se, but I hope things will get better. I know things will get better." When I asked her how she self-identified, she said, "I'm a Pakistani-Canadian, but Canadian first."

Manar's narrative suggests two things. Outside of Pakistan, her presence is a site of contestation; but despite everything she has suffered, she is happy to assert a Canadian identity. While it may be easy to dismiss her assertion as resulting from her experience of trauma, it must be taken seriously as her attempt to fashion a sense of place, and an effort to be somewhere else that might benefit herself and her family. Instead of reading her story as one of defeat, I interpret her narrative as a real articulation of her desire.

Bushra views Pakistan as a carcass of corruption and finds herself claustrophobic upon return, suggesting a deep disappointment with the postcolonial state and a sense of disillusionment that perhaps compels her identification with Canada. How is this sense of disappointment with or betrayal by Pakistan—especially for those who thought Pakistan would give them the equality and dignity they were denied as Muslims in India, or for women like Manar who felt they were not treated as human—reconciled with the humiliation and frustration of poverty and racism in Canada? In a way, this apparent insistence on claiming Canadian-ness can be thought of as a way to resolve earlier disappointments with Pakistan.

Narratives such as Manar's life story suggest the deep, affective purchase of why women change their lives and persist in their struggles, even when the results are not what they expected or even necessarily wanted. Although a trained lawyer, Manar spent time working at a gas station, and although she is now settled in Toronto, she still cannot counsel people according to her level of education and expertise. Her claim to Canadian citizenship can be read as a place-making activity that critiques the differences between living in more- and less-developed countries. It is not a stretch to believe that she continued to think in the back of her mind, "If I had just lived in Canada, my son would not have died." She invoked the notion of freedom in her conversations with me, but it was about freedom from living in a state of abjection. The predicament of postcolonial migrant lives operates under a number of logics: abjection, disposability, or precarity (Rodriguez 2010; Tadiar 2009). It is not surprising that one solution for Manar would be to relocate herself to a place where she imagined there would be regular access to good health care. In these stories, citizenship and security are necessarily and tragically linked. Pakistan arose as a place of the past; even dead and picked over, in Bushra's imagination. With ongoing violence, poor access to health care, fewer resources, limits on women's mobility, and an unstable government, they not only felt disadvantaged as women in Pakistan but also that their overall quality of life was better in resource-filled countries like Canada.

Precarious Citizenship

Gulnaaz was from Karachi and had been living in Canada for a year and a half when we met. She had been a working lawyer in Pakistan for five years before moving to Canada. She moved independently, although she has a brother in New York who helped her while she was unemployed. In order to work as a lawyer, she would need to write "papers" (her term for exams). She was in the process of receiving an evaluation of her credentials from the National Accreditation Committee, which takes approximately six months to one year. The accreditation of foreign credentials is big business in Canada—a feature of the neoliberal state—and, as I explained earlier, there are so many different companies with almost no standardization that professional organizations often do not recognize evaluations, rendering them effectively useless. Once Gulnaaz receives her evaluation, she will be able to take the bar exam, which should take another year. In total she has to take twelve exams at a cost of approximately $600 each, which will take an additional year and a half. An alternate path suggested to her was that she return to university. After being in Canada for eleven months she got a job as a legal assistant, but ultimately left due to harassment from her employer. When she first arrived in Canada she tried odd jobs, including making kebabs. "It was my choice to move here, so I'm still giving Canada a chance." When I asked her whether she also identified as Pakistani, she said, "I was Pakistani, and my origins will always be Pakistani, but I'm a Canadian now."

The sovereignty of the state in an era of global migration has been understood as inextricably bound to questions of territory (Gupta and Sharma 2006); the boundaries of the nation-state become reified through the everyday ways citizens make claims to citizenship. The question of state sovereignty in an era of globalization and global migration has undergone considerable debate in the anthropological literature (e.g., Appadurai 1996; Gupta and Ferguson 2002). As Gupta and Sharma (2006) have argued, globalization is imagined to compromise the national state since it challenges two features that are central to the idea of a national state: territory and sovereignty. The nation-state is imagined to be porous, and those permitted entry are thought to have real and imagined ties to communities elsewhere that would compromise their loyalty. Authors have countered such images of the equation of territory with "a people" (e.g., Appadurai 1996; Gupta 1992). For these women, being unemployed represents a failure of social inclusion, a kind of failed citizenship predicated on the notion that inclusion encompasses economic participation. I referred to this kind of citizenship, one that goes beyond legal papers, in detail in the previous chapter as cultural citizenship, in an attempt to understand the different kinds of claims that immigrant and minority communities make beyond the realm of legal recognition. Early theorists of cultural citizenship stress the necessity of inclusion in multiple spheres of public participation (e.g., Flores and Benmayor 1997; Ong 1999; Rosaldo 1994). The women I spoke with invoked discourses of promise and a better future for their children to understand their liminal, contingent position, sometimes understanding their economic failure as a failure of the state to properly integrate foreign labor, thus critiquing the state, and sometimes blaming themselves. This discourse of promise and a better future for their children indexes a hope in the state with which they still identify. In so doing, they position themselves as morally right, good citizens deserving of full participation in the nation-state.

Precarity throughout this chapter has emerged as a social condition of the contemporary global era. In all the narratives presented here, a socio-economic state of precarity was accompanied by a similar feeling in their social worlds. Berlant (2011) asks, "What does it mean even to propose that a spreading precarity provides the dominant *structure* and *experience* of the present moment, cutting across class and localities? . . . To what degree [is precarity] an economic and political condition suffered by a population or by the subjects of capitalism generally; or a way of life; or an affective atmosphere; or an existential truth about contingencies of living, namely, that there are no guarantees that the life one intends can or will be built" (192)? Gendered narratives of precarity illustrated here demonstrate the ways global processes and social inequality are unevenly distributed. Yet, in the face of this precarity women had a desire to persevere and to survive.

Imagining a Better Life

Shabana tells me,

> Canada has been good to me, because in Pakistan if I had a daughter and my husband left me with nothing, I would have been ruined. Here I had housing, they paid for daycare; Canada helped me. In Pakistan, maybe there wouldn't have been any help for me—the government wouldn't have been there to help me find a home, or help me support my child. . . . There are other things, my mother would have helped at home, but the government there, they don't have the resources, there are no daycares or housing like this [government housing]. It's a third-world country. Even if I had a job, I would have been struggling all my life.

She explains her Canadian nationalism in relation to the differences between living in the global North versus the global South. Not only does daily life have a different quality, but there are resources available to her in Canada that she would not have had in Lahore. However, it is important that we not read these narratives as celebratory accounts of the global North rescuing women of the global South. The wealth and power of the global North is maintained at the expense of those living elsewhere, and often living right there in the global North, contributing to society and perpetuating the nation but undocumented or underpaid.

In the context of Toronto, one must also remember that women like Shabana moved to Canada because they were living in a state of abjection in Pakistan; but then, having moved to Canada, they were victimized again by an inequitable system that marginalizes them economically. Master narratives such as globalization or capitalism tell stories of progress and of becoming, but they also represent a disaggregated set of practices with local manifestations and cultures. One enduring story of capitalism is that of progress, or forward movement, of success and accomplishment based on a meritocracy, a story challenged by the experiences articulated here. In the face of economic and social precarity, when Pakistani immigrant women claim Canadian citizenship it becomes a way for them to imagine their worlds differently. This portrayal of national allegiance represents a very definite understanding of material and economic differences between life in Canada versus life in Pakistan. Questions of belonging exceed the discourse of the nation-state; we need ways of knowing that account for loss, as Manar's story demonstrates, but we also do not want to absolve the state of responsibility for the blatant disregard of life, both within its borders and outside of them. These women's claims to citizenship also stem from a kind of desire—a desire for support or welfare from the state, for equality, and for dignity. The structural context in which this desire emerges complicates the standard narrative of "migrating for a better life." I asked numerous women why they chose to stay and whether they ever thought about returning to Pakistan. I most often heard some version of the following: "I came here for my kids—I hope my children will do better than me." This imagining of a better life for their children was a narrative that appeared throughout my time in Toronto. These kinds of statements could be read as reproducing aspects of the promise of upward mobility inherent in discourses of global migration and multiculturalism, a kind of "Canadian dream." However, I believe that these kinds of hopes function instead to make sense of a precarious and even catastrophic present, a hope of something better for generations to come.

These hopes are not inconsequential; rather, they are political perspectives that provide a kind of commentary on contemporary social life in late capitalism. As Berlant so aptly writes in *Cruel Optimism* (2011), "For many now . . . the traditional infrastructures for reproducing life—at work, in intimacy, politically—are crumbling at a threatening pace" (5). People's everyday existence is now "shaped by crisis in which people find themselves developing skills for adjusting to newly proliferating pressures to scramble for modes of living on" (8). The attachments people forge to an idea of the good life can perform the work of cruel optimism, a hoping for something that is no longer possible. As the process of capitalism figures in the annihilation of the promise of a good life, creating precarious situations for women and their families, holding on to hope is a means to understand and survive the catastrophic present.

The writing of women into history involves redefining and enlarging traditional no-tions of historical significance, to encompass personal, subjective experience as well as public and political activities. Such a methodology implies not only a new history of women, but also a new history.—JOAN SCOTT, *Gender and the Politics of History*

Nadeem was one of the last women I met at the Center. I had been answer-ing phones as a volunteer at the front desk that day because the regular ad-ministrator was out sick. Nadeem did not have an actual appointment, but instead had come to the Center to socialize with other women in the wait-ing area. Clearly frustrated and perhaps lonely, her conversation filled the Center. Suddenly and without warning, her interest turned to me. Who was I? She wanted to know. When I told her, she expressed interest in being interviewed, wanting to be included in the study or at least to have her voice heard and her words documented. She said, "I've been exploited. . . . So much money is wasted every year on studies like this [referring to *Down-wardly Global*], but nothing ever changes. If you don't like what I said, you can erase my interview and not call me again." Nadeem's frustration and her comments raise a critical point about where money and efforts are put ɔes ! and what kinds of change are actually possible.

Multiculturalism's Identity Crisis

In June 2012, Citizenship and Immigration Canada suspended the Federal Skilled Worker Program, which had been the primary route for skilled-worker immigration, bringing in approximately 55,000 people every year. Due to a tremendous backlog, some applicants had been waiting up to eight years to hear about the status of their application; nonetheless, Jason Kenney, then minister of Citizenship and Immigration, declared that applications submitted before February 28, 2008, would be terminated. The program was reopened again in May 2013, but with substantial changes reflecting a more challenging process for applicants. First, there is now a higher minimum threshold for skills in English or French, and immigrants must meet a higher level of proficiency in the Canadian Language Benchmark. Second, more points are given to younger applicants. Third, the new Educational Credential Assessment system was established to measure foreign credentials, though the low success rate of similar programs in the past makes this seem like a hollow gesture. Fourth, those with arranged employment can now have their applications expedited. Finally, more points are awarded to applicants with a spouse who has English-language skills and/or work experience in Canada. As of January 2015, in order to apply for the Federal Skilled Worker Program, prospective immigrants must submit their applications through what is called Express Entry, which enters applicants in a pool from which they may be invited to apply for permanent residence. Drawings to select immigrants happen regularly over the course of each year. Express Entry is the culmination of Kenney's attempt to reform the immigration system so that it more closely resembles that of Australia or New Zealand, known as an "expression of interest" system, in which Citizenship and Immigration Canada could select immigrants based on skills matched to businesses.

Ironically, during this period Canada has also faced a labor shortage. In order to resolve this, Kenney traveled to Ireland in October 2012 to promote immigration to Canada. He attended a recruitment fair in Dublin and appeared on Ireland's *Late Late Show* to discuss the Canadian government's interest in recruiting young Irish men and women to work in Canada. According to the *Toronto Star*, "Kenney said he only has to look around the parliament buildings in Ottawa to see the contributions the Irish made to Canada. 'There are shamrocks (engraved in the stone) that is a reminder that the Irish are one of the founding peoples [of Canada].' "[1] This discourse of founding people is inaccurate; it erases not only the presence of Indigenous people, but even the celebrated Canadian origin-story of settler colonialism. Kenney has repeatedly spoken publicly about terrorists and immigration "queue jumpers," which is even more disconcerting in contrast to his trip to Ireland to seek more white immigrants. This trip exemplifies how multicultural practice often appears self-congratulatory, privileging tolerance over justice and focusing on the axis of margin and center rather than the axis of oppression and suppression.

This book has told a story of the welfare state in decline, the effects of which have caused widespread precarity and uncertainty in the lives of many. The scenes described here—of economic marginalization and government solutions to the problem—present a cartography of downward mobility that many presume to be caused by bureaucratic entanglements. What I have tried to show, however, is that this problem has deeper origins in settler colonial ideologies of governance and rule that are masked by the sanitized language and practice of multiculturalism. The frustrations, anxieties, and desperation that Pakistani Muslim immigrant women experience in Toronto make visible the effects of large-scale social transformations on everyday lives. The experiences of these women challenge the teleologies of success that are reproduced in master narratives of capitalism, globalization, and even multiculturalism, narratives that elide the social production of inequality that are endemic to these processes. The promise of success and the "good life" (Berlant 2011) that dominates these master narratives makes the failures even more devastating. Everyday practices in settlement-services agencies and cultural festivals point to broader social issues that immigrant women deal with in their efforts to succeed in a multicultural society that promises them inclusion, but practices differentiated exclusion.

In the North American context, questions of multiculturalism have overtaken explicit public discussions about race, racism, and racialization. Never a favored topic in Canada, racism and race politics have been marginalized in favor of the sanitized and wholesome language of ethnicity, multiculturalism, and its attendant rhetoric of "equality within a model of difference," revealing the injury and then the erasure of that injury. Such language reproduces a discourse of benevolence and generosity in contrast (from the perspective of the Canadian public eager to distance itself from the United States) to U.S. problems of domestic racism. What is more dangerous about the Canadian approach at this particular historical moment is the way that racism and race-based discrimination are masked by the discourse of the post-racial moment. If Canadian culture is post-racial, then economic inequality must have some other explanation, such as individualized failure to be competitive on the global market.

The stories illustrated throughout this book challenge popular narratives concerning the workings of multiculturalism and globalization. Debates around multiculturalism since the 1970s, at least in Canada, have focused on a perceived tension between giving newcomers a sense of belonging versus emphasizing differences between communities, and therefore promoting the development of ethnic enclaves.[2] This debate often leads to a focus on loyalty to the "new country," which in fact serves to mask the Janus-faced approach to multiculturalism in Canada. Public discourse on this practice describes a relinquishing of cultural imperialism and a celebration of "multi-ness," as demonstrated by cultural festivals or other public celebrations. The reality, however, is that dominant culture decides what forms of difference are acceptable to emphasize and attempts to train away any markers of Otherness that do not serve it. In this book, I have examined regulatory practices that make immigrant bodies legible through a close analysis of the sanitized sensorium, and looked at instances of state-sanctioned diversity in cultural festivals. An examination of these modes of interpellation demonstrates the embodied nature of citizenship in Canada.

The contemporary crisis of multiculturalism is not due to the presence of unassimilated minorities, but rather to the ways that difference is controlled, managed, and contained; liberal multicultural practice creates competing narratives of citizenship, further alienating already marginalized citizens. Rethinking immigrant bodies as central to the making of national identity (rather than as a challenge to it) contradicts the whiteness naturalized as the center and subject of liberal multicultural discourse. Examining the everyday experiences of immigrants as partially included subjects demonstrates the challenges and fractures of reigning notions of citizenship, which promises not only inclusion but equality as well. The body, here the immigrant body, becomes a site of contestation in the making of modern citizen-workers, which reframes globalization not as a smooth process, but as one that state institutions mediate and shape.

The crisis contained within multiculturalism is not about the unassimilability of certain bodies, but is really about the disjuncture between liberal ideologies and marginalizing practices. Rather than ask how incommensurate worlds are made commensurate, Elizabeth Povinelli (2001) asks "how the incommensurateness of liberal ideology and practice is made to *appear* commensurate" (328, emphasis added). Rather than imagining multiculturalism as a means to manage incommensurate social worlds, in the context of Canada it is important to understand how liberal ideologies of equality and difference are made to appear commensurate with exclusionary practices.

These liberal ideologies of equality and difference are at the heart of attempts to govern immigrant populations. In the contemporary era, there is a range of social actors involved in the project of rule; here, I have focused on the contracting out of settlement for new immigrants. This has occurred in other cultural contexts (Rose 1996a; Sharma 2008) in which an increasing range and power of voluntary organizations exist between the state and its citizens. In Canada, the contracting out of settlement services has created a gap between a government that formerly had an international reputation for welfare and care, and its citizens. In particular, the settlement-services sector has helped exacerbate the marginalization of immigrant populations by locating their unemployment not within labor markets, but on their bodies.

Government agencies offer training sessions to teach immigrant women to make themselves more acceptable to white Canadians in order to make them more employable, but the state does not act to curtail the discrimination they face. The Canadian people and their government wish to view themselves as inclusive, multicultural, and anti-racist, yet their policies and practices follow the logics of racial, religious, and gender exclusion. The multiculturalism that Canadians celebrate as a form of universal integration in reality functions to generate and legitimate new forms of exploitation and exclusion. Racial stratification is explained as a product of Pakistani Muslim immigrant women's unfitness for inclusion rather than as the inevitable outcome of cultural assumptions and practices deliberately designed to exclude people designated as Other.

Racializing Muslim Bodies

A challenge to multicultural ideals in Canada emerged in 2010, when Québec introduced Bill 94, the first legislation in North America that places a ban on the niqab in any government building, including high schools and universities. According to an Angus Reid poll, 95 percent of Quebecers, and three out of four not from Québec, approved of Bill 94. Québec Premier Jean Charest said, "Two words: uncovered face. The principle is clear." Christine St-Pierre, cabinet minister, referred to the niqab as "ambulatory prisons," while Louise Beaudoin of the Parti Québécois called any Muslim head coverings examples of "submission of women, of regression, and a subjugation of all our freedoms." Not mentioning the niqab explicitly, the bill states that in government buildings, people must "show their face during the delivery of services," for "security, communication and identification."[3] This is the latest manifestation of the "reasonable accommodations" debate that occurred in 2007. This banning of the niqab and the secular and racial politics that accompany it, are not limited to Québec, a recent poll finding that the majority of Canadians outside of Québec agree with Bill 94, with 77 percent in Ontario.[4] Echoing Ghassan Hage's (2009) paranoid nationalism, in which anxiety is a means of attachment to the state in the presence of dwindling hope, these challenges to the practice of Islam have emerged in times of increasing economic insecurity, so that Muslims have become a demonized Other.

What undergirds this sensorial mode of governance discussed throughout has been a politics of racialization and race-based discrimination. In the post 9/11-period, Muslim has increasingly become a racialized category and thus a basis for race discrimination under the amorphous and growing category of Arab/Muslim/Other/those who look that way. Junaid Rana (2011) has thoughtfully explored the emergence of Muslim as a racial category. He writes, "in the contemporary theory of racializing Muslims into the global racial system, the boundaries of race lie between the body and performances that aim to restrict and subjugate . . ." the Muslim is understood not only as a totalized biological body but also as a cultural and social entity constructed within a number of discursive regimes, including those of terrorism, fundamentalism, patriarchy, sexism, and labor migration (25–26). Thus Muslims emerged as a racial figure, as a body on which global politics is enacted.

According to Omi and Winant, racialization is a historically specific, ideological process by which "the extension of racial meaning [is ascribed] to a previously racially unclassified relationship, social practice, or group" (13). While there is a corporeal relationship to the concept of race, those differences are viewed and interpreted in historically and contextually specific ways (Omi and Winant 2014: 13). David Theo Goldberg (1993) has written on the import of these racial categories, "[race] has established who can be imported and who exported, who are immigrants and who are indigenous, who may be property and who are citizens; and among the latter who get to vote and who do not, who are protected by the law and who are its objects, who are employable and who are not, who have access and privilege and who are (to be) marginalized" (87).

To understand this form of racialization, one must understand its outcomes. Ruth Gilmore (2007) writes, "racism, specifically, is the state-sanctioned or extralegal production and exploitation of group-differentiated vulnerability to premature death" (28). For Gilmore, racism includes not only practices by state actors but elements that fall outside laws, including the realms of affect and the senses for instance. These practices can lead to the production of a racial group. In this case, immigration laws, regulations, and sensorial registers work together to produce the category of Pakistani/South Asian/Muslim/Other. This category then becomes a site of exploitation and discrimination, leading to the death of some members of that racialized group. For instance, in the case of Pakistani/South Asian/Muslim/Other, there is systemic discrimination and even death resulting from changes in practices and policies following 9/11.[5] Thus in this ethnography, these divergent state practices of inclusion and exclusion are intrinsic to the practice of racialization at the heart of multicultural governance that determines and defines the limits of acceptance.

In the post-9/11 period, Muslims as a category have become a racialized group subject to exploitation and discrimination, which in this ethnography has been experienced through unfair labor practices in terms of recognition and hiring, leading to precarity and even poverty. For instance, Zubeidah and her husband (discussed in chapter 1) believed that their Pakistani and Muslim identity became a factor contributing to their family's precarity. Her husband has had a lot of frustration over being treated like a terrorist and has been afraid that it will impact his work, which included collaboration with American companies. Increasingly, he was being stopped at the United States border, where he had been interrogated for three hours and had his fingerprints taken. He was angry that he was being treated like a terrorist, and afraid of losing his job at the same time.

These experiences of discrimination were not Zubeidah and her husband's alone, but were felt by many others. The experiences of two women, Zenith and Najmi, highlight this critical dimension of discrimination based on a racialized identity. I had taken the subway to the end of the line and then a bus another half an hour to reach the foundation's main offices. I was meeting with Zenith, whose work provided community services for seniors, women, and newcomers in North York. We had met on and off at various nonprofits and social events, and she finally agreed to let me sit down with her to discuss her personal experience of migration. The mission of the foundation was to enable members of these groups to "participate in the social, economic and civic life of Canada, by encouraging and engaging them to contribute through their knowledge, skills and experiences in the development and well-being of our neighborhoods and our communities." Dosti, which had formed as an offshoot of this foundation, targeted senior women and was where I met Abida and Bushra. Zenith had been working with the foundation for less than a year in communication, research, facilitating volunteers, and running workshops that would get seniors out of the house, as loneliness and depression were major issues facing the community.

Zenith was born in Quetta, the capital of Balochistan. She had moved to Canada in 1994. She said, "I wanted to move to Canada to primarily push for the future of my kids. We were uncertain of the political situation in Pakistan and we wanted a secure future." She was educated in Pakistan, doing a degree in communications. She is married and has two children. Her husband was in the hotel business, having studied business administration. Both had a lot of trouble finding work when they arrived in Canada. "It was the standard newcomer situation," she said, "we went to workshops and tried to have our degrees evaluated." She had been the primary applicant because she had some knowledge of French, which strengthened their application since it is one of Canada's official languages. During workshop classes she was told to highlight her language experience. "When we got here, we found that the style of résumés were different, but we dealt with it. We were pretty clearly told we didn't have Canadian experience and our credentials were not sufficient." Over and over again she was told that she was overqualified, which to her didn't make sense. "Everything we applied for, we got curt responses and racist remarks," the latter of which she did not want to discuss. "It's a Catch-22," she said, adding, "our credentials are in demand, but we're not considered to have a good background," which I interpreted to mean that on paper her qualifications looked good, yet her Pakistani background was judged to be a negative. "With communications I could work in different fields, education, publishing, advertising, senior management, I could approach different sectors, but I'm overqualified." Her husband experienced the same kinds of things, and she was more willing to talk about the racism he faced: "He had racist remarks in the job search. One was from a high-end head hunter who said, 'All we need is another Indian tragic story,'" in reference to their difficulties finding work. "Another Indian tragic story" was marked by Zenith as a point of racism. Echoing the comments of those discussed in chapter 4, she resisted the conflation of Pakistani with Indian. In this instance, a headhunter referring to her husband as having a tragic Indian story felt like an affront, a dismissal of their experiences based on assumptions surrounding race.

Zenith continued this discussion of the ways race figured in her job search when she spoke of the issue of eye contact. She said, "I had an absence of eye contact because of my own racial discomfort," meaning that for her, she felt uncomfortable making eye contact with white men and women. I did not ask her more about that because she seemed so uncomfortable, but in retrospect it could signify either her own insecurity and vulnerability being on the job market, or her frustration and anger toward gatekeepers. Eventually she started getting contract jobs and attending more workshops at settlement-services agencies. "We asked a lot of questions. English is my language, but it was still difficult." She sought out a number of available resources and marketed her degree in communications toward nonprofit work because she felt she understood the experiences of newcomers. While Zenith was not in a regulated profession, she still faced numerous barriers to her employment, including what she identified as racism. "Now, it's a different climate, it's less socially acceptable to be racist." Or perhaps multiculturalism simply provides a façade for hiding racial injustice.

Racialized bodies become the site upon which these global politics are written and enacted, with the whiteness of multicultural practices attempting to bleach uncontainable difference. Whether in colonial India or contemporary Toronto, these women are subjects and subjected to a historically informed project of empire: of civilizing the native, of disciplining subjects. The sensorial pedagogies that women receive in settlement-services workshops depart from the kinds of (unmarked) self that usually appear in discussions of neoliberal governance, and in them, self-management takes on highly racialized forms. Such regulatory regimes can be traced historically to colonial modernist projects of empire and civilization; in the contemporary era, race, nation, and Otherness have become personalized impediments to be trained away through sensorial pedagogies.

Najmi had more success than many. She had been in Toronto for two years. She was a psychologist in Pakistan and had her advanced degrees measured to be the equivalent to the bachelor's degree by the accreditation service offered by the University of Toronto, rather than by WES, which was discussed in chapter 1. After two years, she counted herself among the lucky. She was able to find work as a substance-abuse counselor, and is now working full time with developmentally disabled people. Her success is perhaps due in part to the fact that counseling, like nursing, is understood as a gendered form of care labor. She said, "I've come across many people from Pakistan who are not working in their fields. I met a woman who has been here longer than me and has an MA in sociology and can't get a job. She didn't have work experience." Najmi pointed to the fact that many employers discriminate against immigrant workers because they do not have Canadian experience and yet to get Canadian experience, one needs to get a job.

Her husband faced race-based discrimination on the basis of a Muslim identity and Muslim identifiers. He is highly educated, having completed an MBA in Pakistan. He had successfully worked for the head office of an international company in Dubai before they moved to Canada. He had sent his résumé to the local offices of this company in Toronto and immediately received an interview. They said they were very interested and would get back to him, but they never did. Eventually he was able to find work in an IT company. Najmi continued:

> The last two years he's had a tough time. He joined a coop program for those who are newcomers with little English. The instructor didn't know what to tell him. The instructor was a white Canadian, said he didn't see anything wrong with his résumé, said it could be because he had a Muslim name so he said he should change it. My husband said no because the next step would be asking him to change his faith, then his skin color. They have to accept him the way he is. They tell you to forget your past here. He didn't do it.

Najmi went on to discuss media representations as influencing public behavior. "Our country is always shown to be [filled with] terrorists, it doesn't reflect well on the community. People generalize from these things—'they're all like that.'" Najmi's comments reflect the racism implicit in the practice of the sanitized sensorium. He was encouraged to change his name for legibility, but felt it would simply be the first step in a larger process of transforming his identity, which he did not want to do.

The sensorium is the site at which the world is interpreted and understood, and thus is critical in understanding the politics of globalization, immigration, unemployment, and the regulation of bodies under such regimes. Sara Ahmed (2004) writes, "Hardness is not the absence of emotion, but a different emotional orientation towards others. The hard white body is shaped by its reactions: the rage against others surfaces as a body that stands apart by its reactions" (4). These kinds of responses, such as rage or disgust, signal the stakes of the sanitized sensorium and must be taken seriously as a site of disciplining and controlling Other bodies because they have material consequences. In order to understand liberal multicultural governance, we must engage questions of affect, the body, and its racialization, which in turn demonstrate how governmental forces are exerted differentially on raced and gendered bodies. The larger public's fear of the smell or look of immigrant bodies results in not only social but economic marginalization and reproduces poverty and social inequality.

The race discrimination Najmi felt in Canada, however, was not enough to make her rethink their decision to migrate. "We came here because of the political situation in Pakistan. I came here as a landed immigrant under the points system. They rate your age, education, your money. Landed immigrants need a lot of money in their accounts." She later added, "I moved because I wanted to give my children a better future, for their education. I was thinking ten to fifteen years down the road in Pakistan. I wanted my children to have an international experience." She had two children, a boy who was twelve and a girl who was eight. Her entire family was against their move, suggesting instead that they later send their children for their education. Despite her family's concerns, she and her husband decided to take a chance: "My husband is a risk taker."

Through her counseling work, she found that this systemic racism has had large-scale effects in the community. In her experience, South Asian immigrants face issues such as depression and substance abuse (alcohol being the most common among adults, while teenagers abuse alcohol and drugs). "The whole family lifestyle changes here; there are odd jobs, odd hours, children are left unsupervised. Landed immigrant parents have a compromised job and standard of living, it puts pressure on children and they're expected to perform better. . . . Teens need guidance; they have cultural conflicts. They get different messages, they can't identify with either culture and their [skin] color is not accepted here, but they're also deviating from their culture at home. In Pakistan, family life is different, the whole family is together; here there's no time because they're so busy." Najmi points to the consequences of unemployment and underemployment, which impact family dynamics, children's care, and one's own personal health. These concerns taken together illustrate the toll that racialization as terrorist Other has taken on individual lives.

This racialization as Muslim, however, is best understood through an intersectional analysis that takes into account the gender and class elements of this process. For instance, racialization is also part of a gendered form of nationalism that produces raced and sexed bodies fit for citizenship. Cynthia Enloe (1989) writes, "nationalism typically has sprung from masculinized memory, masculinized humiliation and masculinized hope. Anger at being 'emasculated'—or turned into a 'nation of busboys'—has been presumed to be the natural fuel for igniting a nationalist movement" (44). Bringing this conception of nationalism to racialization demonstrates that creating a racialized form of citizenship is also at once a process of gendering. In this case, the process of turning upwardly mobile professional women into downwardly mobile service workers includes their ability to perform a kind of sanitized worker, a radical alterity, and a gendered subject—all part of the process of citizen-making.

Sensing Precarity, Belonging, and Citizenship

Racialization is a critical part of this process of downward mobility, and is also importantly gendered. Thus, questions of labor and unemployment are inseparable from questions of the racialization and gendering of subjects, and have implications for citizenship, belonging, and living in a state of precarity. In this way, these women's exclusion from the public sphere of employment demonstrates that the process of making citizens is also a process of racialization and race-making. While this unemployment and underemployment are most often understood publicly as resulting from bureaucratic error, I have suggested instead that it is symptomatic of state restructuring under late capitalism and is sustained by a sensorial regime that produces Otherness. This restructuring moves the terrain of "immigrant integration" toward the gendered immigrant body, so that governmental programs and practices treat unemployment as a problem of the immigrant body and racialized Otherness. State practices then manage these new immigrants through institutionalized multiculturalism that racializes them, further revealing the complex ways that immigration (in particular, labor migration) has come to be managed by neoliberal and multicultural techniques of governance.

How is the greater public to understand itself as benevolent when faced with growing numbers of poor and desperate immigrants? As Ahmed (2000) writes, "What is at stake in the *ambivalence* of such relationships between human and alien is not whether aliens are represented as good or bad, or as 'beyond' or 'within' the human, but how they function to establish and define the boundaries of who 'we' are in their very proximity, in the very intimacy of the relationship between (alien) slime and (human) skin. . . . Aliens allow the demarcation of spaces of belonging: by coming too close to home, they establish the very necessity of policing the borders of knowable and inhabitable terrains" (3). The sensorium demarcates belonging at the limits of the body and its Otherness, yet it is not a one-way process. People respond to the ways they are understood and interpellated.

Women themselves also respond to, act out, and resist these discourses and processes of racialization to make meaning out of state-produced categories of identification. Exploring the ways Pakistani women resist the category of South Asian makes clear the damage of multicultural practices aimed at the governmental category of immigrant integration. Governmental ideologies of citizenship hinder the inclusion of Pakistani women who feel the strain of limited categories of inclusion. That is not to say that some do not see the value in coalition building, or the need to strategically employ these categories when, for instance, applying for a job. However, many feel that community interests are lost and that concerns particular to Muslims are rendered invisible, citing it not as an inclusive category but rather as "a gloss for India."

I have been concerned with the cultural registers through which the unemployed and underemployed come to understand themselves as not simply "professional" and "foreign" but also Canadian and "ethnic." What does it mean to be gendered female, ethnicized Pakistani or "South Asian," and labeled foreign in a place one now calls home? Identity is not a stable category and is relational; thus the experiences of those in diaspora may bear little resemblance to one another as they struggle to belong and become legible in the context of new countries and national imaginaries. Beyond the contextual and material differences between the women I studied and those explored in other South Asian diasporic texts, women come to understand themselves through affective registers and through different identifiers (South Asian, Canadian, Muslim) endemic to global processes and multicultural politics, as they are subject to processes of racialization and de-skilling that turn them from highly mobile middle-class workers into seemingly desperate and poor immigrants. The multicultural state inflicts violence in the name of socializing Pakistani immigrant women for legibility, in the context of a nation-state with an international reputation for its excellent treatment of immigrants and refugees.

Also critical is the politics of representation for transnational Muslim cultures. It is important to expand conversations about Muslim women beyond questions of Islamic practice to examine issues of agency in other areas of their lives. Pakistani Muslim women as workers have largely failed to enter the public or scholarly imaginary. As such, gender has been a central analytic in my effort to problematize the category of the highly mobile high-tech worker in order to examine a particular type of mobile subject.[6] Focusing on the dilemma of professional women expands what we know about gender and labor in the global economy.[7] It shifts focus away from images of women laboring as domestic workers, nannies, and factory workers to examine a broader range of social experiences, particularly for "third-world" women.[8] The prism of the unemployment of immigrant women captures changes in governance, multicultural ideologies, transnationalism, subject formation, and political and economic struggles taking place in the contemporary world.

In that vein, it is also important to consider not only the kinds of ethnography produced about "third-world women" but also the kinds of questions being asked. For instance, Gayatri Spivak (1988) and Chandra Mohanty et al. (1991) inquire who constitutes the subject of anthropological research and the subject/object of the anthropological gaze. Who has the authority and who constitutes the category "third-world woman"? Who is entitled to have a voice? Attempts to give voice to a subaltern Other necessarily have two inherent problems: first, the assumption of cultural solidarity among a homogenous subaltern; second, a dependence on Western intellectuals to speak for subalterns. As Mohanty argues, "Scholars often locate 'third world women' in terms of the underdevelopment, oppressive traditions, high illiteracy, rural and urban poverty, religious fanaticism, and 'overpopulation' of particular Asian, African, Middle Eastern, and Latin American countries. Corresponding analyses of 'matriarchal' black women on welfare, 'illiterate' Chicana farmworkers, and 'docile' Asian domestic workers also abound in the context of the United States" (5–6). Yet, another kind of representation of third-world woman is possible, that of the professional worker. The experiences documented here demonstrate the power of representation, as the sensorial regimes to which women are subjected presume racialized and Orientalist conceptions of Otherness that have material consequences.

The sanitized sensorium is not limited in practice to Canada; it is a global phenomenon, as evidenced by the appearance of sensorial and affective requirements for workers in other cultural contexts, particularly in order to be legible on the global stage. For instance, research on call-center workers in India illustrates how they must present themselves in a way that is translatable to a larger American audience, while still being on the other end of the phone (e.g., Aneesh 2015; Mankekar 2015). Aneesh (2015) has examined the ways call-center work in India neutralizes racial and ethnic difference because workers must not betray their location. Also in the South

Asian context, culture has been mobilized in the production of migrant IT professionals who represent a "global Indianness" (e.g., Radhakrishnan 2011; Upadhya 2008). In the East Asian context, the erasure of bodily smell has been tied to globalization and modernity (Iwabuchi 2002). As these examples illustrate, in order to be legible as a global worker, one must be subject to the sanitized sensorium. Workers' names, accents, smells, and clothing are transformed in order to approximate a white Western subject, which is the global norm they are judged against. Possessing a neutral accent or a scentless body is the currency of global labor regimes. Processes of globalization produce everyday inequities, particularly when the economic needs of the state are balanced with cultural desires. That is, the state needs differentiated levels of labor but is unable to deal with difference. Women suffer downward mobility because of this tension.

Thinking through the question of gender and women's experiences can provide a more nuanced critique of global capitalism and an understanding of citizenship that moves beyond the realm of the legal to explore its intimate, affective, sensorial, and everyday dimensions. Examining these reveals the hidden aspects of global power and how women are gendered and racialized. When government think tanks and international development organizations contend with issues of immigrant labor, smelly bodies do not arise as the issue. Rather, the World Trade Organization, for instance, suggests that if we break down barriers, resources will go to where they are needed. There is a contradiction between the economic logic of capital, the flat world of Thomas Friedman (2005), and the realities that all capital is embedded in cultural networks, which means that histories of racism and imperialism become reinscribed in the new era. Because the Canadian state is formally multicultural, it does not have to have a reciprocal relationship to culture; thus it hides the Anglo-male Protestant dominance and reinscribes global social inequities. With an understanding of the function and practice of the sanitized sensorium, we can bring together the political economy of labor regimes with the realm of the intimate and affective to reveal how they have become mutually constitutive features of late capitalism.

Nadeem, whose story begins this conclusion, critically drew attention to the fact that seemingly endless resources are funneled into studying the foreign-trained-professionals problem, and yet little change actually occurs. Nadeem's frustration makes me return again to this question of racialization and value. If racialization (through multiculturalism) produces some bodies as valuable and some bodies as valueless, then these women's participation in settlement agencies will only confound their marginalization as they learn the terms of their conditional belonging. Nadeem felt exploited by global politics that would render her a victim of precarious employment. I wish I had a better answer for her, or that there were resources that would actually help change her life circumstances. The issue that undergirds social problems such as this is that there is a global racial hierarchy that presumes some bodies are worth more than others, and renders some bodies disposable on the global market.

This book is about what it means to live in a state of precarity and liminality, the affective dimensions of not knowing how to make ends meet or what is going to happen next. How does one quantify the experience of feeling hopeless or desperate? Examining anthropological theories of the state and governance, the anthropology of the senses, and the production of a global body allows us to think through some of these questions. People are not simply subject to global forces, however; in my work the women very much talked back. In response to these global forces that make them downwardly mobile, they sought to position themselves as deserving and morally right citizens. Articulating a discourse of a promising future became a way to understand their present circumstances; engaging with a kind of hope and optimism emerged as a way to maintain dignity when they are not able to live well or care for their families in the ways they wanted. In this context, hope and the promise of a better life become a way out of a catastrophic present. Living in a state of precarity and fear in this moment was rendered intelligible, as a promising future appeared phantom-like yet possible.

1. At present, there are two broad categories under which one may immigrate to Canada: as a worker or as a sponsored family member or refugee. In the first case, one may apply as a skilled worker, a Québec-selected skilled worker, a provincial nominee, for a start-up visa, as self-employed, or as a caregiver. There are three categories of "skilled workers": Federal Skilled Worker, Canadian Experience Class, and Federal Skilled Trades program. Of the 250,000 permanent residents arriving in Canada every year, approximately 60 percent enter in the "independent" economic class. Of that group, one-third (or 50,000) are the principal skilled immigrants the Canadian government strives to attract (Keung 2008).

2. Original data calculation by Dr. Murtaza Haider of Ryerson University using data from the 2006 census. Personal correspondence, May 20, 2012. According to Statistics Canada, the low income cut-off (LICO) is the income limit below which one uses more of their income on necessities such as food, shelter, and clothing.

3. The efficacy of the term "immigrant" has been debated in scholarly work on globalization and transnationalism, suggesting that it fails to accurately describe the mobile subject. While Roger Rouse (1995) suggests "im/migrant," scholars of South Asian communities abroad largely engage with discourses of diaspora in order to describe the mobility of subjects. I shift between these terms through this book in order to emphasize different aspects of migration and mobility.

4. This book is based on ethnographic fieldwork I have been doing in both Pakistan and Canada since 2002. Specifically, I conducted 125 interviews with government officials, nonprofit workers, mullahs, and Pakistani Muslim women ranging in age from their twenties to their sixties. All of the women identify with Pakistan in some way, and the vast majority identify as Muslim.

5. The government of Canada conducted a study of fifty thousand cab drivers in Canada and found that one in three taxi drivers is born in India or Pakistan. Among them they found doctors, engineers, and architects. "Who Drives a Taxi in Canada?," last modified on May 28, 2012, http://www.cic.gc.ca/english/resources/research/taxi /seco2.asp#s2-2. See also "Overqualified Immigrants Really Are Driving Taxis in

Canada," *Globe and Mail*, May 10, 2012, http://www.theglobeandmail.com/globe
-debate/editorials/overqualified-immigrants-really-are-driving-taxis-in-canada
/article4106352/.

6. Toronto, as a global city, is a compelling site to explore transnational processes that have more often been studied in other urban centers such as New York, London, and Tokyo. See Brah 1996; Leonard 1992; Ong 2003; Prasad 2000; Raj 2003; Sassen 1991; Shukla 2003; Van Der Veer 1995.

7. In Pakistan, teachers are not considered professional in the same way as doctors, engineers, or lawyers; however, in the context of Toronto, teaching is also a regulated profession that requires a license to work.

8. A March 18, 2016 article in the *New York Times* titled, "As Women Take Over a Male-Dominated Field, the Pay Drops," by Claire Cain Miller, argues that work that is done by women is not valued as highly as work done by men.

9. In contrast to Pakistani women, Indian women in Toronto have higher labor-force participation rates at 70 percent, and lower unemployment rates at 10 percent (Ornstein 2006). These statistics are from a report by Canadian sociologist Michael Ornstein and were the most current statistics at the time of my research. In 2011, the Canadian government conducted the voluntary National Household Survey instead of conducting the mandatory census. The sampling frame, questionnaire, and non-response rates differ significantly and make any comparison with the previous census years impossible. "European" is a census category used by the Institute for Social Research in its analysis of the racialization of poverty in Toronto (Ornstein 2006).

10. "Annual Report to Parliament on Immigration, 2011," last modified on October 27, 2011, http://www.cic.gc.ca/english/resources/publications/annual-report-2011 /section2.asp. Almost half of Toronto's population (49.97 percent) is foreign born, compared to 36 percent in New York and 39.7 percent in Los Angeles (U.S. Census Bureau, "Statistical Abstract of the United States: 2012," accessed November 15, 2013, http://www.census.gov/compendia/statab/2012/tables/12s0038.pdf).

11. "Immigration and Ethnocultural Diversity in Canada," *Statistics Canada*, Analytical products 2011, http://www12.statcan.gc.ca/nhs-enm/2011/as-sa/99-010-x/99 -010-x2011001-eng.cfm.

12. Original data calculation by Dr. Murtaza Haider of Ryerson University using data from the 2006 census. Personal correspondence, May 20, 2012.

13. See Reitz 2001. In 2006, immigrants' salaries in Canada were 21 percent below average; for recent immigrants, salaries were 56 percent below average. Further, the earnings gap between male immigrants and those born in Canada was $15,000 or 26 percent in Toronto. "Immigrants Get Fewer Jobs, Earn Less," *CBC News*, December 19, 2011, http://www.cbc.ca/news/business/immigrants-get-fewer-jobs-earn-less-1 .1092938.

14. While 66 percent of immigrants with a university degree find some type of work within six months, very few find work in their professional fields within five years.

15. Frances Woolley, "'Visible Minority': A Misleading Concept That Ought to Be Retired," *Globe and Mail*, June 10, 2013, http://www.theglobeandmail.com

/globe-debate/visible-minority-a-misleading-concept-that-ought-to-be-retired
/article12445364/.

16. Omi and Winant (2014) have described racialization as a historically specific and ideological process whereby racial meanings are ascribed to a previously "racially unclassified relationship, social practice, or group" (13). David Theo Goldberg (1993) has discussed the import of racial categories that serve to determine inclusion and exclusion.

17. Toronto Community Housing, "About Us," accessed November 27, 2013, http://www.torontohousing.ca/about.

18. Elaine Carey, "High-Rise Ghettos: In Toronto, Visible Minorities Are Pushed into 'Pockets of Poverty,'" *Toronto Star*, February 3, 2001, M1–M2.

19. Carey, "High-Rise Ghettos."

20. The non-European population in Canada increased from 5 percent in 1971 to 40 percent in 2001 (Ornstein 2006: iii).

21. "York University study reveals the true face of poverty," *yFile, York University's Daily News*, October 3, 2006, http://www.yorku.ca/yfile/archive/index.asp?Article=6102.

22. "The persistance of racial inequality in Canada," *Toronto Star*, March 20, 2012, http://www.thestar.com/opinion/editorialopinion/2012/03/20/the_persistence_of_racial_inequality_in_canada.html.

23. This book builds on critical studies of multiculturalism in both Canadian (e.g., Abu-Laban 2002; Amit-Talai 1996; Kymlicka 1995; Taylor 1994) and other multicultural contexts (Ahmed 2004; Asad 1993; Maira 2009; Moallem and Boal 1999; S. Shankar 2008; Zizek 1997).

24. "Sarkozy Speaks Out against Burka," *BBC News*, June 22, 2009, http://news.bbc.co.uk/2/hi/8112821.stm.

25. "Merkel Says German Multicultural Society Has Failed," *BBC News*, October 17, 2010, http://www.bbc.com/news/world-europe-11559451.

26. "State Multiculturalism Has Failed, Says David Cameron," *BBC News*, February 5, 2011, http://www.bbc.com/news/uk-politics-12371994.

27. Government of Canada, "Canadian Multiculturalism Act," accessed November 17, 2013, http://laws-lois.justice.gc.ca/eng/acts/C-18.7/page-1.html.

28. Moallem and Boal (1999) write, "multicultural nationalism operates on the fault line between a universalism based on the notion of an abstract citizenship that at the same time systematically produces sexualized, gendered and racialized bodies, and particularistic claims for recognition and justice by minoritized groups" (245). These multicultural politics are informed by immigration policies targeted toward producing a certain kind of population.

29. In 1961 visible minorities composed 3 percent of the population of Toronto (Siemiatycki and Isin 1997: 78). Before 1961, 90 percent of Canadian immigrants were from Europe (Abu-Laban 1998: 80). However, as Western Europe recovered from World War II in the late 1950s and 1960s, emigration from those regions effectively stopped, thus creating a need to re-envision Canada's model of immigration (Troper 2003).

30. Toronto provides an interesting case study for immigration because of the speed at which it became so dramatically racially and ethnically diverse. From the founding of the city in the late eighteenth century, Toronto was dominated by a British, Protestant population. Jewish populations, being the largest ethnic group, experienced massive discrimination in the early part of the twentieth century (Lemon 1985; Siemiatycki and Isin 1997). International migration transformed the constitution of the city's population in an incredibly short period of time. The first significant influx of immigrants following colonization arrived between 1846 and 1849 as a result of the Irish potato famine, and by 1851 the Irish constituted Toronto's largest ethnic population. In 1931, 81 percent of the population of Toronto self-identified as of British origin (Siemiatycki et al. 2003: 373).

31. "Gatineau's Values Guide for Immigrants Stirs Controversy," Ingrid Peritz, *Globe and Mail*, December 4, 2011, http://www.theglobeandmail.com/news/politics/gatineaus-values-guide-for-immigrants-stirs-controversy/article2259694/.

32. Peritz, "Gatineau's Values Guide."

33. In the context of South Asian American studies, there is a rich collection of ethnographic texts that deals with South Asian American experiences involving the politics of citizenship and belonging (Afzal 2014; Maira 2002: 2009; Rana 2011; Rudruppa 2004; Shankar 2008; Shukla 2003).

34. This section title is a reference to Behar, *The Vulnerable Observer*.

1. Bodies and Bureaucracies

1. These transformations in Canadian immigration policies are also intertwined with U.S. immigration histories. For instance, as Nayan Shah (2011) has demonstrated, American and Canadian immigration policies at the turn of the twentieth century "experimented with developing a 'white' political democracy and forging racial apartheid by subordinating, segregating, and exploiting nonwhite 'races'" (3). Post 1965, U.S. immigration law promoted family reunification over granting immigration to skilled workers. For instance, in 1987, 75 percent of those entering as legal immigrants to the United States migrated under family reunification, in contrast to 4 percent as skilled workers. George J. Borjas, "The U.S. Takes the Wrong Immigrants," *Wall Street Journal*, April 5, 1990, A18, http://www.hks.harvard.edu/fs/gborjas/publications/popular/WSJ040590.htm.

2. Nine factors were established for independent applicants, totaling a possible one hundred points; each applicant was required to achieve fifty. Three classes of immigrants were established: family, independent, and refugee. Five criteria qualified as "long term": education, occupational demand, skills, age, and personal qualities (up to seventy points). Four criteria were considered "short term": arranged employment, knowledge of English or French, a family member living in Canada, and the general atmosphere of employment opportunities in Canada (up to thirty points).

3. The investor stream of immigrants is for those with a net worth of at least $500,000 who are willing to commit to investing their money in Canada for a period of time.

4. The period between the 1950s and the early 1980s was defined by the rise of the welfare state in Canada and the implementation of Canadian multicultural policy, which initiated a different framework for integrating new immigrants in Toronto (Siemiatycki et al. 2003: 413). Trends in social policy until the mid-1970s moved toward expanding most forms of state social support to reduce economic risks to Canadians (Struthers and Montigny 1999). Federal funding was slowly withdrawn from social programs; the common state discourse was that reduced social spending was good for Canadians, even those living below the poverty line for whom dependency on social assistance over individual autonomy has supposedly resulted in the decline in "traditional family values." The reduction of social assistance was part of a "wider campaign to 'remoralize' the family and to rehabilitate a work ethic perceived to be under siege through the enticements of an overly generous welfare state" (Struthers and Montigny 1999). Immigrants have paid the price of this economic restructuring and moralizing process.

5. Distinct from assimilation and segregation, integration is imagined to be, according to Citizenship and Immigration Canada, "a process of mutual adjustment by both newcomers and society. This approach sets us apart from many other countries. Newcomers are expected to understand and respect basic Canadian values, but society is also expected to understand and respect the cultural differences newcomers bring to Canada. Rather than expecting newcomers to abandon their own cultural heritage the emphasis is on finding ways to integrate differences within a pluralistic society" (as cited in Abu-Laban 2004: 136).

6. The immigration system in Canada has also been criticized for its inflexibility compared to the pre-screening processes of Australia, New Zealand, and the United Kingdom, designed to meet short-term labor needs (Harding 2003).

7. "Planning to Work in Canada? An Essential Workbook for Newcomers," Section C, Finding a Job in Canada, accessed October 23, 2015, http://www.cic.gc.ca/english /pdf/pub/workbook-national.pdf.

8. While teachers are not considered professional in Pakistan in the same way that medical professionals are, in Canada teaching is a regulated profession and prospective teachers must go through regulatory boards in order to work.

9. "Building a New Life in Ontario: A Guide for Newcomers," accessed November 15, 2013, http://www.ontarioimmigration.ca/prodconsum/groups/csc/@oipp /documents/document/oi_professions_english.pdf.

10. Katherine Harding, "A Leap of Faith," *Globe and Mail*, January 8, 2003, A7.

11. In 2003, the PEO began offering provisional licenses that are valid for one year; however, engineers need four years of experience working as an engineer anywhere in the world in order to obtain a provisional license. Further, earnings are shaped by one's country of origin and the origin of their credentials, rather than their ability to perform particular tasks (Boyd and Thomas 2001).

12. In order to be licensed, applicants must (a) be Canadian citizens or permanent residents; (b) have a bachelor's degree in engineering from a Canadian university program, or, if they were trained outside of Canada, their credentials must be assessed by

the PEO through examinations and interviews; (c) have four years of work experience, with at least twelve months in Canada under the direction of a licensed professional engineer; (d) pass the Professional Practice Exam; (e) be proficient in English; and finally, (f) be "of good character and reputation" as determined by the PEO (Girard and Bauder 2007: 41–42).

13. All amounts refer to Canadian dollars unless specifically noted.

14. In 2006, the Government of Ontario premier, Dalton McGuinty, established Global Experience Ontario or GEO, which functions essentially as a referral service. The GEO is "a hub of resources and support for newcomers to navigate through the complex system of licensure and registration in Ontario" (Ministry of Citizenship and Immigration 2006: para. 1). Ontario Citizenship and Immigration Minister Mike Colle was quoted as saying, "We've listened to newcomers who have said that one of the major barriers they face is getting accurate and accessible information about registration practices in regulated professions" (Ministry of Citizenship and Immigration 2006: para. 1). The GEO is simply another referral tool that provides little practical assistance.

15. In 2001, the Chretien government began a "Strengthening Settlement Capacity Project" and committed $95 million to the Voluntary Sector initiative (Abu-Laban 2004: 137). The result is "an integration system in which the provincial governments will perform the key planning and administrative roles and the federal government will be limited to setting and enforcing principles and standards, and providing funding for settlement and integration programs" (Garcea, cited in Abu-Laban 2004: 138). Through this process, the settlement-services sector entered the domain of governance through collaboration with voluntary, private, and public actors in the "design and achievement of government objectives in a matter that shares policy formation, risk and operational planning, and that may replace program delivery by state employees with those of third parties" (Phillips, cited in Abu-Laban 2004: 137).

16. Intrinsic to this directive to be flexible was a range of affects including positivity and independence. Positivity in this context seemingly suggests there will be events that may cause one to react negatively, such as mistreatment in the workplace or workplace discrimination. In the face of systemic barriers, or cultural practices such as racial discrimination, the solution proposed in the workshop is to be positive. This question of affect is taken up in the next chapter on nursing.

17. The next chapter, on nursing, explores an exception to this model.

2. Pedagogies of Affect

1. While teaching is also a "feminized field," the images of Asian women (e.g., docile, deferent) do not line up the same way in terms of expectations for nurses.

2. Legislation governing nursing in Ontario is set out in the Nursing Act of 1991 and the Regulated Health Professions Act of 1991. The Nursing Act established seven requirements for registration as an RN or RPN in Ontario, http://www.cno.org/Global /docs/prac/41064_fsNursingact.pdf. Lawyers similarly must have their credentials recognized by the National Committee on Accreditation (NCA) before they can enter

the licensing process. They must take tests, and often courses. The NCA may also refuse qualification altogether. The appeals process costs $280.

3. Sanitizing Citizenship

1. Neil MacDonald, "The Barbaric Cultural Practice of Election Pronouncements," *CBC News*, October 6, 2015, http://www.cbc.ca/news/politics/canada-election-2015 -neil-macdonald-muslims-1.3257892.

2. Sean Kilpatrick, "'Old Stock Canadians' Comment Gives Chills to Professor," *Toronto Star*, September 18, 2015, http://www.thestar.com/news/canada/2015/09/18 /old-stock-canadians-phrase-chills-prof-ignites-twitter.html.

3. It is important to note that in this analysis I am primarily focusing on the federal policy of multiculturalism.

4. "Part 6 Editorial: Strike Multiculturalism from the National Vocabulary," *Globe and Mail*, October 8, 2010, http://www.theglobeandmail.com/news/national/time -to-lead/multiculturalism/part-6-editorial-strike-multiculturalism-from-the-national -vocabulary/article1748958/.

5. The Canadian nation-state is conceived as a "settler nation" in which the English and French are discursively constructed as the center in legislation, erasing the presence of Indigenous populations. All other racial and ethnic groups are peripheral in relation to English and French Canadians. However, French Canadians—not only in Québec but throughout Canada—have felt increasingly marginalized and have disputed their seeming equation with other "ethnic" groups. In 1995, a referendum among the Québec population decided in a vote of 51 to 49 percent against the separation of Québec from the rest of Canada—a decision that Québec premier Lucien Bouchard "blamed" on the "ethnic vote." "Québec Rejects Separation," *Migration News* 2 (12) (December 1995), http://migration.ucdavis.edu/mn/more.php ?id=814_0_2_0.

6. See, for example, Abu-Laban 2002; Amit-Talai 1996; Berlant and Warner 1994; Breton 1986; Kymlicka 1995; Razack 1998; Taylor 1994; Walcott 2003.

7. "The Persistence of Racial Inequality in Canada," *Toronto Star*, March 20, 2012, http://www.thestar.com/opinion/editorialopinion/2012/03/20/the_persistence_of _racial_inequality_in_canada.html.

8. It is important not to equate the social position of Indigenous populations with those of racial and ethnic minority groups. This comparison between the Indigenous population in Canada and the Black population in the United States is meant only to highlight how those in power in these two national contexts treat those deemed Other.

9. "Canada's Race Problem? It's Even Worse than America's. For a Country So Self-Satisfied with Its Image of Progressive Tolerance, How Is This Not a National Crisis?" *Maclean's*, January 22, 2015. On November 24, 2014, a grand jury in Ferguson, Missouri, decided not to indict police officer Darren Wilson, who fatally shot Michael Brown, an eighteen-year-old black man, on August 9, 2014. Protests and unrest erupted in response to the shooting and intensified after the grand jury's decision.

10. Amsin McMahon, "Why Fixing First Nations Education Remains So Far Out of Reach: Aboriginal Youth Face a Fate That Should Horrify Canadians and There's No Obvious Fix," *Maclean's*, August 22, 2014, http://www.macleans.ca/news/canada/why-fixing-first-nations-education-remains-so-far-out-of-reach/.

11. "Kenney Says Homegrown Terrorism a 'Reality' in Canada," Mark Kennedy, *Ottawa Citizen*, March 8, 2015. In March 2015, Jason Kenney said, "Today, homegrown terrorism is not a remote concept, but sadly a Canadian reality," arguing that in the past Canadians have been able to avoid such threats because of "our geographic remoteness, our prosperity and our peaceful pluralism, and the generous dispensation of the American security umbrella."

12. The "Toronto 18" consisted of a group of immigrant and Canadian-born self-described Muslims who were planning a series of bombings in southern Ontario.

13. In February 2015, three teenage British Muslim girls (Khadiza Sultana, Amira Abase, and Shamina Begum) left London to join ISIS, an act that drew international attention to the increasing number of single young women in their teens and early twenties joining ISIS. "Jihad and Girl Power: How ISIS Lured 3 London Girls," *New York Times*, Katrin Bennhold, August 17, 2005, http://www.nytimes.com/2015/08/18/world/europe/jihad-and-girl-power-how-isis-lured-3-london-teenagers.html.

14. This area is still dominated by the canonical (and deeply problematic) work of political scientist Susan Okin, whose "Is Multiculturalism Bad for Women?" (1997) insists that in modern liberal states, minority rights trump the rights of women—to the latter's detriment. Okin thus reinscribes colonial notions about the savagery of "Other" men and evokes the colonial imperative that Gayatri Spivak (1988) articulates concisely as that of white men saving brown women from brown men.

15. I term the smells discussed here "South Asian" to highlight the ways that popular Canadian understandings of cultural difference, in this case, homogenize people from the subcontinent.

16. In 2002, the Canadian government named May Asian Heritage Month in Canada, but in Ontario it is South Asian Heritage Month.

17. On July 15, 2013, Kenney became minister of Employment and Social Development and minister for Multiculturalism. On February 9, 2015, he was named minister of National Defence.

18. It is important to note that Jason Kenney has only targeted particular South Asian communities, harnessing the deep Islamophobia in diasporic Hindu and Sikh communities to forge strategic political alliances and support. However, his comments are crucial in understanding the government's construction of the South Asian diaspora and who counts as its members.

19. *Masti* is also a term used in India by men who have sex with men to refer to casual sexual encounters, although this definition never arose in my ethnographic fieldwork.

20. In 2012, the festival was taken on the road and hosted an event in Dubai, after years of being courted by countries such as Singapore, Britain, and the United Arab Emirates, all of which have fraught relationships with their Indian and Pakistani minority communities.

21. "Canada Celebrates Its Multiculturalism and Diversity," *Integration, Building Inclusive Societies*, United Nations Alliance of Civilizations, July 23, 2010, http://www.unaoc.org/ibis/2010/07/23/canada-celebrates-its-multiculturalism-and-diversity/.

22. Eid Festival website, Muslim Association of Canada, accessed November 25, 2013, http://www.gtaeid.com/.

4. Racializing South Asia

1. For example, José Muñoz (1999) has theorized disidentification, in which people might strategically use a proscribed subject position, sometimes rejecting it outright, sometimes identifying with parts of the category, and sometimes using it to subvert that subject position, thus "disidentifying" with the category in response to the way it identifies them.

2. Coll (2013) writes, "Cultural citizenship as an analytic frame offers an important position from which to highlight the situation of certain groups of citizens who, though formally entitled to full legal political rights, are socially recognized neither as first-class citizens nor as contributors to the vernacular meanings of citizenship as it plays a role in day-to-day life in the United States" (5). See also Maira 2009; Shankar 2008; Siu 2005.

3. This research also builds on important anthropological analyses of diaspora that have grappled with understanding identity in an era of increased global migration (e.g., Axel 2001; Ewing 2008; Khan 2004; Maira 2002; Ong 1999; Siu 2005), as well as studies of the South Asian diaspora (e.g., Bhachu 1995; Brah 1996; Gopinath 2005; Khan 2004; Leonard 2007; Shukla 2003; Van Der Veer 1995; Vertovec 2000; Werbner 1999), and the relationship between area studies and diaspora studies. Dipesh Chakrabarty (1998) published a seminal work in this conversation on the benefits of bringing together area studies and work on the South Asian diaspora. To his analysis I suggest another benefit to bringing these areas together. Studying "South Asians" in a new geopolitical territory allows for the examination of communalism outside of South Asia and questions of Partition and violence. Instead, in the context of the liberal settler multicultural state, an examination of communal tension reveals the role of the colonial state in not only perpetuating but also sustaining divisions within communities.

4. Bowen 2007; Fernando 2010; Grewal 2013; Werbner 2002.

5. Haroon Siddiqui, "Children of the Raj," *Toronto Star*, October 15, 1992, E8.

6. Siddiqui, "Children of the Raj."

7. Barbara Keddy, "Terror in an OHC lobby: Pakistani family attacked by youths," *Globe and Mail*, May 14, 1980.

8. Marina Jiménez, "Do Ethnic Enclaves Impede Integration?" *Globe and Mail*, February 8, 2007, A8.

9. In August 1947, India gained independence from Britain and became two sovereign nation-states: India and Pakistan. Partition was a bloody event; approximately one million people died in riots all over northern India, and approximately ten to

twelve million people lost their homes. It was followed by the overwhelming silence of citizens not wanting to acknowledge the violence at the heart of the nation.

10. The Canadian government in 2008 announced $30 million in new funding per year to support local arts, heritage festivals, and events "to engage Canadians in their communities through the expression, celebration and preservation of local culture," accessed November 15, 2013, http://www.pch.gc.ca/pgm/dcap-bcah/fest-eng.cfm.

5. The Catastrophic Present

1. See Boris and Parreñas 2010; Choy 2003; Ehrenreich and Hochschild 2002; Kang 2010; Parreñas 2001.

2. Status of Women Canada, Government of Canada, "Fact Sheet: Economic Security," "Women's Representation and Participation in the Labour Force," last modified February 25, 2015, http://www.swc-cfc.gc.ca/initiatives/wesp-sepf/fs-fi/es-se-eng.html.

3. Catherine Rampell, "Women's Unemployment Surpasses Men's," *New York Times*, January 4, 2013, http://economix.blogs.nytimes.com/2013/01/04/womens-unemploy ment-surpasses-mens/?_r=0.

4. Mike Adler, "Muslim Seniors in Scarborough Feeling Neglected, Angry and Abused: Survey," *Scarborough Mirror*, February 10, 2012, http://www.insidetoronto .com/news-story/74616-muslim-seniors-in-scarborough-feeling-neglected-angry-and -abused-sur/.

Conclusion

1. Richard J. Brennan, "Canada woos Irish Immigrants in Search of Jobs," *Toronto Star*, October 7, 2012, http://www.thestar.com/news/canada/2012/10/07/canada _woos_irish_immigrants_in_search_of_jobs.html.

2. "Editorial: Strike multiculturalism from the national vocabulary," *Globe and Mail*, October 8, 2010, last updated August 23, 2010, http://www.theglobeandmail .com/news/national/time-to-lead/multiculturalism/part-6-editorial-strike -multiculturalism-from-the-national-vocabulary/article1748958/.

3. Martin Patriquin and Charlie Gillis, "About Face: A Bill Banning the Niqab— Supported by a Majority of Canadians: How Did Our Multicultural, Tolerant Nation Get Here?" *Maclean's*, April 7, 2010, http://www.macleans.ca/news/canada/about -face/.

4. Patriquin and Gillis, "About Face."

5. This has been explored by several theorists including Puar 2007; Rana 2011; Razack 2002. I have also explored post-9/11 discrimination elsewhere; see Ameeriar 2012.

6. Here I seek to build on materialist studies of women migrating for labor that have focused on sex work, factory work, or domestic labor from the Philippines or the Caribbean (Bakan and Stasiulis 1997; Ehrenreich and Hochschild 2002; Fernandez-Kelly 1983; Lamphere et al. 1993; Parreñas 2001), to examine the experiences of professional working women in masculinist grand narratives of globalization (Freeman 2001).

7. For studies of gender and work, see Boris and Parreñas 2010; Ducey 2010; Hochschild 1983; McElhinny 2007. Many authors have also explored the relationship between
gender and transnationalism (e.g., Anzaldúa 1999; Glick-Schiller et al. 1995; Gopinath
2005; Grewal 2005; Grewal and Kaplan 1997). Because of the ways the global assembly
line operates, theories of gendered transnational labor migrations have tended to focus
on a particular set of mobile subjects (e.g., working-class women laboring in factories
or providing care in homes). These works also tend to focus on the United States and
Europe, while few explore the politics of Canada and the global city of Toronto.

8. Immigrant women as professionals have been underrepresented in academic discourse and understandings of working women in global markets, and descriptions of
high-tech workers have generally focused on the experience of men. Catherine Choy's
(2003) text on Filipino nurses in the United States is a notable exception, as is Carla
Freeman's (2000) ethnography of high-tech workers in Barbados.

Abu-Laban, Yasmeen. 1998. "Keeping 'Em Out: Gender, Race, and Class Biases in Canadian Immigration Policy." In *Painting the Maple: Essays on Race, Gender, and the Construction of Canada*, edited by Veronica Strong-Boag, Sherrill Grace, Avigail Eisenberg, and Joan Anderson. Vancouver: University of British Columbia Press.

Abu-Laban, Yasmeen. 2002. "Liberalism, Multiculturalism and the Problem of Essentialism." *Citizenship Studies* 6 (4): 459–82.

Abu-Laban, Yasmeen. 2004. "Jean Chretien's Immigration Legacy." *Review of Constitutional Studies* 9: 133–50.

Abu-Laban, Yasmeen, and Christina Gabriel. 2002. *Selling Diversity: Immigration, Multiculturalism, Employment Equity, and Globalization*. Toronto: University of Toronto Press.

Abu-Laban, Yasmeen, and Daiva Stasiulis. 1992. "Ethnic Pluralism under Siege: Popular and Partisan Opposition to Multiculturalism." *Canadian Public Policy* 18 (4): 365–86.

Abu-Lughod, L. 1990. "The Romance of Resistance: Tracing Transformations of Power through Bedouin Women." *American Ethnologist* 17 (1): 41–55.

Afzal, Ahmed. 2014. *Lone Star Muslims: Transnational Lives and the South Asian Experience in Texas*. New York: NYU Press.

Ahmad, Farah, Angela Shik, Reena Vanza, Angela Cheung, Usha George, and Donna Stewart. 2004. "Voices of South Asian Women: Immigration and Mental Health." *Women and Health* 40 (4): 113–30.

Ahmed, Sara. 2000. *Strange Encounters: Embodied Others in Postcoloniality*. New York: Routledge.

Ahmed, Sara. 2004. *The Cultural Politics of Emotion*. New York: Routledge.

Akbari, Ather. 1999. "Immigrant 'Quality' in Canada: More Direct Evidence of Human Capital Content, 1956–1994." *International Migration Review* 33 (1): 156–75.

Alboim, Naomi, and Elizabeth McIsaac. 2007. "Making the Connections: Ottawa's Role in Immigrant Employment." *Immigration and Refugee Policy* 13 (2). http://irpp .org/wp-content/uploads/assets/research/diversity-immigration-and-integration /making-the-connections/vol13no3.pdf.

Alexander, Jacqui and Chandra Mohanty. 1997. *Feminist Genealogies, Colonial Legacies, Democratic Futures*. New York and London: Routledge.

Allison, Anne. 2013. *Precarious Japan*. Durham, NC: Duke University Press.

Althusser, Louis. 1971. *Lenin and Philosophy and Other Essays*. New York: Monthly Review Press.

Ameeriar, Lalaie. 2012. "The Gendered Suspect: Women at the Canada-U.S. Border after September 11." *Journal of Asian American Studies* 15(2).

Amit-Talai, Vered. 1996. "The Minority Circuit: Identity Politics and the Professionalization of Ethnic Activism." In *Resituating Identities: The Politics of Race, Ethnicity, and Culture*, edited by Vered Amit-Talai and Caroline Knowles, 89–114. Toronto: University of Toronto Press.

Anderson, Benedict. 1991. *Imagined Communities: Reflections on the Origin and Spread of Nationalism*. Reprint ed. London: Verso. Orig. pub. 1983.

Aneesh. A. 2015. *Neutral Accent: How Language, Labor, and Life Become Global*. Durham, NC: Duke University Press.

Anisef, P., and M. Lanphier. 2003. *The World in a City*. Toronto: University of Toronto Press.

Anzaldúa, Gloria. 1999. *Borderlands/La Frontera: The New Mestiza*. San Francisco: Aunt Lute Books.

Appadurai, Arjun. 1996. *Modernity at Large: Cultural Dimensions of Globalization*. Minneapolis: University of Minnesota Press.

Arat-Koc, Sedef. 1999. "Neo-liberalism, State Restructuring and Immigration: Changes in Canadian Politics in the 1990s." *Journal of Canadian Studies* 34 (2): 31–56.

Aretxaga, Begona. 2003. "Maddening States." *Annual Review of Anthropology* 32: 393–410.

Asad, Talal. 1993. *Genealogies of Religion: Discipline and Reasons of Power in Christianity and Islam*. Baltimore: Johns Hopkins University Press.

Asad, Talal. 2003. *Formations of the Secular: Christianity, Islam, Modernity*. Stanford, CA: Stanford University Press.

Authier, Amber. 2002. "Cultures Blend at Harbourfront Centre." http://www.harbourfrontcentre.com/press/rhythms2002_masala.htm.

Axel, Brian Keith. 2001. *The Nation's Tortured Body: Violence, Representation, and the Formation of a Sikh "Diaspora."* Durham, NC: Duke University Press.

Axel, Brian Keith. 2002. "National Interruption: Diaspora Theory and Multiculturalism in the UK." *Cultural Dynamics* 14 (3): 235–56.

Axel, Brian Keith. 2004. "The Context of Diaspora." *Cultural Anthropology* 19 (1): 26–60.

Bahri, Deepika, and Mary Vasudeva. 1996. *Between the Lines: South Asians and Postcoloniality*. Philadelphia: Temple University Press.

Bakan, Abigail, and Davia Stasiulis, eds. 1997. *Not One of the Family: Foreign Domestic Workers in Canada*. Toronto: University of Toronto Press.

Balibar, Étienne, and Immanuel Wallerstein. 1991. *Race, Nation, Class: Ambiguous Identities*. London: Verso.

Bannerji, Himani. 1993. *Returning the Gaze: Essays on Racism, Feminism and Politics*. Toronto: Sister Vision Press.

Bannerji, Himani. 2000. "The Paradox of Diversity: The Construction of a Multicultural Canada and 'Women of Color.'" *Women's Studies International Forum* 23 (5): 537–60.

Barry, Andrew, Thomas Osborne, and Nikolas Rose. 1996. *Foucault and Political Reason: Liberalism, Neo-liberalism, and Rationalities of Government*. Chicago: University of Chicago Press.

Basch, Linda, Nina Glick Schiller, and Cristina Szanton-Blanc. 1994. *Nations Unbound: Transnational Projects, Postcolonial Predicaments, and Deterritorialized Nation-States*. Langhorne, PA: Gordon and Breach.

Basran, G. S., and Z. Li. 1998. "Devaluation of Foreign Credentials as Perceived by Visible Minority Professional Immigrants." *Canadian Ethnic Studies* 30 (3): 6–23.

Bauder, Harald. 2003. "'Brain Abuse,' or the Devaluation on Immigrant Labour in Canada." *Antipode* 35 (4): 699–717.

Baumann, Gerd. 1996. *Contesting Culture: Discourses of Identity in Multiethnic London*. Cambridge, UK: Cambridge University Press.

Behar, Ruth. 1997. *The Vulnerable Observer: Anthropology that Breaks Your Heart*. New York: Beacon Press.

Berlant, Lauren. 2007. "Nearly Utopian, Nearly Normal: Post-Fordist Affect in *La Promesse and Rosetta*." *Public Culture* 19 (2): 273–301.

Berlant, Lauren. 2011. *Cruel Optimism*. Durham, NC: Duke University Press.

Berlant, Lauren, and Michael Warner. 1994. "Introduction to 'Critical Multiculturalism.'" In *Multiculturalism: A Critical Reader*, edited by David T. Goldberg, 107–13. Oxford, UK: Blackwell.

Bernal, Victoria. 1994. "Gender, Culture, and Capitalism: Women and the Remaking of Islamic 'Tradition' in a Sudanese Village." *Comparative Studies in Society and History* 36 (1): 36–67.

Bernal, Victoria. 2004. "Eritrea Goes Global: Reflections in Nationalism in a Transnational Era." *Cultural Anthropology* 19 (1): 3–25.

Bhachu, Parminder. 1995. "New Cultural Forms and Transnational South Asian Women: Culture, Class, and Consumption among British Asian Women in the Diaspora." In *Nation and Migration: The Politics of Space in the South Asian Diaspora*, edited by Peter Van Der Veer, 222–44. Philadelphia: University of Pennsylvania Press.

Bhattacharjee, Ananya. 1992. "The Habit of Ex-Nomination: Nation, Woman, and the Indian Immigrant Bourgeoisie." *Public Culture* 5 (1): 19–44.

Binder, Leonard. 1986. "Islam, Ethnicity and the State in Pakistan." In *The State, Religion and Ethnic Politics: Afghanistan, Iran and Pakistan*, edited by Ali Banuazizi and Myron Weiner. Syracuse, NY: Syracuse University Press.

Bissoondath, Neil. 1994. *Selling Illusions: The Cult of Multiculturalism in Canada*. Toronto: Penguin.

Blackburn, Carole. 2009. "Differentiating Indigenous Citizenship: Seeking Multiplicity in Rights, Identity, and Sovereignty in Canada." *American Ethnologist* 36 (1): 66–78.

Block, Sheila, and Grace-Edward Galabuzi. 2011. "Canada's Colour Coded Labour Market: The Gap for Racialized Workers." Ottawa, ON: Canadian Centre for Policy Alternatives and Wellesley Institute.

Boris, Eileen, and Rhacel Parreñas. 2010. *Intimate Labors: Cultures, Technologies, and the Politics of Care*. Stanford, CA: Stanford University Press.

Bourdieu, Pierre. 1977. *Outline of a Theory of Practice*. Cambridge, UK: Cambridge University Press.

Bourdieu, Pierre. 1984. *Distinction: A Social Critique of the Judgment of Taste*. Cambridge, MA: Harvard University Press.

Bowen, John. 2007. *Why the French Don't Like Headscarves: Islam, the State, and Public Space*. Princeton: Princeton University Press.

Boyd, Monica, and Grant Schellenberg. 2008. "Re-accreditation and the Occupations of Immigrant Doctors and Engineers." Statistics Canada. Last modified November 21. http://www.statcan.gc.ca/pub/11-008-x/2007004/10312-eng.htm.

Boyd, Monica, and Derrick Thomas. 2001. "Match or Mismatch? The Employment of Immigrant Engineers in Canada's Labor Force." *Population Research and Policy Review* 20 (1–2): 107–33.

Brah, Avtar. 1996. *Cartographies of Diaspora: Contesting Identities*. London: Routledge.

Breton, Raymond. 1986. "Multiculturalism and Canadian Nation-Building." In *The Politics of Gender, Ethnicity, and Language in Canada*, edited by Alan Cairns and Cynthia Williams, 27–66. Toronto: University of Toronto Press.

Brown, Jacqueline Nassy. 1999. "Black Liverpool, Black America, and the Gendering of Diasporic Space." *Cultural Anthropology* 13 (3): 291–325.

Brown, Judith. 2006. *Global South Asians: Introducing the Modern Diaspora*. Cambridge, UK: Cambridge University Press.

Bryce-Laporte, R. 1981. "The New Immigration: The Female Majority." In *Female Immigrants to the United States: Caribbean, Latin American, and African Experiences*, edited by Delores Mortimer and Roy S. Bryce-LaPorte. Washington: Smithsonian Institution Press.

Burke, Timothy. 1996. *Lifebuoy Men, Lux Women: Commodification, Consumption, and Cleanliness in Modern Zimbabwe*. Durham, NC: Duke University Press.

Butler, Judith. 2009. *Frames of War: When is Life Grievable?* London and New York: Verso.

Calliste, Agnes. 1993. "Women of 'Exceptional Merit': Immigration of Caribbean Nurses to Canada." *Canadian Journal of Women and Law* 6 (1): 85–103.

Canadian Heritage, Government of Canada. 2008. "Funding for Festivals to Support Arts and Heritage, Build Stronger Communities." Last modified April 8, 2011. http://www.pch.gc.ca/pgm/dcap-bcah/fest-eng.cfm.

Castells, Manuel. 1996. *The Rise of the Network Society*. London: Blackwell.

Chakkalalkal, A., and J. Harvey. 2001. "Access for Foreign-Trained IT Professionals: An Exploration of Systemic Barriers to Employment." Toronto: Job Start and Skills for Change.

Chakrabarty, Dipesh. 1998. "Reconstructing Liberalism? Notes toward a Conversation between Area Studies and Diasporic Studies." *Public Culture* 10 (3): 457–81.

Challinor, A. E. 2011. "Canada's Immigration Policy: A Focus on Human Capital." Migration Policy Institute. Accessed November 27, 2013. http://www.migration information.org/Profiles/display.cfm?ID=853.

Chatterjee, Partha. 1997. *The Nation and Its Fragments: Colonial and Postcolonial Histories*. Delhi: Oxford University Press.

Choy, Catherine. 2003. *Empire of Care: Nursing and Migration in Filipino American History*. Durham, NC: Duke University Press.

Chua, Jocelyn. 2011. "Making Time for the Children: Self-Temporalization and the Cultivation of the Antisuicidal Subject in South India." *Cultural Anthropology* 26 (1): 112–37.

Chui, Tina. 2011. "Immigrant Women." *Statistics Canada* (July): 5–36. http://www.statcan.gc.ca/pub/89-503-x/2010001/article/11528-eng.pdf.

Citizenship and Immigration Canada, Government of Canada. 2006. "Immigration Representatives: What If I Have a Complaint?" Accessed November 23, 2013. http://www.cic.gc.ca.

Citizenship and Immigration Canada. 2007. Accessed November 23, 2013. http://www.cic.gc.ca.

Citizenship and Immigration Canada. 2008. Accessed November 23, 2013. http://www.cic.gc.ca.

Citizenship and Immigration Canada. 2011. "Annual Report to Parliament on Immigration." Last modified October 27, 2013. http://www.cic.gc.ca/english/resources/publications/annual-report-2011/section2.asp#archived.

City of Toronto. 2007. "Arts, Heritage, Culture, History: The Modern Metropolis from 1951." http://www.toronto.ca/culture/history/history-1951-onward.htm.

City of Toronto. 2013. "Toronto's Racial Diversity." Accessed November 26, 2013. http://www.toronto.ca/toronto_facts/diversity.htm.

Classen, C. 1993. *Worlds of Sense: Exploring the Senses in History and across Cultures*. London: Routledge.

Classen, Constance, David Howes, and Anthony Synnott. 1994. *Aroma: The Cultural History of Smell*. London: Routledge.

Clifford, James. 1997. *Routes: Travel and Translation in the Late Twentieth Century*. Cambridge, MA: Harvard University Press.

Cohn, Bernard S. 1987. *An Anthropologist among the Historians and Other Essays*. Delhi: Oxford University Press.

Coll, Kathleen. 2013. *Remaking Citizenship: Latina Immigrants and New American Politics*. Stanford: Stanford University Press.

College of Nurses of Ontario. 2007. "Nursing Standards." http://www.cno.org/prac/index.htm.

Collins, Jane L. 2003. *"Threads: Gender, Labor, and Power in the Global Apparel Industry*. Chicago: University of Chicago Press.

Colour of Poverty. 2013. "Fact Sheet #1: Understanding the Racialization of Poverty in Ontario; An Introduction in 2007." Learning and Violence. Accessed November 12, 2013. http://www.learningandviolence.net/lrnteach/material/Poverty FactSheets-aug07.pdf.

Cook-Lynn, Elizabeth. 1997. "Who Stole Native American Studies?" *Wicazo Sa Review* 12 (1): 9–28.

Coronil, Fernando. 2000. "Towards a Critique of Globalcentrism: Speculations on Capitalism's Nature." *Public Culture* 12 (2): 351–74.

Correia, Eugene. 2003. "Immigration Dilemmas." *Frontline* 20 (16), http://www.frontline.in/static/html/fl2016/stories/20030815001006200.htm.

Coulter, Kendra. 2009. "Women, Poverty Policy, and the Production of Neoliberal Politics in Ontario, Canada." *Journal of Women, Politics, and Policy* 30 (1): 23–45.

Coulthard, G. S. 2007. "Subjects of Empire: Indigenous Peoples and the 'Politics of Recognition' in Canada." *Contemporary Political Theory* 6 (4): 437–60.

Crapanzano, Vincent. 1985. *Waiting: The Whites of South Africa*. New York: Random House.

Cumming, Peter A., Enid L. D. Lee, and Dimitrios G. Oreopoulos. 1989. *Access! Report of the Task Force on Access to Professions and Trades in Ontario*. Ontario Ministry of Citizenship.

Damasco, Valerie. 2012. "The Recruitment of Filipino Healthcare Professionals to Canada in the 1960s." In *Filipinos in Canada: Disturbing Invisibility*, edited by R. S. Coloma, B. S. McElhinny, J. P. C. Catungal, E. Tungohan, and L. M. Davidson, 97–122. Toronto: University of Toronto Press.

D'Antonio, Patricia. 1993. "The Legacy of Domesticity: Nursing in Early Nineteenth-Century America." In *Nurses' Work: Issues across Time and Place*, edited by Patricia D'Antonio, E. Baer, S. Rinker, and J. Lynaugh. New York: Springer Publishing.

Das Dasgupta, Shamita. 1998. *A Patchwork Shawl: Chronicles of South Asian Women in America*. New Brunswick, NJ: Rutgers University Press.

Das Gupta, Monisha. 2006. *Unruly Immigrants: Rights, Activism, and Transnational South Asian Politics in the United States*. Durham, NC: Duke University Press.

Das Gupta, Tania. 1996. "Anti-Black Racism in Nursing in Ontario." *Studies in Political Economy* 51: 97–116.

Das Gupta, Tania. 2009. *Real Nurses and Others: Racism in Nursing*. Halifax, ON: Fernwood Press.

Das Gupta, Tania, Rebecca Hagey, and Jane Turritin. 2007. "Racial Discrimination in Nursing." In *Interrogating Race and Racism*, edited by Vijay Agnew. Toronto: University of Toronto Press.

Davies, Margery. 1982. *Woman's Place Is at the Typewriter: Office Work and Office Workers 1870–1930*. Philadelphia: Temple University Press.

Dean, Mitchell. 1999. *Governmentality: Power and Rule in Modern Society*. Thousand Oaks, CA: Sage.

Department of Canadian Heritage. 2002. "Speaking Notes for the Honourable Sheila Copps, Minister of Canadian Heritage, Address to a Meeting of the Canada–France Chamber of Commerce." http://www.canadianheritage.gc.ca/pc-ch/notes/2003-02-04_e.cfm.

Department of Canadian Heritage. 2007. "Canadian Multiculturalism: An Inclusive Citizenship." http://www.pch.gc.ca/progs/multi/inclusive_e.cfm.

Desh Pardesh Fonds. 2007. "Inventory of Desh Pardesh Fonds." Clara Thomas Archives, York University, Toronto. Last modified November 26, 2008. http://archivesfa.library.yorku.ca/fonds/ON00370-f0000522.htm.

Dhingra, Pawan. 2007. *Managing Multicultural Lives: Asian American Professionals and the Challenge of Multiple Identities*. Stanford, CA: Stanford University Press.

Douglas, Mary. 2002. *Purity and Danger: An Analysis of Concepts of Pollution and Taboo*. Routledge Classics ed. New York: Routledge. Orig. pub. 1966.

Dua, Enakshi, Narda Razack, and Jody Nyasha Warner. 2005. "Race, Racism and Empire: Reflections on Canada." *Social Justice* 32 (4): 1–10.

Du Bois, W. E. B. 2008. *The Souls of Black Folk*. Rockville, MD: ArcManor. Orig. pub. 1903.

Ducey, Ariel. 2010. "Technologies of Caring Labor: From Objects to Affect." In *Intimate Labors: Cultures, Technologist, and the Politics of Care*, edited by Eileen Boris and Rhacel Parreñas, 18–32. Stanford, CA: Stanford University Press.

Dusenbery, Verne. 1995. "A Sikh Diaspora? Contested Identities and Constructed Realities." In *Nation and Migration: The Politics of Space in the South Asian Diaspora*, edited by Peter Van Der Veer, 17–42. Philadelphia: University of Pennsylvania Press.

Ehrenreich, B., and A. Hochschild, eds. 2002. *Global Woman: Nannies, Maids, and Sex Workers in the New Economy*. New York: Henry Holt.

Elyachar, Julia. 2012. "Before (and After) Neoliberalism: Tacit Knowledge, Secrets of Trade, and the Public Sector in Egypt." *Cultural Anthropology* 27 (1): 76–96.

Enloe, Cynthia. 1989. *Bananas, Beaches, and Bases: Making Feminist Sense of International Politics*. Berkeley: University of California Press.

Ewing, Katherine. 1983. "The Politics of Sufisim: Redefining the Saints of Pakistan." *Journal of Asian Studies* 42 (2): 251–68.

Ewing, Katherine, ed. 2008. *Being and Belonging: Muslims in the United States since 9/11*. New York: Russell Sage Foundation.

Ferguson, James. 1999. *Expectations of Modernity: Myths and Meanings of Urban Life on the Zambian Copperbelt*. Berkeley: University of California Press.

Fernandez-Kelly, Maria. 1983. *For We Are Sold, I and My People: Women and Industry in Mexico's Frontier*. Albany: State University of New York Press.

Fernando, Mayanthi. 2010. "Reconfiguring Freedom: Muslim Piety and the Limits of Secular Law and Public Discourse in France." *American Ethnologist* 37 (1): 19–35.

Fish, Stanley. 1997. "Boutique Multiculturalism, or Why Liberals Are Incapable of Thinking about Hate Speech." *Critical Inquiry* 23 (2): 378–96.

Flores, William, and Rina Benmayor. 1997. *Latino Cultural Citizenship: Claiming Identity, Space, and Rights*. Boston: Beacon Press.

Flynn, Karen. 2009. "Beyond the Glass Wall: Black Canadian Nurses, 1940–1970." *Nursing History Review* 17 (1): 129–52.

Foucault, Michel. 1977. *Discipline and Punish*. New York: Vintage.

Foucault, Michel. 1978. *The History of Sexuality, Volume 1*. New York: Vintage.

Foucault, Michel. 1982. *The Archaeology of Knowledge and the Discourse on Language*. New York: Pantheon.

Foucault, Michel. 1991. "Governmentality." In *The Foucault Effect: Studies in Governmentality*, edited by Graham Burchell, Colin Gordon, and Peter Miller, 87–104. Chicago: University of Chicago Press.

Fraser, Nancy. 2009. "Feminism, Capitalism, and the Cunning of History." *New Left Review* 56: 97–117.

Freeman, Carla. 2000. *High Tech and High Heels in the Global Economy: Women, Work, and Pink-Collar Identities in the Caribbean*. Durham, NC: Duke University Press.

Freeman, Carla. 2001. "Is Local: Global as Feminine: Masculine? Rethinking the Gender of Globalization." *Signs* 26 (4): 1007–37.

Freud, Sigmund. 1953. "Mourning and Melancholia." In *The Standard Edition of the Complete Psychological Works of Sigmund Freud, Volume XIV (1914–1916): On the History of the Psycho-Analytic Movement, Papers on Metapsychology and Other Works*, edited by J. Strachey, 237–358. London: Hogarth Press. Orig. pub. 1917.

Friedman, Thomas L. 2005. *The World Is Flat: A Brief History of the Twenty-First Century*. New York: Farrar, Straus and Giroux.

Ganguly, Keya. 2001. *States of Exception: Everyday Life and Postcolonial Identity*. Minneapolis: University of Minnesota Press.

Garcea, J. 1998. "Bicommunalism and the Bifurcation of the Immigration System." *Canadian Ethnic Studies* 30 (3): 149–72.

Gates, Henry Louis, Jr. 1993. "Beyond the Culture Wars: Identities in Dialogue." *Profession* 93: 6–11.

Gellner, Ernest. 2006. *Nations and Nationalism*. 2nd ed. Oxford, UK: Blackwell. Orig. pub. 1983.

George, Rosemary. 1997. "From Expatriate Aristocrat to Immigrant Nobody: South Asian Racial Strategies in the Southern Californian Context." *Diaspora* 6 (1): 30–61.

Ghosh, Amitav. 1988. *The Shadow Lines*. London: South Asia Books.

Ghosh, Amitav. 1994. *In an Antique Land: History in the Guise of a Traveler's Tale*. New York: Vintage.

Gilmore, Ruth Wilson. 2007. *Golden Gulag: Prisons, Surplus, Crisis, and Opposition in Globalizing California*. Berkeley: University of California Press.

Gilroy, Paul. 1993. *The Black Atlantic: Modernity and Double Consciousness*. Cambridge, MA: Harvard University Press.

Girard, Erik R., and Harald Bauder. 2007. "Assimilation and Exclusion of Foreign Trained Engineers in Canada: Inside a Professional Regulatory Organization." *Antipode* 39 (1): 35–53.

Glick-Schiller, Nina, Linda Basch, and Cristina Szanton Blanc. 1995. "From Immigrant to Transmigrant: Theorizing Transnational Migration." *Anthropological Quarterly* 68 (1): 48–63.

Global Experience Ontario, Government of Canada. 2008. http://www.ontarioimmig ration.ca/English/geo.asp.

Globe and Mail. 2010. "Part 6: Editorial: Strike Multiculturalism from the National Vocabulary." *Globe and Mail*, October 8. Last updated August 23, 2012. http:// www.theglobeandmail.com/news/national/time-to-lead/multiculturalism

/part-6-editorial-strike-multiculturalism-from-the-national-vocabulary/article
1748958/.

Goldberg, David Theo. 1993. *Racist Culture: Philosophy and the Politics of Meaning.*
Cambridge, MA: Blackwell.

Goldberg, David Theo. 2002. *The Racial State.* Oxford, UK: Blackwell.

Goldstein, Tara. 1995. "'Nobody Is Talking Bad': Creating Community and Claiming Power on the Production Lines." In *Gender Articulated: Language and the Socially Constructed Self*, edited by Kira Hall and Mary Bucholtz, 375–400. New York:
Routledge.

Gopinath, Gayatri. 2005. *Impossible Desires: Queer Diasporas and South Asian Public
Cultures.* Durham, NC: Duke University Press.

Gordon, Suzanne. 2002. "Following Doctors' Orders." *The Nation.* March 4.

Gordon, Suzanne. 2009. *Nursing Against the Odds: How Health Care Cost Cutting,
Media Stereotypes, and Medical Hubris Undermine Nurses and Patient Care.* New
York: Cornell University Press.

Grady, P. 2009. "The Impact of Immigration on Canada's Labour Market." *Fraser
Forum* (December). http://www.global-economics.ca/ImpactofImmigrationon
CanadasLabourMarket.pdf.

Grandin, Greg. 2009. *Fordlandia: The Rise and Fall of Henry Ford's Forgotten Jungle
City.* New York: Metropolitan.

Gregory, S., and R. Sanjek, eds. 1994. *Race.* New Brunswick, NJ: Rutgers University
Press.

Grewal, Inderpal. 2005. *Transnational America: Feminisms, Diasporas, Neoliberalisms.*
Durham, NC: Duke University Press.

Grewal, Inderpal, and Caren Kaplan, eds. 1997. *Scattered Hegemonies: Postmodernity and Transnational Feminist Practices.* Minneapolis: University of Minnesota
Press.

Grewal, Zareena. 2013. *Islam is a Foreign Country: American Muslims and the Global
Crisis of Authority.* New York: NYU Press.

Guevarra, Anna. 2010. *Marketing Dreams, Manufacturing Heroes: The Transnational
Labor Brokering of Filipino Workers.* New Brunswick, NJ: Rutgers University Press.

Gupta, Akhil. 1992. "The Song of the Nonaligned World: Transnational Identities and
the Reinscription of Space in Late Capitalism." *Cultural Anthropology* 7 (1): 63–79.

Gupta, Akhil. 1995. "Blurred Boundaries: The Discourse of Corruption, the Culture
of Politics, and the Imagined State." *American Ethnologist* 22 (2): 375–402.

Gupta, Akhil. 2005. "Imagining Nations." In *A Companion to the Anthropology of Politics*, edited by David Nugent and Joan Vincent, 267–81. London: Blackwell.

Gupta, A., and J. Ferguson. 1997. *Culture, Power, Place: Explorations in Critical Anthropology.* Durham, NC: Duke University Press.

Gupta, A., and J. Ferguson. 2002. "Spatializing States: Toward an Ethnography of
Neoliberal Governmentality." *American Ethnologist* 29 (4): 981–1002.

Gupta, Akhil, and Aradhana Sharma. 2006. "Globalization and Postcolonial States."
Current Anthropology 47 (2): 277–307.

Hage, Ghassan. 2003. *Against Paranoid Nationalism: Searching for Hope in a Shrinking Society.* Sydney: Pluto Press.

Hage, Ghassan. 2009. "Waiting Out the Crisis: On Stuckness and Governmentality." In *Waiting*, edited by Ghassan Hage, 97–106. Carlton, AU: University of Melbourne Press.

Hale, Charles. 2002. "Does Multiculturalism Menace? Governance, Cultural Rights and the Politics of Identity in Guatemala." *Journal of Latin American Studies* 34 (3): 485–524.

Hall, Stuart. 1993. "Cultural Identity and Diaspora." In *Colonial Discourse and Postcolonial Theory: A Reader*, edited by Patrick Williams and Laura Chrisman, 392–403. New York: Columbia University Press.

Hall, Stuart. 1997. *Representation: Cultural Representations and Signifying Practices.* London: Sage.

Hartmann, Heidi. 1997. "The Unhappy Marriage of Marxism and Feminism: Towards a More Progressive Union." In *The Second Wave: A Reader in Feminist Theory*, edited by Linda Nicholson, 97–122. New York: Routledge. Orig. pub. 1979.

Harvey, David. 1990. *The Condition of Postmodernity.* Oxford, UK: Blackwell.

Hasnat, Naheed. 1998. "Being 'Amreekan': Fried Chicken versus Chicken Tikka." In *A Patchwork Shawl: Chronicles of South Asian Women in America*, edited by Shamita Das Dasgupta, 33–45. New Brunswick, NJ: Rutgers University Press.

Henry, Miriam, and Suzanne Franzway. 1993. "Gender, Unions, and the New Workplace: Realizing the Promise?" In Belinda Probert and Bruce W. Wilson eds., *Pink Collar Blues: Work Gender and Technology.* Melbourne: Melbourne University Press.

Herzfeld, Michael. 1993. *The Social Production of Indifference: Exploring the Symbolic Roots of Western Bureaucracy.* Chicago: University of Chicago Press.

Hobsbawm, E. J., and T. O. Ranger. 1983. *The Invention of Tradition.* New York: Cambridge University Press.

Hochschild, Arlie. 1983. *The Managed Heart: Commercialization of Human Feeling.* Berkeley: University of California Press.

Hochschild, Arlie, with Anne Machung. 2012. *The Second Shift: Working Families and the Revolution at Home.* New York: Penguin.

Hyde, Alan. 2006. "Offensive Bodies." In *The Smell Culture Reader*, edited by Jim Drobnick, 53–58. New York: Berg.

Immigration and Refugee Protection Act. 2002. "Immigration and Refugee Protection Regulations." Accessed November 18, 2013. http://laws-lois.justice.gc.ca/eng/regulations/SOR-2002-227/FullText.html.

Islam, N. 1989. "Naming Desire: Shaping Identity." In *A Patchwork Shawl: Chronicles of South Asian Women in America*, edited by Shamita Das Dasgupta, 72–96. New Brunswick, NJ: Rutgers University Press.

Ismael, Shereen. 2006. *Child Poverty and the Canadian Welfare State: From Entitlement to Charity.* Edmonton: University of Alberta.

Israel, Milton. 1994. *In the Further Soil: A Social History of Indo-Canadians in Ontario.* Toronto: University of Toronto Press.

Iwabuchi, Koichi. 2002. *Recentering Globalization: Popular Culture and Japanese Transnationalism*. Durham, NC: Duke University Press.

Jameson, F. 1992. *Postmodernism, or, The Cultural Logic of Late Capitalism*. Durham, NC: Duke University Press.

Jung, Moon-Ho. 2006. *Coolies and Cane: Race, Labor and Sugar in the Age of Emancipation*. Baltimore, MD: Johns Hopkins University Press.

Kallen, E. 1982. "Multiculturalism: Ideology, Policy and Reality." *Journal of Canadian Studies* 17: 51–63.

Kang, Miliann. 2010. *The Managed Hand: Race, Gender, and the Body in Beauty Service Work*. Berkeley: University of California Press.

Kaplan, Caren, Norma Alarcon, and Minoo Moallem. 1999. *Between Woman and Nation: Nationalisms, Transnational Feminisms, and the State*. Durham, NC: Duke University Press.

Kearney, M. 1986. "From the Invisible Hand to Visible Feet: Anthropological Studies of Migration and Development." *Annual Review of Anthropology* 15: 331–61.

Kearney, M. 1995. "The Local and the Global: The Anthropology of Globalization and Transnationalism." *Annual Review of Anthropology* 24: 547–65.

Keung, Francine. 2007. "A City of Unmatched Diversity." *Toronto Star*, December 5. http://www.thestar.com/news/gta/2007/12/05/a_city_of_unmatched_diversity.html.

Keung, N. 2008. "Australia, New Zealand Fine-Tuned Screening: Skilled People Processed in Just 6 to 12 Months." *Toronto Star*, May 26. http://www.thestar.com/article/429913.

Khan, Aisha. 1995. "Homeland, Motherland: Authenticity, Legitimacy, and Ideologies of Place Among Muslims in Trinidad." In *Nation and Migration: The Politics of Space in the South Asian Diaspora*, edited by Peter Van Der Veer, 93–131. Philadelphia: University of Pennsylvania Press.

Khan, Aisha. 2004. *Callaloo Nation: Metaphors of Race and Religious Identity among South Asians in Trinidad*. Durham, NC: Duke University Press.

Khan, Tanya Sabena. 2012. "A Part of and Apart from the Mosaic: A Study of Pakistani Canadians' Experiences in Toronto during the 1960s and 1970s." PhD thesis, McGill University.

King, Gary, and Christopher J. L. Murray. 2001. "Rethinking Human Security." *Political Science Quarterly* 116 (4): 585–610.

Kingfisher, C. 2002. *Western Welfare in Decline: Globalization and Women's Poverty*. Philadelphia: University of Pennsylvania Press.

Kipfer, S., and R. Keil. 2002. "Toronto Inc? Planning the Competitive City in the New Toronto." *Antipode* 34 (2): 227–64.

Klein, Naomi. 2000. *No Logo*. Toronto: Vintage Canada.

Kohrman, Matthew. 2005. *Bodies of Difference: Experiences of Disability and Institutional Advocacy in the Making of Modern China*. Berkeley: University of California Press.

Koshy, Susan. 1998. "Category Crisis: South Asian Americans and Questions of Race and Ethnicity." *Diaspora* 7 (3): 285–320.

Krishnan, Raghu. 2003. "Remembering Anti-Racism: Can Identity Politics Make a Comeback?" *This Magazine* 36 (4): 26, 3p.

Kurien, Prema. 2007. *A Place at the Multicultural Table: The Development of an American Hinduism.* New Brunswick, NJ: Rutgers University Press.

Kwon, June. 2015. "The Work of Waiting: Love and Money in Korean Chinese Transnational Migration." *Cultural Anthropology* 30 (3): 477–500.

Kymlika, Will. 1995. *Multicultural Citizenship: A Liberal Theory of Minority Rights.* Oxford, UK: Oxford University Press.

Lamont, Michèle. 2000. *The Dignity of Working Men: Morality and the Boundaries of Race, Class and Immigration.* Cambridge, MA: Russell Sage Foundation.

Lamphere, L., and A. Stepick. 1994. *Newcomers in the Workplace: Immigrants and the Restructuring of the US Economy.* Philadelphia: Temple University Press.

Lamphere, L., P. Zavella, F. Gonzales, and P. Evans. 1993. *Sunbelt Working Mothers: Reconciling Family and Factory.* Ithaca, NY: Cornell University Press.

Law, L. 2001. "Home Cooking: Filipino Women and Geographies of the Senses in Hong Kong." *Ecumene* 8: 264–83.

Leonard, Karen. 1992. *Making Ethnic Choices: California's Punjabi Mexican Americans.* Philadelphia: Temple University Press.

Leonard, Karen. 2007. *Locating Home: India's Hyderabadis Abroad.* Stanford, CA: Stanford University Press.

Lévi-Strauss, C. 1983. *The Raw and the Cooked: Mythologiques*, Vol. 1, trans. J. Weightman and D. Weightman. Chicago: University of Chicago Press. Orig. pub. 1964.

Lewellen, Ted. 2002. *The Anthropology of Globalization: Cultural Anthropology Enters the 21st Century.* Westport, CT: Bergin and Garvey.

Low, Kelvin. 2005. "Ruminations on Smell as a Sociocultural Phenomenon." *Current Sociology* 53: 397–417.

Low, Kelvin. 2006. "Presenting the Self, the Social Body, and the Olfactory: Managing Smells in Everyday Life Experiences." *Sociological Perspectives* 49 (4): 607–31.

Lowe, Lisa. 1996. *Immigrant Acts: On Asian American Cultural Politics.* Durham, NC: Duke University Press.

Lowry, Michelle. 2002. "Creating Human Insecurity: The National Security Focus in Canada's Immigration System." *Refuge* 21 (1): 28–39.

Lutz, Catherine. 1995. "The Gender of Theory." In *Women Writing Culture*, edited by Ruth Behar and Deborah Gordon. Berkeley: University of California Press.

Lutz, C., and L. Abu-Lughod, eds. 1990. *Language and the Politics of Emotion.* Cambridge, UK: Cambridge University Press.

Lutz, C., and G. White. 1986. "The Anthropology of Emotions." *Annual Review of Anthropology* 15: 405–36.

Mahmood, Saba. 2001. "Feminist Theory, Embodiment, and the Docile Agent: Some Reflections on the Egyptian Islamic Revival." *Cultural Anthropology* 16 (2): 202–36.

Mahmood, Saba. 2005. *The Politics of Piety: The Islamic Revival and the Feminist Subject.* Princeton: Princeton University Press.

Maira, Sunaina. 2002. *Desis in the House: Indian American Youth Culture in NYC.* Philadelphia: Temple University Press.

Maira, Sunaina. 2009. *Missing: Youth, Citizenship, and Empire after 9/11*. Durham, NC: Duke University Press.

Man, G. 2004. "Gender, Work and Migration: Deskilling Chinese Immigrant Women in Canada." *Women's Studies International Forum* 27 (2): 135–48.

Manalansan, Martin. 2006. "Immigrant Lives and the Politics of Olfaction in the Global City." In *The Smell Culture Reader*, edited by Jim Drobnick, 41–52. New York: Berg.

Mankekar, Purnima. 2015. *Unsettling India: Affect, Temporality, Transnationality*. Durham, NC: Duke University Press.

Martin, Emily. 1994. *Flexible Bodies: Tracking Immunity in American Culture from the Days of Polio to the Age of AIDS*. Boston: Beacon Press.

Massey, Dorinne. 1994. *Space, Place, and Gender*. Minneapolis: University of Minnesota Press.

Mauss, M. 1968. "Techniques of the Body." *Economy and Society* 2 (1): 70–88. Orig. pub. 1934.

McBride, Stephen. 1999. "Toward Permanent Insecurity: The Social Impact of Unemployment." *Journal of Canadian Studies* 34 (2): 13–30.

McCaskell, Tim. 2005. *Race to Equity: Disrupting Educational Inequality*. Toronto: Between the Lines Press.

McElhinny, Bonnie, ed. 2007. *Words, Worlds, Material Girls: Language and Gender in a Global Economy*. Berlin: Mouton de Gruyter.

McElhinny, Bonnie. 2010. "The Audacity of Affect: Gender, Race, and History in Linguistic Accounts of Legitimacy and Belonging." *Annual Review of Anthropology* 39: 309–28.

McGowan, Rima. 1999. *Muslims in the Diaspora: The Somali Communities of London and Toronto*. Toronto: University of Toronto Press.

Melamed, Jodi. 2011. *Represent and Destroy: Rationalizing Violence in the New Racial Capitalism*. Minneapolis: University of Minnesota Press.

Ministry of Citizenship and Immigration. 2006. "McGuinty Government Opening Doors for International Professionals" (press release). Government of Ontario website, December 18. http://news.ontario.ca/archive/en/2006/12/18/McGuinty -Government-Opening-Doors-for-International-Professionals.html.

Mirchandani, K. 2012. *Phone Clones: Authenticity Work in the Transnational Service Economy*. Ithaca, NY: ILR Press.

Mitchell, Katharyne. 2001. "Transnationalism, Neo-liberalism, and the Rise of the Shadow State." *Economy and Society* 30 (2): 165–89.

Mitchell, Katharyne. 2004. *Crossing the Neoliberal Line: Pacific Rim Migration and the Metropolis*. Philadelphia: Temple University Press.

Moallem, Minoo, and Iain A. Boal. 1999. "Multicultural Nationalism and the Poetics of Inauguration." In *Between Woman and Nation: Nationalisms, Transnational Feminisms, and the State*, edited by Caren Kaplan, Norma Alarcon, and Minoo Moallem. Durham, NC: Duke University Press.

Mohanty, Chandra, Ann Russo, and Lourdes Torres, eds. 1991. *Third World Women and the Politics of Feminism*. Bloomington: Indiana University Press.

Molé, Noelle. 2012. "Hauntings of Solidarity in Post-Fordist Italy." *Anthropological Quarterly* 85 (2): 371–96.

Moodley, K. 1983. "Canadian Multiculturalism as Ideology." *Ethnic and Racial Studies* 6 (3): 320–31.

Muehlebach, Andrea, and Nitzan Shoshan. 2012. "Introduction, AQ Special Collection: Post-Fordist Affect." *Anthropological Quarterly* 85 (2): 317–44.

Muñoz, José. 1999. *Disidentifications: Queers of Color and the Performance of Politics.* Minneapolis: University of Minnesota Press.

Muñoz, José Esteban. 2009. *Cruising Utopia: The Then and There of Queer Futurity.* New York: New York University Press.

Muslim Association of Canada. 2009. "Eid Festival: 28 Years of Tradition." http://www.gtaeid.com/.

Ng, Roxana. 2006. "Learning to be Good Citizens: Informal Learning and the Labour Market Experiences of Professional Chinese Immigrant Women. Final Report for the Centre of Excellence on Research on Immigration and Settlement." Toronto: Ontario Institute for Studies in Education, University of Toronto.

Ochs, E., and B. Schieffelin. 1989. "Language Has a Heart." *Text* 9 (1): 7–25.

Okin, Susan. 1997. "Is Multiculturalism Bad for Women?" *Boston Review* 22 (October–November): 25–28.

Omi, Michael, and Howard Winant. 2014. *Racial Formation in the United States.* 3rd ed. New York: Routledge.

O'Neill, Bruce. 2014. "Cast Aside: Boredom, Downward Mobility, and Homelessness in Post-Communist Bucharest." *Cultural Anthropology* 29 (1): 8–31.

Ong, Aihwa. 1987. *Spirits of Resistance and Capitalist Discipline: Factory Women in Malaysia.* Albany: State University of New York Press.

Ong, Aihwa. 1999. *Flexible Citizenship: The Cultural Logics of Transnationality.* Durham, NC: Duke University Press.

Ong, Aihwa. 2003. *Buddha Is Hiding: Refugees, Citizenship, the New America.* Berkeley: University of California Press.

Ong, Aihwa. 2006. *Neoliberalism as Exception: Mutations in Citizenship and Sovereignty.* Durham, NC: Duke University Press.

Ontario Council of Agencies Serving Immigrants. 2008. "Immigrants Need More Than Credentials Recognition." http://www.ocasi.org.

Ontario Immigration, Government of Ontario. 2005a. "Before You Arrive." http://www.ontarioimmigration.ca/en/before/index.htm.

Ontario Immigration. 2005b. "Work in Your Profession." http://www.ontarioimmigration.ca/en/working/OI_HOW_WORK_PROF.html.

Ornstein, Michael. 2006. *Ethno-Racial Groups in Toronto, 1971–2001: A Demographic and Socio-Economic Profile.* Toronto: York University, Institute for Social Research.

Palumbo-Liu, David. 1999. *Asian/American: Historical Crossings of a Racial Frontier.* Stanford, CA: Stanford University Press.

Parreñas, R. S. 2001. *Servants of Globalization: Women, Migration, and Domestic Work.* Stanford: Stanford University Press.

Parreñas, R. S. 2005. *Children of Global Migration: Transnational Families and Gendered Woes*. Stanford, CA: Stanford University Press.

Phillips, S. 2000. "More than Stakeholders: Reforming State-Voluntary Relations." *Journal of Canadian Studies* 35 (4): 182–202.

Povinelli, Elizabeth. 1999. "Settler Modernity and the Quest for an Indigenous Tradition." *Public Culture* 11: 19–47.

Povinelli, Elizabeth. 2001. "Radical Worlds: The Anthropology of Incommensurability and Inconceivability." *Annual Review of Anthropology* 30: 319–34.

Povinelli, Elizabeth. 2002. *The Cunning of Recognition: Indigenous Alterities and the Making of Australian Multiculturalism*. Durham, NC: Duke University Press.

Prasad, Vijay. 2000. *The Karma of Brown Folk*. Minneapolis: University of Minnesota Press.

Procupez, Valeria. 2012. "Inhabiting the Temporary: Patience and Uncertainty among Urban Squatters in Buenos Aires." In *The Anthropology of Ignorance*, edited by Casey High, Ann H. Kelly, and Jonathan Mair, 163–88. New York: Palgrave Macmillan.

Puar, Jasbir. 2007. *Terrorist Assemblages*. Durham, NC: Duke University Press.

Radhakrishnan, Smitha. 2011. *Appropriately Indian: Gender and Culture in a New Transnational Class*. Durham, NC: Duke University Press.

Raj, Dhooleka. 2003. *Where Are You From? Middle-Class Migrants in the Modern World*. Berkeley: University of California Press.

Ralston, Helen. 1996. *Lived Experience of South Asian Immigrant Women in Atlantic Canada: The Interconnections of Race, Class, and Gender*. New York: Edwin Mellen Press.

Rana, Junaid. 2011. *Terrifying Muslims: Race and Labor in the South Asian Diaspora*. Durham, NC: Duke University Press.

Rana, Jyoti. 2005. "What Is MMM?" http://www.masalamehndimasti.com/index.php ?option=com_content&task=view&id=5&Itemid=9.

Razack, Sherene. 1998. *Looking White People in the Eye: Gender, Race, and Culture in Courtrooms and Classrooms*. Toronto: University of Toronto Press.

Razack, Sherene. 2002. *Race, Space, and the Law: Unmapping a White Settler Society*. Toronto: Between the Lines Press.

Reitz, Jeffrey. 2001. "Immigrant Skill Utilization in the Canadian Labour Market: Implications of Human Capital Research." *Journal of International Migration and Integration* 2 (3): 346–78.

Richmond, Ted. 1996. "Effects of Cutbacks on Immigrant Service Agencies—Results of an Action Research Project." Toronto: City of Toronto Public Health Department.

Richmond, Ted, and John Shields. 2004. "Third Sector Restructuring and the New Contracting Regime: The Case of Immigrant Serving Agencies in Ontario." *Policy Matters* 3 (February): 2–7. Toronto: Joint Centre of Excellence for Research on Immigration and Settlement.

Rodrigue, Dylan. 2010. *Suspended Apocalypse: White Supremacy, Genocide, and the Filipino Condition*. Minneapolis: University of Minnesota Press.

Rodriguez, Robyn. 2010. *Migrants for Export: How the Philippine State Brokers Labor to the World*. Minneapolis: University of Minnesota Press.

Rofel, Lisa. 1999. *Other Modernities: Gendered Yearnings in China after Socialism*. Los Angeles: University of California Press.

Rosaldo, Michelle. 1984. "Toward an Anthropology of Self and Feeling." In *Culture Theory: Essays on Mind, Self, and Emotion,* edited by R. A. Shweder and R. A. LeVine, 137–57. Cambridge, UK: Cambridge University Press.

Rosaldo, Renato. 1993. *Culture and Truth: The Remaking of Social Analysis*. Boston: Beacon Press.

Rosaldo, Renato. 1994. "Cultural Citizenship and Educational Democracy." *Cultural Anthropology* 9 (3): 402–11.

Rosaldo, Renato. 1997. "Cultural Citizenship, Inequality, and Multiculturalism." In *Latino Cultural Citizenship: Claiming Identity, Space, and Rights*, edited by William Flores and Rina Benmayor, 27–38. Boston: Beacon Press.

Rose, N. 1996a. "Governing 'Advanced' Liberal Democracies." In *Foucault and Political Reason: Liberalism, Neo-liberalism, and Rationalities of Government*, edited by Andrew Barry, Thomas Osborne, and Nikolas Rose, 37–64. Chicago: University of Chicago Press.

Rose, N. 1996b. *Inventing Our Selves: Psychology, Power, and Personhood*. Cambridge, UK: Cambridge University Press.

Rouse, Roger. 1995. "A Thinking Through Transnationalism: Notes on the Cultural Politics in the Contemporary United States." *Public Culture* 7 (2): 353–402.

Rudrappa, Sharmila. 2004. *Ethnic Routes to Becoming American: Indian Immigrants and the Cultures of Citizenship*: New Brunswick, NJ: Rutgers University Press.

Safran, William. 2005. "The Jewish Diaspora in a Comparative and Theoretical Perspective." *Israel Studies* 10 (1): 36–60.

Said, Edward. 1978. *Orientalism*. New York: Random House.

Sassen, Saskia. 1991. *The Global City: New York, London, Tokyo*. Princeton, NJ: Princeton University Press.

Sassen, Saskia. 1996. *Losing Control? Sovereignty in an Age of Globalization*. New York: Columbia University Press.

Sassen, Saskia. 1998. *Globalization and Its Discontents: Essays on the New Mobility of People and Money*. New York: New Press.

Scott, Joan Wallach. 1988. *Gender and the Politics of History*. New York: Columbia University Press.

Sedgwick, E. 2003. *Touching Feeling: Affect, Pedagogy, Performativity*. Durham, NC: Duke University Press.

Seremetakis, C. Nadia. 1994. *The Senses Still*. Chicago: University of Chicago Press.

Sexton, Patricia. 1982. *The New Nightingales: Hospital Workers, Unions, New Women's Issues*. New York: Enquiry Press.

Shah, Nayan. 2001. *Contagious Divides: Epidemics and Race in San Francisco's Chinatown*. Berkeley: University of California Press.

Shankar, Lavina, and Rajini Srikanth, eds. 1998. *A Part, Yet Apart: South Asians in Asian America*. Philadelphia: Temple University Press.

Shankar, Shalini. 2008. *Desiland: Teen, Culture, Class, and Success in Silicon Valley*. Durham, NC: Duke University Press.

Sharma, Aradhana. 2008. *Logics of Empowerment: Development, Gender, and Governance in Neoliberal India*. Minneapolis: University of Minnesota Press.

Shaw, Alison. 2000. *Kinship and Continuity: Pakistani Families in Britain*. New York: Routledge.

Shields, J., and E. Mitchell. 1998. *Shrinking the State: Globalization and the Reform of Public Administration*. Halifax, NS: Fernwood.

Shukla, Sandhya. 1997. "Building Diaspora and Nation: The 1991 'Cultural Festival of India.'" *Cultural Studies* 11 (2): 296–315.

Shukla, Sandhya. 2001. "Locations for South Asian Diasporas." *Annual Review of Anthropology* 30: 551–72.

Shukla, Sandhya. 2003. *India Abroad: Diasporic Cultures of Postwar America and England*. Princeton, NJ: Princeton University Press.

Siemiatycki, M., and E. Isin. 1997. "Immigration, Diversity and Urban Citizenship in Toronto." *Canadian Journal of Regional Science* 20 (1): 73–102.

Siemiatycki, M., T. Rees, R. Ng, and K. Rahi. 2003. "Integrating Community Diversity in Toronto: On Whose Terms?" In *The World in a City*, edited by Paul Anisef and Michael Lanphier, 373–456. Toronto: University of Toronto Press.

Simpson, Audra. 2014. *Mohawk Interruptus: Political Life across the Borders of Settler States*. Durham, NC: Duke University Press.

Siu, Lok. 2005. *Memories of a Future Home: Diasporic Citizenship of Chinese in Panama*. Stanford, CA: Stanford University Press.

Slyomovics, Susan. 1994. "New York City's Muslim World Day Parade." In *Nation and Migration: The Politics of Space in the South Asian Diaspora*, edited by Peter Van Der Veer, 157–77. Philadelphia: University of Pennsylvania Press.

Smith, Andrea. 2012. "Indigeneity, Settler Colonialism, White Supremacy." In *Racial Formation in the Twenty-First Century*, edited by Daniel HoSang, Oneka La-Bennett, and Laura Pulido. Berkeley: University of California Press.

Spivak, Gayatri. 1988. "Can the Subaltern Speak?" In *Marxism and the Interpretation of Culture*, edited by Cary Nelson and Lawrence Grossberg, 271–313. Urbana: University of Illinois Press.

Standing, Guy. 2011. *The Precariat: The New Dangerous Class*. New York: Bloomsbury Academic.

Stasiulis, Daiva. 1999. "Relational Positionalities of Nationalisms, Racisms, and Feminisms." In *Between Woman and Nation: Nationalisms, Transnational Feminisms, and the State*, edited by Caren Kaplan, Norma Alarcón, and Minoo Moallem, 182–218. Durham, NC: Duke University Press.

Statistics Canada. 2006a. "Place of birth for the immigrant population by period of immigration, 2006 counts and percentage distribution, for Canada, provinces and territories—20% sample data." Last modified March 27, 2009. http://www12.statcan.gc.ca/census-recensement/2006/dp-pd/hlt/97-557/T404-eng.cfm?Lang=E&T=404&GH=4&GF=1&SC=1&S=1&O=D.

Statistics Canada. 2006b. "Place of birth for the immigrant population by period of immigration, 2006 counts and percentage distribution, for census metropolitan areas and census agglomerations—20% sample data." Last modified March 27, 2009.

http://www12.statcan.ca/census-recensement/2006/dp-pd/hlt/97-557/T404-eng
.cfm?Lang=E&T=404&GH=8&GF=932&SC=1&S=1&O=D.

Statistics Canada. 2009a. "Immigrant Population by Place of Birth and Period of Immigration (2006 Census)." Last modified October 14. http://www.statcan.gc.ca/tables-tableaux/sum-som/101/cst01/demo24a-eng.htm.

Statistics Canada. 2009b. "Visible Minority of Person." Last modified December 18, 2012. http://www.statcan.gc.ca/concepts/definitions/minority-minorite1-eng.htm.

Statistics Canada. 2011. "Immigration and Ethnocultural Diversity in Canada: National Household Survey." Catalogue no. 99-010-X2011001. http://www12.statcan.gc.ca/nhs-enm/2011/as-sa/99-010-x/99-010-x2011001-eng.pdf.

Stevenson, Winona. 1998. "Ethnic Assimilates Indigenous: A Study in Intellectual Neocolonialism." *Wicazo Sa Review*: 33–51.

Stewart, Kathleen. 2007. *Ordinary Affects*. Durham, NC: Duke University Press.

Stiell, Bernadette, and Kim England. 1999. "Jamaican Domestics, Filipina Housekeepers and English Nannies: Representations of Toronto's Foreign Domestic Workers." In *Gender, Migration and Domestic Service*, edited by Janet Henshall Momsen, 43–60. London: Routledge.

Stoler, Ann. 2002. *Carnal Knowledge and Imperial Power: Race and the Intimate in Colonial Rule*. Berkeley: University of California Press.

Stoler, Ann. 2004. "Affective States." In *A Companion to the Anthropology of Politics*, edited by David Nugent and Joan Vincent, 4–20. Oxford, UK: Blackwell.

Stoller, Paul. 1989. *The Taste of Ethnographic Things: The Senses in Anthropology*. Philadelphia: University of Pennsylvania Press.

Struthers, James, and Edgar-André Montigny. 1999. "Families, Restructuring and the Canadian Welfare State." *Journal of Canadian Studies* 34 (2): 5–12.

Sutton, David. "Food and the Senses." 2010. *Annual Review of Anthropology* 39: 209–23.

Synnott, Anthony. 1991. "A Sociology of Smell." *Canadian Review of Sociology and Anthropology* 28: 437–59.

Tadiar, Neferti. 2009. *Things Fall Away: Philippine Historical Experience and the Makings of Globalization*. Durham, NC: Duke University Press.

Taylor, Charles. 1994. "The Politics of Recognition." In *Multiculturalism*, edited by Amy Gutmann, 25–74. Princeton, NJ: Princeton University Press.

Taylor, Charles. 2004. *Modern Social Imaginaries*. Durham, NC: Duke University Press.

Taylor, Leslie Ciarula. 2008. "City Immigration Policy Proposed." *Toronto Star*, May 24. http://www.thestar.com/news/gta/2008/05/24/city_immigration_policy_proposed.html.

Thomson, K., R. Addis, S. Stead, and N. Campbell. 2002. "The Gatekeeper and the Immigrants." *Globe and Mail*, July 20.

Ticktin, Miriam. 2008. "Sexual Violence as the Language of Border Control: Where French Feminist and Anti-immigrant Rhetoric Meet." *Signs* 33 (4): 863–89.

Tololyan, Khachig. 1996. "Rethinking Diaspora(s): Stateless Power in the Transnational Moment." *Diaspora* 5 (1): 3–36.

Toronto Community Housing, Government of Ontario. 2013. "About Us." Accessed November 27, 2013. http://www.torontohousing.ca/about.

Tran, Kelly, Jennifer Kaddatz, and Paul Allard. 2005. *South Asians in Canada: Unity through Diversity*. Ottawa: Statistics Canada. Catalogue No. 11-008.

Troper, Harold. 2003. "Becoming an Immigrant City: A History of Immigration into Toronto since the Second World War." In *The World in a City*, edited by Paul Anisef and C. Michael Lanphier, 19–62. Toronto: University of Toronto Press.

Tsing, Anna. 2001. "The Economy of Appearances." *Public Culture* 12 (1): 115–44.

Tsing, Anna. 2005. *Friction: An Ethnography of Global Connection*. Princeton, NJ: Princeton University Press.

Tsing, Anna. 2009. "Supply Chains and the Human Condition." *Rethinking Marxism* 21 (2): 148–76.

Tuan, Mia. 1998. *Forever Foreigners or Honorary Whites? The Asian Ethnic Experience Today*. New Brunswick, NJ: Rutgers University Press.

Upadhya, Carol. 2008. "Management of Culture and Managing Through Culture in the Indian Software Outsourcing Industry." In *In an Outpost of the Global Economy: Work and Workers in India's Information Technology Industry*, edited by Carol Upadhya and A. R. Vasavi, 101–35. London: Routledge.

Van Der Veer, Peter, ed. 1995. *Nation and Migration: The Politics of Space in the South Asian Diaspora*. Philadelphia: University of Pennsylvania Press.

Vertovec, Steven. 2000. "Religion and Diaspora." In *New Approaches to the Study of Religion: Textual, Comparative, Sociological, and Cognitive Approaches*, edited by Peter Antes, Armin Geertz, and Randi Ruth Warne, 275–304. Berlin: Verlag de Gruyter.

Vora, Kalindi. 2010. "The Commodification of Affect in Indian Call Centers." In Boris and Parreñas, *Intimate Labors*, 33–48.

Vora, Neha. 2013. *Impossible Citizens: Dubai's Indian Diaspora*. Durham, NC: Duke University Press.

Walcott, Rinaldo. 2003. *Black Like Who? Writing Black Canada*. Toronto: Insomniac Press.

Werbner, Pnina. 1999. "Global Pathways: Working Class Cosmopolitans and the Creation of Transnational Ethnic Worlds." *Social Anthropology* 7 (1): 17–37.

Werbner, Pnina. 2002. "The Place which Is Diaspora: Citizenship, Religion and Gender in the Making of Chaordic Transnationalism." *Journal of Ethnic and Migration Studies* 28 (1): 119–34.

Winston, Iris. 2011. "Nursing Shortages a National Concern." *Postmedia News*, February 18. http://www.canada.com/health/Nursing+shortages+national+concern/4288871/story.html.

Yanagisako, Sylvia. 2002. *Producing Culture and Capital: Family Firms in Italy*. Princeton, NJ: Princeton University Press.

Young, Iris Marion. 1990. *Justice and the Politics of Difference*. Princeton, NJ: Princeton University Press.

Zaman, Habiba. 2006. *Breaking the Iron Wall: Decommodification and Immigrant Women's Labor in Canada*. Lanham, MD: Lexington Books.

Zietsma, Danielle. 2006. "The Canadian Immigrant Labour Market in 2006: First Results from Canada's Labour Force Survey." ISSN: 1914–6299. Last modified September 10, 2007. http://www.statcan.gc.ca/pub/71-606-x/71-606-x2007001-eng.htm.

Žižek, Slavoj. 1997. "Multiculturalism, or, The Cultural Logic of Multinational Capitalism." *New Left Review* 225 (September–October): 28–51.

INDEX

identity politics, 12. *See also* politics of recognition; visible minority

ideology, 18, 52–53, 69, 139; gendered, 53, 73, 136; multicultural, 4, 11–12, 15, 23, 50, 73, 83, 87, 94, 102–3, 155–58, 165–66, 171n16; racialized, 29, 34, 53, 73. *See also* multiculturalist policy; feminized labor

immigration. *See* citizenship; integration; labor migration

imperialism, 3, 22, 77, 161, 167; cultural, 76–77, 156

inclusion, 3–5, 13–15, 19, 22, 28, 32–34, 50, 69, 77, 88–93, 97–105, 109–110, 114–18, 124, 130, 149, 155–59, 165, 171n16. *See also* exclusion; systemic barriers

incommensurability, 23, 37–38, 52, 76, 129, 156

India, 37–39, 44, 60, 64, 95–96, 104–5, 112, 115, 121–22, 140, 144, 147, 161, 165, 169n5, 176n19, 177n9. *See also* diaspora; Partition; "South Asian"

Indigenous, 31, 80–82, 93, 115, 136, 154, 175n5, 175n8

individual, 6–7, 14, 32–34, 37, 39, 41, 45, 47, 63, 79, 87, 91–92, 94, 104, 114, 123, 128–29, 142, 155, 163, 173n4

integration, 2–4, 6, 8, 12–13, 16, 19, 26, 29, 31–35, 53, 88, 91, 94, 99, 108, 112, 149, 157, 164–65, 173n5, 174n15. *See also* assimilation

interpellation, 3–4, 23, 55, 99, 103, 123–24, 129, 165

interview, 85–86, 90–91, 100, 105, 108, 121, 143, 146, 162

intimate labor, 6, 22, 54–55, 62–64, 71, 74, 117, 167

investor stream immigration, 31, 172n3

ISIS (Islamic State), 81, 176n13

Islam, 11, 99, 103, 110–12, 129, 146, 158, 165. *See also* Islamophobia; Muslim; Muslim problem; secularism

Islamophobia, 11, 176n18

Kenney, Jason, 93–94, 154, 176n11, 176n17, 176n18

Keynesian economics, 31, 136

Kymlicka, Will, 79, 94

labor. *See* capitalism; care work; class; intimate labor; labor migration; market; wage labor

labor migration, 12, 31, 115–18, 131, 158, 164, 179n7

Lastman, Mel, 99

Leitch, Kellie, 78

Lévi-Strauss, Claude, 92

liberalism, 4–7, 11, 17, 22–24, 45, 70, 74–76, 79–84, 88, 91, 94, 97–99, 104, 109, 117–18, 124–25, 156, 162, 176n14, 177n3. *See also* governance; neoliberalism

Little India, 2, 95–96, 107

Lorde, Audre, 124

market, 5, 7, 15, 19, 28, 30, 32–33, 35, 39, 41, 45, 50, 53, 55–56, 62, 64, 67–68, 76, 82, 87, 91, 96, 99, 109, 128–31, 143, 155, 157, 161, 168, 179n8. *See also* capitalism; class; neoliberalism

Masala, Mehndi, Masti (MMM), 95, 101, 116–19. *See also* difference; festivals

masculinity, 49–50, 136–37

masculinized labor, 49, 53–56, 60, 62, 64, 67, 69, 86, 100, 131, 163. *See also* feminized labor

Massey, Doreen, 130

Massumi, Brian, 14

material barriers, 29, 34; markers of difference, 14, 18, 75, 151; interests and conditions, 6, 12, 22, 29, 80, 90, 123, 125. *See also* ideology; systemic barriers

Mauss, Marcel, 18

mehndi, 2, 95

melancholia, 72

Metis, 115

middle-class, 16, 21, 39, 43, 72, 108, 116, 133, 145, 165

migration. *See* labor migration

minority, 6, 8–12, 31, 52, 77, 79, 81, 90, 94–95, 97, 99, 103–4, 111, 113, 116, 124, 149, 156, 171n28, 171n29, 175n8, 176n14, 176n20. *See also* model minority; visible minority

Mississauga, 10, 121

mobility. *See* downward mobility; upward mobility

model minority, 99

Mohanty, Chandra, 123, 166

Statistics Canada, 8–10, 58, 95, 169n2,
170n11
Stewart, Kathleen, 135
Stoler, Ann, 17, 83
Stoller, Paul, 13
structural barriers. *See* systemic barriers
subaltern, 81, 166
subjectivity, 50, 55, 84, 89, 105, 118, 131.
See also individual
survival jobs, 4, 6–7, 16, 19, 27, 41, 60, 67,
89, 146. *See also* wage labor
systemic barriers, 3, 8, 28–29, 34, 37–38,
57–59, 67, 82, 91, 99, 102, 139, 161,
174n14, 174n16

Taylor, Charles, 79, 94, 104
temporality, 66, 85, 130, 141
temporary labor, 27, 39–41
terrorism, 142, 154, 158–59, 162–63, 176n11
Ticktin, Miriam, 91
time-space compression, 130
tolerance, 11, 13, 76, 78–80, 92, 97–98, 112,
124, 155. *See also* Barbaric Cultural Practices Act (2008); politics of recognition
Toronto. *See* housing projects; municipal-
ity; Ontario
Toronto 18: 81, 176n12
Toronto Star, 10, 106, 154
transnational, 7, 12, 15, 21, 31, 68, 73, 103,
115, 129, 131, 137, 141, 165–66, 169n3,
170n6, 179n7
Trudeau, Pierre, 11
Tsing, Anna, 136–37

underemployment, 1, 4, 6, 34, 70, 129–30,
137, 163–65
United Nations, 9, 80, 97, 142

United States, 36, 113, 146; corporate
logic in, 40; gender politics in, 61, 124,
136, 166, 179n7, 179n8; racial politics
in, 7, 9, 11–12, 21, 80, 106–8, 114, 116,
124, 155, 159, 166, 172n1, 175n8, 177n2,
179n8
universality, 5, 17–18, 21, 33, 47, 87, 91,
171n28
University of Toronto, 34, 36, 106–8, 111,
161
upward mobility, 4, 8, 21, 87, 113, 127, 129,
151. *See also* downward mobility
Urdu, 134

visibility/invisibility, 9, 23, 91, 102, 109, 117,
125, 165
visible minority, 9, 94–95

wage labor, 10, 17, 30, 38, 40, 55, 71–72,
131–32, 136. See *also* survival jobs
Wallerstein, Immanuel, 80, 125
War on Terror, 110, 142
welfare state, 17, 27, 31, 33, 43–45, 51, 136,
151, 155, 157, 173n4
West, 11, 22–23, 56, 63–64, 77, 85, 88,
103–6, 121
white and whiteness, 8–12, 16–18, 27, 32,
47, 49–51, 57, 62–63, 79, 81, 87, 89,
91–92, 100, 108, 118, 139–41, 154, 156–57,
161–62, 167, 172n1, 176n14
World Education Services (WES), 34,
36–37, 161
World Trade Organization, 167

York University, 10

Žižek, Slavoj, 79, 98